The Tamil Country:
Transition From Feudalism to Imperialism
(A.D. 1751 to 1816)

The Tamil Country:
Transition From Feudalism to Imperialism
(A.D. 1751 to 1816)

Author

V. Ranjan

Lecturer in History, Scott Christian College, Nagercoil

SERIALS PUBLICATIONS

NEW DELHI (INDIA)

First Published - 2009

ISBN: 978-81-8387-235-5

Published by

SERIALS PUBLICATIONS
4830/24, Prahlad Street, Ansari Road
Darya Ganj, New Delhi-110002 (India)
Phone : 23245225 Fax : 91-11-23272135
E-mail: serials@satyam.net.in

CONTENTS

PREFACE

The present treatise **The Tamil Country: Transition from Feudalism to Imperialism 1751 to 1816** is the outcome of the Doctoral work carried out by me under the supervision and scholarly guidance Dr. B. Maria John, Professor of History, Manonmaniam Sundaranar University, Tirunelveli.

The year 1751 represented a turning point in the history of the relation between the central authority represented by the Nawab of Arcot and the Feudal interests represented by the Poligars and Zamindars. Threatened by common foes, the Nawab and the English East India Company forged a close alliance. After their combined victory over the French and the Nevayets, they directed their attention against the auxiliary powers. The Nawab supported by the British, occupied Vellore, Tanjore, Sivaganga and Ramand, but gained no significant victory over the Poligars. The Madras Government of the English East India Company there upon proceeded against these powers on their own, which was called 'significant' and assumption of revenue authority over the Carnatic. In 1792 the Company through a settlement with the Nawab, brought the Poligars under its direct authority and launched against them a series expeditions.

The auxiliary powers reacted to the emerging situation that threatened their survival. They formed alliances among themselves and sought the support of the French as well as Mysore. As a result there broke out military operations on a large scale. Between 1792 and 1806 they were suppressed and brought under the authority of the British. Through the Revenue and Judicial Regulations, the British by 1816 destroyed the Feudal authority and brought the country under a unified system. This transition was of considerable significance to the political, social and economic life of the people.

I express my sincere thanks and record my deep sense of gratitude to Prof. Fr. K. Rajayyan M.M., M.Lit., A.M., Ph.D., for his scholarly directions and suggestions in selecting the topic for my research.

I express my torrential-flowing and profound thanks to my guide and supervisor Dr. Maria John for his valuable and generous.

I owe a deep sense of gratitude to beloved Father late Mr. P. Vethamoni, Lilly, my sons R. Lijish Ranj, R. Lijin Ranj and my daughter R. Littja Rani for their love and encouragement. I express my sincere thanks to my father-in-law Mr. R. Sathianesan, my mother-in-law Mrs. A. Kochuthresia and my brother-in-law Mr. R. S. Vincent for their support.

I express my sincere gratitude to my brother-in-law advocate P. Jayaraj and advocate P. Dharmaraj, secretary, CSI Diocese of Kanyakumari, for their constant encouragement.

I also thank my Professor, P. Justin Sundardhas, Dr. V. Yesudhason, Dr. Marthunathu, Prof. B. Mariadhasan, Dr. T. S. Emmanuel, N. M. Christian College, Marthandam and Dr. Chellakumar Rose, Principal, Scott Christian college, Nagercoil for their encouragement. I also convey my thanks to the authorities of the Tamil Nadu archives, Chennai for having permitted me to collect valuable records on the topic. I extend my thanks to Dr. Sundaraj, Tamil Nadu archives, Chennai for his timely help.

I am indebted to the staff of the Kerala State archives, Trivandrum; Manuscript Library, Chennai; Jesuits Archives, Senbaganoor, Kodaikanal and Scott Christian College Library, Nagercoil for having kindly supplied me the necessary records.

I express my sincere thanks to Serials Publications, New Delhi for the neat execution of this work.

V. Ranjan

INTRODUCTION

The Tamil Country, situated in the southern region of peninsular India is the home of the Tamils. Across the centuries it experienced varied political systems, whether it was tribalism, oligarchy, monarchy, feudalism or imperialism. Feudalism is identified with medieval Europe, but it was not confined either to the medieval period or to Europe. In one form or other it existed and flourished across the World. The Tamil Country was no exception. Feudalism is defined in different ways. In a political sense it is a decentralised structure of society in which private individuals exercised governmental authority over the population, who depended upon them for protection and living. Such a polity existed side by side with the central authority, either depending upon it or not depending upon it.[1] In an economic sense it was a method of holding land, the land lord giving land to the tenants for cultivation in return for services. Such a system in varied dimensions flourished in different regions, including the land of the Tamils.

The Tamil Country, known as Tamilagam in the distant past, extended from Kanyakumari in the south to Tiruvenkatam, a mountain range of the Eastern Ghats, in the north and from the Arabian Sea in the west to the Bay of Bengal in island of Sri Lanka by the Sixth Century B.C. The Tamil Kingdoms particularly of the Pandyas the east. The present day Tamil Nadu, Kerala and the Chittore District of Andhra Pradesh formed parts of the Tamil Country, otherwise referred to as Tamilakam or Dravida. Recent researches indicate that there existed Tamil habitations in the and the Cholas extended their survey to which island.[2] However, the situation changed as a result of migrations and invasions. The western region of Tamilakam developed a cultural identity of its own with Malayalam as its language and become Kerala. With the Telugu settlement in the northern region adjoining the Tiruvenkadam Hills, Chittore and southern Nellore became parts of the Telugu speaking Andhra Desa. The rest of Tamilakam was constituted into a separate state in 1956, when the provinces of India were reorganized on linguistic basis and is at present called Tamil Nadu.[3]

Situated north of the equator with in the tropics Tamil Nadu with an area of 130357 square kilometers has retained it's Tamil identity. The eastern and southern shores are washed away by the seas. Though natural harbours are seldom, the land adequate rainfall. As a result terrible heat regions and renders life miserable in summer seasons. In November-December during winter the North East Monsoon brings in rain, that itself through cyclones and tempests causing considerable damage to life and property. The river systems are the Pennar, Kaverai, Vaigai, and Tampraparni but except the second all are dry during the most part because of its location on the high way of the seas between the East and West has attracted the attention of foreign traders, missionaries and invaders from the distant past. The coast is noted for its fishing grounds and pearl banks. The two mountain systems, the Eastern Ghats and the Western Ghats join at Nilgiris, making its terrain picturesque. However, as a rain shadow area the state seldom receives of the year. Total rainfall is about forty inches, quite inadequate for a tropical area. As a result the people living in most of the state are to make a precarious living, depending upon the monsoons which are not very dependable. Poverty, insecurity and labour intensive farming have contributed to the rise of moneylenders, middlemen, and chieftains exercising considerable influence on the economy of the common people.

Most of the population belong to the Dravidian stock, while the rest to the Adi Dravida and Aryan groups. Tamil is the popular language, yet a large section of the inhabitants has Telugu as their mother tongue. Most of the people follow Hindu religion, while others with Islam or Christianity. In early times Janism and Buddhism flourished in the Tamil Country, but they declined with the rise of Brahmanical of Hinduism by the nineth century. The Hindu society was caste based and as such it did not recognise equality of men. While the caste system contributed to distinctions among the people, the concept of fatalism created a situation favourable for the preservation of caste distinctions. When the ideal of human dignity and human equality, was lacking, it served as a philosophical justification for the acceptability of the idea of high and low. In consequence, the inhabitants were prepared to accept the status that they had.

The political life of the people was marked by ups and downs as in case of other peoples. The inscriptions in different languages-Tamil, Prakrit, Kannada, Telugu, Sanskrit and Persian as well as literary sources usually in Tamil, English and French shed light on the changing fortunes of the powers. Colin Mackenzie, Robert Sewell, V.Rangacharya, Burges and Natesa Sastri and a host of other scholars through their pains taking effort collected many of the records for preservation of historical evidences.[4] For the medieval period most of the sources are in Persian and Marathai languages. As many of these records are lost, it is not possible to have a comprehensive idea about the political situation of the period. The evidences that have survived restrict their scope to revenue and military transactions, as the state was yet to take a keen interest on socio-economic activity.

The Persian sources and the Marathi records that have survived, are preserved in Tamil Nadu State Archives, Madras, and Saraswathi Mahal Library at Thanjavur. The European records are much relevant to the study of the nature and extent of feudalism that developed and flourished in the Tamil Country through the subject was not treated as such. The Factory Records of the Dutch, the Danes, the French and the British tell of the local chiefs, but their primary concern was commercial transaction. However, as the British gained Political ascendancy, their records deal much about the feudal lords of the period, particularly the poligars and the zamindars of particular reference are their records coming under the categories of Political consultations, of the Board of Revenue, Military Consultations and the Sundries, belonging to different departments. However, all that they contain cannot be taken as true and balanced for at the most they represent different versions.

These sources throw considerable light on the making of the political system. They tell not only of the rulers but also of the feudatories and the land grants made by the rulers to varied agencies, contributing to the rise of a feudal order. The historical period of Tamilakam when rainfall is about forty inches, quite inadequate the Sanga begins with the Sangam Age, that is identified with the first three centuries of the Christian Era m classics were believed to have been composed.[5] The early history of the Tamils was centered on three ruling houses the Pandyas, the Cholas and the Cheras-collectively known as the *Muvendar* or three Crowned Kings. Madurai in the south, Thanjavur on the banks of the Kaveri and Vanchi on the west coast served as the respective centers of their authority. As these rulers established their empires, they had their capitals in different provinces too. In fact the historical trends in the Tamil Country were centered on the vicis situdes in the political fortunes of the three powers until external forces moved into the scene. The tradition is that the Early Pandays ruled over a vast empire but due to a deluge, a part of their country was lost to the sea. Nedunjelian II, the greatest among them, ruled over the country by 210 A.D. He defeated the Cholas and the Cheras and established the supremacy of the Pandyas over the Tamil Country. However, the Cholas led by their ruler Karikalan, asserted their authority over the Tamil Country, with the decline of the Pandyas. Among the powers of the Sangam age the Cheras were noted for their daring exploits. Senguttuvan, the most powerful of the Early Cheras, created a vast empire in South India and led expeditions to the north. However, frequent conflicts among the Tamil powers weakened them and prepared the ground for the Kalabra conquest by 250 A.D.

During the Sangam period monarcy appeared as an indispensable institution and it was endowed with absolute powers. The king was to give protection to his people and to safeguard their welfare. In the Sangam Literature there are no references to any popular resistance to the will of the monarch. This was because peace between the ruler and the ruled was stressed upon as that between father and son. Yet different chieftains held possession of vest tracts of land and exercised an independent or semi independent authority. Among them are mentioned the chiefs of Viyalur and Kalukar in the central region and the tribal lords of Velir, the Banaes, the Muttaraiyars and Kodumbalur.[6] Also there are references to Pari of Parambu, Cari of Kovalur and Adigaiman of Tagadur. These feudatories usually professed loyalty to one king or the other of the three ruling dynasties and served them in command of their levies. They had their strong holds in inaccessible terrains supported by their private forces, they maintained their influence. For want of information it is not possible to ascertain the nature of their relations with their subject population.

The Kalabras, who conquered Tamilakam from the Muvendar the Pandays, the Cheras and the Choles of the Sangam period, ruled over the Tamil County for three centuries. Believed to be of Kannada descent, they established themselves on the hill tracts of the north and subsequently moved into the plains. The ruling powers, the Pandyas and the Pallavas, sought to check their advance but were overwhelmed. With their seat of power at Kaveripatnam, the Kalabras subdued the three powers and extended their sway to Sri Lanka. They gave political unity to the Tamil Country and reorganised the administration on the basis of division and sub-division of their territories. The Kalbras retained possession to the land until they suffered defeat in their wars against the Pandyas and the Pallavas during the sixth century A.D. In view of the general paucity of source material it is not possible to know the feudal situation.

The period that followed witnessed the revival of the local powers-the Pandyas, the Pallavas, the Cheras and the Cholas. By 575 A.D. the Pandyas of Madurai and the Pallavas of Kanchi asserted their independence. Raja Simha, the ruler of the Pandyas, occupied Kongu Nadu in the north from the Pallavas, while another prince, Nedunjeliyan, suppressed the feudatories and consolidated his authority. The Pallavas in the meantime established themselves in the northern region of the Tamil Country and expended their conquests in the north. This brought them into a prolonged conflict with the Chalukyas of Vatapi, marked by invasions and counter invasions. The stuggle culminated in the Chalukya conquest of Kanchi and it led to the decline of the Pallavas. Though the Pallavas made their exit from power, they bequeathed a proud legacy of cultural achievements in architecture, arts and fine arts.

In the ninth century A.D., the Cholas taking advantage of the conflict between the Pandayas and the Pallavas, gained possession of the Kaveri delta. Before long, they occupied Tondaimandalm in the north and Kongu Nadu in the northwest. By 910 A.D. the Chola forces sacked Madurai and invaded the southern island of Sri lanka. The greatest among the imperial Cholas were Raja Raja I (985-1012 A.D) and Rajendra I (1012-1042 A.D) Under their able leadership the Cholas embarked upon imperial expansion and maritime glory. They conquered the most of the western coast from the Cheras and the northern region of Sri Lanka. As a result, the Cholas gained control of the western trade. As the Cheras and the Sinhalese sought to join in an alliance against the Cholas, Rajendra Chola found it essential to send a second expedition to the island. Accordingly the Chola army marched from Elam in Sri Lanka to the south, defeated the Sinhala forces, captured King Mahindra V. as prisoner and annexed the island with Empire by 1017 A.D. After this victory Rajendra Chola supported by the Chalukyas of Vengi, took the field against the Chalukyas of Vatapi, but suffered reverses. In a second battle he defeated the Chalukyas and made the Tungabhadra region secure. As the ruler of Kalinga supported the Western Chalukyas in this war the Cholas found it essential to undertake a major expedition to Orissa too. After defeating the Kalinga forces, the Chola army invaded Bengal and gained a victory oner the rulers, Dharmapala and Mahipala. To commemorate these exploits Rajendra Chola bulit a new capital and called it Gangai Konda Cholapuram. In the mean time there erupted a conflict over trade with Sri Vijaya in South East Asia. As the restrictions imposed upon Chola trade appeared humiliating a naval expedition was sent to the eastern islands. Kataram, the capital of Sri Vijaya, was sacked and the island was made a province of the Empire. This daring venture culminated in a good will mission to China in the interest of promoting trade. Military exploits and naval expeditions made the Empire extensive and wealthy. However, this trend could not be sustained by the later rulers. Internal conflicts and religious feuds between the Vaishnavites and Savites weakened the Empire. By 1279 the Pandyas defeated the Cholas and took possession of Thanjavur. This marked the end of the Chola Empire.

The political system of the Tamil Country under the Pallavas, the Cholas and the Pandyas was Marked by a feudal character. The empire was divided into *mandalams* or provinces province into districts or *Kottams* and district into groups of villages or madus. The Uttaramerur and Ukkal Inscriptions throw light on the working of local bodies. The head of the *nadu* was the *nattar.* As the villages and the *nadus* enjoyed local autonomy, the local chiefs wielded much influence and authority over the inhabitants. There are references to feudatories and tributaries. They collected taxes from the local people, gave them protection to the central authority. Thus the inscriptions dated in the third and twelfth years of Kulothunga Chola's region found at Kongur and Kiranur give the names of Sundaram Nilaiyudaiya Perumal, Udaiyar Viranarayana and Chola Narayana pallavarayan.[7] The inscriptions of Virarajendra Chola brings to light the names of several feudatories. Among them are mentioned Solem Lankeswaradeva and Uttama Chola Pallavarayann. In general these chieftains were called *samantas.*[8] The advent of Brahminical religion in the Tamil Country and the ascendancy of a Hindu priestly class contributed to the rise of a class of landlords, adding a new dimension to what could be called feudalism. The practice of making land grants to the Brahmin priests and their religious establishments called mutts marked a significant step towards feudalising the local economy. Such a custom was sanctified by the injunctions as laid down in the *Dharamasastras,* the didactic portions of the epics of *Ramayana* and *Mahabharata* and the *Puranas.*[9] In fact the *Anusaṣana Parva* of the Mahabharata devotes a whole chapter to the praise of making gifts of land to the Brahmins. Such a dictum was accepted by the rulers of India particularly after the fifth century A.D. If the Guptas adopted this practice in North India the Pallavas in the South. The Cholas, the Pandyas and even the rulers of petty states followed suit. The practice proceeded to such and extent that the rulers even up their administrative rights. Thus the state transferred to the donees all sources of revenue and surrendered administrative rights to the chieftains. Such a system prepared the ground for the rise of religious feudalism with the priests assuming the role of feudal lords.[10] The villages that were granted to the Brahmins either for their own benefit or to the temples for meeting expanses of wonshief were called *brahmadeya* and *devadana* respectively. The Brahmins collected the taxes from the inhabitants and even imposed forced labour, yet were not required to pay taxes to the rulers. In consequence the state lost a good part of the income while the Brahmin nobles lived a life of ease and comfort.[11] The rulers also granted villages to their relatives, vassals and officials, as a result of which the peasants were to pay rent for land and to render labour to these lords. In fact in medieval period land grants were considered as a regular mode of payment for religious and secular services almost all over the sub-continent.

The process of creating a class of landlords progressed together with the growth Brahmanical influence. The practice first surfaced in the western region of penisular India in the early period of the Christian Era, in central India by the fourth century, in eastern India by the fifth century, in Kalinga, in the sixth century, in Assam, in the seventh century, in the Tamil Country in the eight century and in Kerala in the ninth century.[12] Feudalism as a process of administrative decentralisation and political disintegration continued to work in the country. However, as a religious factor it suffered a check with the advent of the Muslim powers, for they cherished no consideration for what was ordained in the *Dharma sastras.*

Early in the fourteenth century the forces of the Sultanate of Delhi appeared in the far south. The expedition led by Malik Kafur, a general in the service of Sultan Ala-ud-din Khilji (1296-1316) after defeating the Yadavas of Devagiri, the Kakathyiyas of Warrangal and the Hoysalas of Dwarasamudra, entered the Tamil Country in 1311. The invading forces took a route so as to cover the great temples of Chidambaram, Srirangam, Madurai and Rameswaram. While the local rulers, the Pandyas, escaped to the wilderness, the Afghans looted the temples and bazaars. This expedition was followed by more of invasions, one by Khusru Khan and another by Uluz Khan. The invasions led to the rise of Madurai Sultanate by 1335. The Sultanate had a chequered history marked by frequent wars against the Hindu powers until it was destroyed by the forces of Vijayanagar in about 1378.[13]

Harihara II (1379-1406) the third ruler of Vijayanagar, organised the Tamil Country into a *mahamandala* or division under a *mahamandaleswara* or viceroy.

The capital of the division was located at Mullagal and subsequently at Chandragiri, situated on the southern slopes of the Thiruvenkadam Hills. The forces of Vijayanagar subdued the local powers, particularly the Sambuvarayas and the Afghans. However the emperor encountered wide spread resistance from the Tamil powers he sought to counter the opposition and to consolidate his authority, by instituting a feudal order spearheaded by what were called the *nayankars.* They entrusted the administration of territories with the nayankars in return for military service. Also they sought to accommodate the early ruling houses in the system. There survived local chieftains in possession of tracts of land but now they received regularisation of their status on condition of giving their loyalty. In addition as the inscriptions of the period indicate, the rulers resumed land grants to the Brahmins, creating a class of religious lords. A combination of these trends in the socio-political system tended to strengthen the feudal order in the land.

Krishna Deva Raya (1509-1530), the greatest of the sovereigns of Vijayanagar, reorgainsed the administration of the Tamil Country. He created a province in the extreme south with Madurai as the capital and Visvanatha Nayak as the governor. Achyuta Raya (1530-1542), the brother and successor of Krishna Deva Raya, formed Thanjavur into a separate province with Thanjavur as capital and Sevvappa Nayak as governor. Apart from them there came into existence the nayakships of Vellore and Senji. As auxiliary powers the nayaks asserted a semi-independent status in the sixteenth century when the Empire entered the path of decline.

Despite the ascendancy of the Nayak powers, the expeditions sent by Bijapur, Golkonda, Mysore the Maraths and the Moghuls greatly altered the political situation in the Tamil Country. On the decline of the Bahmini Kingdom in the Deccan it disintegrated into five sultanates-Bijapur, Golkonda, Ahmadnagar, Berar and Bidar. The combined forces of these sultanates won a signal victory over the army of Vijayanagar in the battle near Talikotta in 1565. This gave the signal to the disintegration of Vijayanagar Empire. While Bijapur and Golkonda occupied the northern region of the Tamil Country, the Nayaks of Madurai, Thanjavur and Senji established their independence in the southern region. The other feudatories, particularly of Vellore, Ramnad and Sivaganga, too gained a status of independence. There followed the Moghal invasion of Arcot and the Maratha occupation of Senji in 1677 and Thanjavur in 1676. The advent of the European powers added to the complexity of the socio- political trends. The resultant situation enabled the feudatories to consolidate their influence. It also contributed to the rise of feudal powers as at Vellore and Jinji. The Marathas in Tamil Country as per the *Sastras* made liberal donation of land to the temples and to the Brahmin habitats called *agraharas*. Such a Policy strengthened the feudal trends at work, creating more of lords and more of tenants.

Between the years 1685 and 1688 the forces of the Moghul Emperor, Aurangzeb(1656-1707), conquered Bijapur and

Golkonda and extended their influence in the Tamil region. Zulficar Khan, the Moghul general, received contributions from the Nayak and Maratha Powers,[14] Zulficar Khan was appointed Nawab or deputy of the Emperor with headquarters at Arcot in 1694. On the decline of the Moghul Empire, Sadat-ullah-Khan, a successor of Zulficar Khan, asserted his independence at Arcot. He belonged to the Navayet Dynasty. Nevayets ruled over Arcot up to 1744, When Anwar-ud-din usurped power and established the rule of his house, in the Wallajahs. The conflict between the Nevayets and the Wallajahs not only weakened the central authority at Arcot but also contributed to the ascendancy of the feudal powers. It also invited foreign intervention, the French on the side of the Nevayets represented by Chanda Sahib, while the English on the side of the Wallajahs represented by Mohammad Ali. The consequent civil war known in history as the second Carnatic War(1751-1756) marked a turning point in the history of feudalism as well as imperialism. To finance the war the Nawab of Arcot required money for which he turned to the feudal powers—the nayaks and the poligars. However, money could be collected only by force for which he required the support of the British. The more the support he took, the moredependent he became to the English East India Company. In consequence a commercial power, as the Company was, transformed itself into a political and imperial power, fighting a war in alliance with the Nawab for the suppression of the feudal forces.

Administration

By mid eighteenth century administration of the country presented no uniformity or order. Sovereignty rested with the Moghul Emperor and subsequently with the Nawab, but the sub-ordinate chiefs known as rajas, nayaks and poligars exercised a large degree of independence in their respective territories. Such political division, whether big or small, ruled by a prince of significant or insignificant note, was called *samastan*. Thus Thanjavur and Ramnad were referred to as *Samstans*. The government of samstan was called the circar.[15] In each province there were two establishments-one revenue and the other military, as in the Mughal Empire. The *amuldar* handled the revenue administration, while the *foujdar* the military establishment.[16] In a princely state the *rajah* handled the administration. He was assisted by a council of advisers or chiefs, usually consulted for decisions of policy.[17] Nevertheless the minister, know as *sirkeel* in Thanjavur, Karyakarta in Pudukkottai and dewan or pradhani in the Marava states of Ramnad and Sivaganga served as the chief adviser to the rajah. The other principal officers were the military commander, the chief revenue administrator, the finance secretary, the chief accountant and the royal secretary. The correspondence was carried on in Persian, the official language, though Marathi and Tamil were also in use.[18] This administrative institutions, whether they were in the provinces or in the feudal estates in their working , were left without checks and balances.

Each province had sub-divisions called by different names-*taluk* in the circar country and the Marava palayams *subah* in Thanjavur, *valanadu* in Pudukkottai and *nadu* in Kallar Nadu. The chief administrator of the district was the tahsildar, also known as *taluqdar, killedar, amil* and even as *subedar* while in a poligar estate he was the poligar. In Kallar nadu a council of elders presided by a tribal chief called *nattar* managed the administration. Each district consisted of groups of villages known as *parganas* or *mahans.*[19]

No regular or uniform method of remunerating the public servants remained in force. The servants received salaries, rent free lands or jagir,[20] the right to collect fees on certain goods passing through a place or a share of the taxes as their allowance.[21] In jagirs the administrators called *jagirdars* exercised vast powers as feudal lords in their estates did.[22] Certain trends in the governmental system are to be noted. The political set up inclined toward absolutism. The rajah or the poligar succeeded to power by the right of inheritance. The inhabitants favoured kingships, though in Kallar Nadu they obeyed the council of elders. The Maravas venerated the *setupati,* ruler of Ramnad, considering him as the guardian of the sacred waters and the Pagoda of Rameswaram.[23] The chief officers at times, accumulated for themselves the allotments made for paying their servants and left the latter free to exact their allowances from the ryots. These practices rendered the administration oppressive. The inhabitants as a result turned to the local chiefs for protection.[24]

All the chiefs of any consequence maintained their own armed establishments. The nayaks, nawabs, jagridars, rajahs poligars and amuldars kept bodies of regular forces or bands of armed med. The sovereign, did not enforce this right as his prerogative. The military establishment of the nawab or the rajah consisted of infantry, cavalry, carriage-bullocks, a few elephants and often a corps of artillery. The troops were of two categories, the regulars in the service of the rulers and the irregulars furnished by subordinate chiefs now and then.[25]

Different forms of tenure remained in force, of which some were joint and others individual. The joint tenures were the *Veesabudi,* and the *aumani,* while the individual one were the *rendal* and the *poligari*. Under joint tenure the peasants held the lands under common assessment. The veesabudi was a village assessment by which the peasants by arrangement among themselves paid the assessed tax for the whole area in ready money. The-*aumani* too was a village settlement by which the cultivators shared the produce in such a proportion as to make good the total assessment for the village. These forms did not very much in substance, for the villages were treated as units and the landholders were collectively held responsible for the payment of tax. The individual tenures were based upon the principle of individual responsibility. The nayaks, poligars and renters collected taxes and paid a fixed amount to sovereign. While the nayak and the poligar held the estates on a hereditary basis with right to alienate any part of it, the renders held the land for a settled term with no right to alienate any part there of.[26]

The assessment on land varied from to time. The Hindu law of ancient India permitted the state to collect one-sixth and even one-fourth of the produce as its share. On the otherhand the Mohammadan law allowed the ruler to take one half of the produce as his share and from the infidels more. However, these concepts seldom found their beneficial application in the administration of the land. The accepted principle of the country was to share the produce in the ratio 50:50. This was done after making a deduction of 5 per cent on account of the expense of harvest. A local tax paid to the villages claimed about 25 per cent of the ryot's share of the produce. The rest went to the peasants. In practice these principles too never found any strict observance. In fact the economic and political considerations caused fluctations in the rates of division. The rulers allowed to the peasants up to 58 per cent of the produce of the lands that were subject to water logging and up to 60 per cent in the lands irrigated by wells.[27] Yet in practice the share of the peasants worked at a very low level. To promote exaction, the revenue servants applied force and violence day after day. In every public office whips, scourges, thumb screws and other instruments of ordeals were regularly and freely applied on the unhappy subjects.[28] In short the ryot the husbandman, the manufacturer, the artificer, and every other inhabitant lived at the mercy of these ministers of exaction, whether it was in a feudal estate or circar lands.[29] Yet in consideration of communal identity and local affinity many of the inhabitants turned to the feudal powers for succour.

Though the collection of taxes was effected through force and violence, the rulers made no attempt to practice rigid economy or to enforce strict check on spending. There was no idea of budget. The feudal chiefs, amuldars and revenue officials who collected the taxes met the items of expenditure on the spot and sent to the ruler if at all any balance remained.[30] This naturally gave scope for corruption. The ancient privileges of the chiefs and concessions granted to religious institutions were rated much higher than what were warranted. The titles of expenses were so joined as to afford pleas and means of secreting and appropriating a great part of the revenue to purposes other than those appeared reasonable.[31] These practices betrayed an almost neglect of financial accountability and gave latitude for every species of fraud.

Judical administration received no serious attention of the rulers, though the feudal lords and public servants heard and settled the cases. The chiefs were the principal judges of their respective estates. In Kallar Nadu the headman and the council of elders administered justice. In the province this was not really a part of the duty of the amuldar or renter. Still he assumed this function evidently because it served his vested interests.[32] The administration of justice was indeed haphazard and marked by irregularity and abuse. The general form and content of jurisprudence was to overrate the pretensions of the superior castes, thus ignoring the principle of equality before law.[33] The poor were refused protection against the despotic violence of the influential people. Any person who wielded some power, tied up and tortured the unfortunate inhabitants on the most frivoulous pretenses but no law took him to task. In the absence of any respect for human rights, the administration of justice was clubbed with revenue. No judicial training was provided. Judges were recruited from the different sections of the population without any discrimination as to their previous training and employment. Judicial service was open to men of different shades, ranging from the clerks to military and revenue officers. Jagirdars, bankers, and physicians occupied the judicial offices, though the Hindu Jurisprudence requires that the judges should be pandits who studied law. Thus the renters and amuldars who had no knowledge of jurisprudence were given the right to decide cases in a crude and summary way. These circumstances together with depredations by free booters made it essential for the inhabitants to seek the protection of feudal lords and render to them services. It was in such a situation the feudal institutions emerged and flourished.[34]

Source of Information

This thesis draws its inspiration from source materials that are available both in Tamil and English. The available materials are classified as Primary as well as Secondary sources. Among the primary sources the epigraphical records and the Madras Government Records constitute the primary source of information for the history of history of British relation with the Tamil country. Next in importance come the Diaries,

Reports and various district Collectorate Records. District Manuals, Gazetters and the Handbooks prepared by the public officials and Tamil Districts largely form secondary sources.

The Records of the Madras Government kept preserved in the Tamil Nadu Archives, Chennai, furnish a wide range of information. They come under different categories, the principal of which are the Proceedings of the Madras Council, Fort St. David Consultations, Sundries, Country Correspondence and Despatches to and from England. The proceedings of the Madras Council called Consultation furnish a comprehensive account of the various official transactions including the views of the members and their decisions. The Sundries form a miscellaneous collection of records related to political or commercial affairs. The branch of records called the country correspondence enclose among other things English translations of the letters written mostly in Marathi, Persion and Tamil sent to and received from the rulers of the Tamil Country or agents of the English East India Company. Despatches from London to Madras contain instructions of the Board of Directors to the Madras Council and their letters of approval or disapproval of what thier representatives at Madras did or proposed to do. Despatches from Madras to London, on the other hand, deal in general with the official proceedings of the Madras Council. Reports relating to the political and military activities of the native rulers complied with the collectorate records of Tamil districts have been sources of infalliable guidance for this scholarly venture. Various facts available in the records of different departments are also utilised for making an estimate of this study.

Another important source material is the Private Diaries of Ananda Ranga Pillai, originally written in Tamil, but translated into English and published in twelve volumes between 1904 and 1924 by the Government of Madras enclose notices on military events, political transactions , commercial policy, social habits and family matters.

The Jesuits Letters kept preserved in the Jesuit Archives, Shenbaganur, Kodaikannal, furnish a wide range of information. The Jesuits Annual Letters are available in the form of La

Mission Du Madura in four volumes. Originally, these letters were written in Latin and were translated with French by Father J. Bertrand of the society of Jesus. Some of the relevent portions of the La Mission Du Madura have been translated into English by R.Sathiyanatha Aiyar. This material has been of immense value to have a perception of the feudalistic elements of the *Nayankara* and *Palaiyakara* systems.

The different branches of the sources furnish wholesome accounts of the British transactions with the Native rulers. But they are not free from bias. The occurance of coloured statements, twisted accounts, flattering pleasantries, false claims and mutal accusations demand caution. However, through the application of criticism of evidence and corroboration of facts, it has been found possible to reconstruct the history of the Tamil country. Though misscellaneous Tamil ballads, celebrating the historical events, contribute to the study of the palaiyakaras in regard to their military system. Works like *Ramappaiyan Ammani, Panjalamkurichi Azhivucharithirakummi, Sivagangai Charithirakummi, Kattabomman Varalaru* and *Khan Sahib Sandai* throw light not only on the Socio-economic life of the period but also on the military activities of Palaiyakars.

Among the Secondary sources no work seems to have so far made an attempt to study the history of The Tamil Country's transition from feudalism to imperialism. Yet it cannot be denied that a few published works deal to a much limited extent with one aspect or other of the history of the Tamil country. Among them are to be mentioned R.Sewell's *A Forgotten Empire,* R.Sathiyanatha Aiyar's *History of the Nayaks of Madura,* Fr. Hentry Hera's *The Aravidu Dynasty of Vijayanagara,* T.V. Mahalingam's *Sounth Indian Polity,* A. Krishnaswami's *The Tamil Country Under Vijayanayar,* R. Caldwell's *A History of Tinnevelly,* H.R. Pate's *Tinnevelly Gazetteer,* K. Rajayyan's *Rise And Fall of The Poligars of Tamil Nadu, South Indian Rebellion, A history of British Diplomacy in Tanjore and History of Madurai* have been well-defined sources of ample information for a proper reconstruction of the historical facts. Gazetteers, Manuals Journals, Weeklies and Dailies have also provided valuable information for validation a host of historical facts. A critical analysis and a comparative study of these different sources and the corroboration of evidences, give a full fleged accounts to finalise this thesis.

Notes and References

1. E.M. Burns and P.L. Ralph (1964), *World Civilizations,* Vol. I, 3rd Edition, Norton and Co. INC. New York, pp. 407-8.
2. Ponnambalam Regupathy (1987), *Early settlements in Jaffna,* Madras , pp. 179-81.
3. In 1956 South Travancore in Kerala was merged with the Tamil areas. The reorgainsed state was called Madras State and since 1957 as Tamil Nadu. (B. Maria John, *Linguistic Reorganisation of Madras Presidency,* Nagercoil, 1994, pp. 78-93.)
4. Colin Mackenzie noted down the inscriptions in his *Collections,* Robert Sewell in his *Lists of Antiquities,* V. Rangacharya in his *Inscriptions of the Madras Presidency* and Burgess and Natesa Sastri in their *Tamil and Sanskrit Inscriptions.* Their works are found of inestimable value for historical research.
5. Among the historians there are differences of opinion on the age of Tamil classics. However on the basis of a comparative study of Sangam literature with the Thevarem Songs and the synchronism of Senguttuvan, the Chera prince, and Gajabahu of Sri Lanka this conclusion about the chronology of Sangam classics, that is first to third centuries is arrived at. Sangam is form the word *sanga* which means academy. Pathupattu on Ten Idylls, Ettuthohai or the Eight Anthologies, the Tirukkural, Silappadikaram and Manimekalai are the well known works of the classical period of the Tamils.
6. M.S. Govindasamy (1965), *The Role of Feudatories in Pallava History,* Annamalai University, Annamalainagar, pp. 1, 38, 71-112.
7. K.V. Subrahmanya Aiyer (1967), Historical Sketches of Ancient Dekhan, Vol. II, The Co-operative Printing Press, Coimbatore, p. 72.
8. *Ibid.,* p. 80.
9. Dharma Sastras enunciate customary laws and practices. They held forth threats of terrible punishments for any infringement of duties. While Ramayana deals with the exploits of Sri Rama, Mahabharata with the war between two Aryan tribes, Kauravas

and Pandavas. The Puranas, another literature of the Aryans, tell of creation of world, geneology of gods, ages of Manu and history of dynastics.

10. R.S. Sharma (1980), *Indian Feudalism*, The MacMillan Co., Madras, pp. 1-5.
11. K. Rajayyan (1993), *Early Tamil Nadu*, Ratna Publications, Rajambadi, Madurai, p. 65.
12. R.S. Sharma, *op.cit.*, p. 215.
13. Kumara Kampana, son of Emperor Bukka Raja of Vijayanagar, defeated the forces of the Sultanate in the battles, fought at Srirangam and Madurai and destroyed the Mohammadan power in the far south.
14. According to the political tradition of the land, payment of a feudal contribution did not mean acceptance of a status of vassalage. In fact an auxiliary power refused payment when he felt himself so powerful and yielded when he appeared helpless.(Madras Council, Military Consultations, 6 May 1771, Vol. 39, pp. 382-383.)
15. Burhan *Tuzak-i-Walajahi*, Madras, 1939, Part I, pp. 131-132 and Part IV, p. 187 (ed. by M.H. Nainar, S.).
16. J. Sarkar, *The Mughal Administration*, p. 58.
17. Military Country Correspondence, Fort St. George, 17 July 1791, Vol. 42, p. 55.
18. Madras Council, Revenue Consultations, February 1796, para 83.
19. B.S. Ward, *Geograhical and Statistical Memoir of the Provinces of Madurai and Dindigul*, Madras, 1895, Vol. III, P. 60.
20. The word *Jagir* means an allowance of land given in lieu of many in order to enable one to meet his public or private charges.
21. The Muhgal Emperors made it a practice to grant large districts as jagirs to influential men and ask them to maintain a fixed number of troops supported by the revenue theron. It was in fact an aspect of the Poligar system. Lord Hobart, the governor of Fort St,Geroge, when he asked the Nawab to assign territory for maintaining an army for the defence of the Cornatic,cited the example of jagir. (Madras Council, Military Consultations, 23 October 1795). In the subsidiary system of lord Wellesley the same principle in a magnified proportion could be noted.

22. Report on the Triuvendipuram Farm, 1775, p. 7.
23. Military Sudries, 13 August 1784, Vol. 66, p. 17.
24. Fort St. Geroge (1787), Military Country Correspondence, 10 April, Vol. 36, p. 65.
25. Radhakrishna Iyer (1916), A General History of the Pudukkottai State, Pudukkottai, p. 241.
26. Madras Council, Revenue Consultations, 4 September 1799, Vol. 96, para 1-7.
27. Selections from the Records of the Collectorate of Tirchinopoly, 1867, p. 34.
28. Fort St. Geroge (1785), Military Sundries, Vol. 66, p. 226.
29. *Ibid.*, p. 218.
30. Persian Records, State Archives Madras, Bundle 9, No. 95.
31. Proceedings of the Committees of Assigned Revenue, 27 May 1782.
32. Proceedings of the Board of Assigned Revenue, 20 November 1780.
33. Fort St. Geroge, Military Sundry Book, Vol. 40, P. 93.
34. Madras Council, Military Consultations, 9 November 1790, Vol. 140, p. 4135.

FOREWORD

Dr. V. Ranjan in the present treatise "The Tamil Country: Transition from Feudalism to Imperialism A.D. 1751 to 1816", discusses the history of the relation between the central authority represented by the Nawab of Arcot and the Feudal interests represented by the Poligars and Zamindars. The Madras Government of the English East India Company through a settlement with the Nawb in 1792 brought the poligars under its direct authority and launched against them a series of expeditions. In 1816 the British destroyed the feudal authority and brought the country under a unified system. This transition was of considerable significance to the political, social and economic life of the people. Awarded Ph.D. degree in 2000 the work represent a significant and original contribution to historical scholarship on South India.

Endowed with high academic attainment and considerable experience in research Dr. V. Ranjan was eminently qualified to undertake a project of this kind. As a research scholar in the Department History, Manonmaniam Sundaranar University, Tirunelveli, he gained specialization that the mobilized for data collection and analysis. Accordingly he visited the Jesuits Archives, Shembaganur, Kodaikanal, Kerala State Archives, Trivandrum and Tamilnadu Archives, Chennai and made a comprehensive and patient study of original source. A glance at the work suggests that he made an interpretative study of research material and presented them cogently from the Tamil country: Transition from Feudalism to Imperialism. The entire work is well documented and properly illustrated. Language is pleasant to read what adds to the credit of the author is that he has adhered to historical method.

The work consists of Ten chapters in addition to Introduction and Conclusion, while Nayankara System is examined in chapter I, poligars and their overlords, feudal orders of the poligars, conflict of interests and British Intervention in chapter II to V. The British Daul system stresses and strains drift to Imperial Sway. Resistance movement and its violent end are discussed in chapter II to VIII. The British Revenue settlement Zamindari to Ryotwari and law and order system are discussed in chapter IX to X. These trends and issues are discussed in this work with historical objectivity.

Being an in-depth study of the history of the Tamil country: Transition to Feudalism to Imperialism, the work is intimate relevance to the promotion of social understanding, cultural and political integration. As such this is an essential contribution for the benefit of scholars and administrators. Dr. V. Ranjan deserves credit for bringing out this work in its present form for the benefit of scholars and readers.

Place: Tirunelveli
Date: 30-4-2008

B. Maria John,
M.A., M.A., M.Phil, Ph.D.
Director & Professor of History
Centre for Gandhian Studies
Manonmaniam Sundaranar University
Tirunelveli-627012

CHAPTER - 1

NAYANKARA SYSTEM

In the Evolution of a feudal system in the Tamil Country the organisation of the Nayankara system represented a significant event. By 1465 A.D. the forces of Vijayanagar Empire overran the southern region, defeated the Sambuvarayas of Tondaimandalam and the Afghans of Madurai and annexed the Tamil provinces. In view of the local opposition the Emperors needed the support of loyal chiefs, who were ready to serve them in times of war as well as in peace. Also they wanted to win over the allegiance of local chieftains and descendants of ancient ruling houses for the consolidation of their authority. These considerations led them to reorganise the administration on a feudal basis and the result was the rise of the Nayankara system. However, with the decline of Vijayanagar Empire the Nayankara system transformed itself into the independent Nayak monarchies of Jinji, Thanjavur and Madurai.

The Vijayanagar inscriptions frequently refer to the term *Nayankara*. Which is an abbreviation of *amaranayankara*, which in turn is composed of the words *amara, nayaka* and *kara*. 'Amara' was used to denote command of a thousand foot soldiers and subsequently it was taken to mean a grant of land by the sovereign to a feudal chief-whether he was a *nayaka* or a *poligar*. Nayaka was a lord or chief and *kara* was probably an office. In short *amaranayaka* referred to an estate granted to a chief for military service. Nearly three fourths of the land in the Tamil country was held by the military chiefs on *Nayankara* tenure. The Emperor of Vijayanagar divided the territory into what were called *amarams* or *nayakkattanams* and granted them to his chieftains in condition of military service. This practice was based upon the medieval doctrine that the king was the owner of all the land in his country and as such he had the right to divide into estates and distribute them among his dependents. Nuring a foreign traveller, has observed "All the land belongs to the king and from his hand the captains hold it. They make it over to the husbandmen who pay 9/10 of the income to their Lord and they have no land of their own, for the kingdom belongs entirely to the king".[1]

In return for the grant of an estate the nayaka was required to provide for the defence of the kingdom. He remitted half of the revenue from his estate to the Emperor and with the rest of the revenue he maintained a fixed number of armed men, horses and elephants for service to the ruler in times of war. Usually he collected nine tenths of the gross produce of the land as his share and permitted the tenants to retain, only one tenth. As a result the nayaks lived in luxury while the tillers of the soil in perpetual poverty. In the opinion of the foreign traveller Nuniz the nayaks paid about half of their gross income to the state. "the lands, they say yield of hundred and twenty lakhs of which they must pay sixty to the king and the rest they retain for the pay of the soldiers and the expanses of the elephants which they are obliged to maintain".[2] In fact the nayaks had to maintain a certain number of foot men, horses and elephants and contribute their services to the Emperor, in times of war. In addition to these. on ceremonial occasions like the birth of a child or a wedding in the imperial household the nayaks, as it was the practice with the barons of medieval Europe, had to make costly presents and attend the functions. Paes tells "Whenever a son happens to be born to this king or a daughter, all the nobles of the kingdom offer him great presents of money and jewels of price and so they do him every year on the day of his birth."[3] These manifold customs and services demanded proper representation. of the feudatories in the capitalcity. Accordingly, the nayaks stationed two officers at the imperial court, a military agent in charge of the feudal army and a representative called *sthanapati* to safeguard the interests of his master in the court and to keep the nayak informed of the developments in the capital.

In return for the collections that the nayaks made, they had to render certain services to the inhabitants. As guardians of peace and order they were to give protection to the people against invaders, freebooters and robbers, defect crimes and administer justice. The police duties were entrusted to the subordinate chiefs called the Poligars. They were also expected to clean the forests, provide for irrigation and promote cultivation. Yet it cannot be denied that their administration was marked by oppression and exaction without which it was not possible for them to raise the resources as required for their pomp and imperial demands.[4]

The Emperor appointed governors called *mahamandaleswares* for territorial divisions called *rajyas*. As representatives of the Emperor, they controlled the nayaks and supervised the maintenance of feudal lords. In fact the Emperor sought to exercise his control over the nayaks through his own governors and through the representatives of the nayaks in his court. Yet they were left free in the internal administration of their estates.

Krishna Deva Raya (1509-1580 A.D) on his accession as Emperor of Vijayanagar found the nayaks of the Tamil Country in a state of insubordination. Therefore he sent an army against the nayak powers, subdued them, collected tribute-and reorganised the administration. He divided the Tamil Country into three nayakships-Jinji extending from Nellore in the north to river Kollidam in the south, Thanjavur spread over the Kaveri delta and Madurai extending from the Kaveri in the north to the seas in the south. The tribute from the nayakships was refixed at one third of the produce instead of one half and worked out the poliger system into a feudal organisation.[5] By this process he sought to develop an internal cheek the feudal set up. By the time of emperor Achyuta Raya (1529-1542 A.D) there come into existence some 200 nayaks-major as well as minor powers. Among them three emerged to provenience they were Jinji, Thanjavur and Madurai, for they had vast territories and extensive resources. Under these feudal lords the Tamil

Country had a chequered history, marked by conflicts and wars. There came conflicts with the imperial power as well as wars among themselves. If the nayaks failed in their duties, the Emperor could not be enforced when he himself became weak and his survival depended upon the auxiliary powers. As mentioned earlier, in 1565 the Bahmini sultans of the Deccan administered a severe defect on Vijayanagar in the battle field near Tailkota. Since then they conquered the northern provinces and forced the rulers of Vijayanagar to flee to Penukonda. The consequent decline of the imperial system extended an opportunity to the nayaks to assert their independence. The nayankara system lost its feudal character, when it transformed itself into a monarchical order. Since this transformation, the lesser nayaks called the Poligars came to occupy the status of the nayaks as a feudal order in the nayak polity.

The following account brings out the role of the nayak powers and sheds light on the nature and extent of the transformation.

Nayak Monarchies

Jinji, otherwise known as Senji or Gingee, occupied Tondaimandalam-the northern region of the Tamil Country. Because of its strategic location the generals of Vijayanagar built a fort on an old Chola foundation and made it the seat of their power. As it grew into an important station, Emperor Krishna Deva Raya made it the headquarters of the province, with Vaiyappa Nayak as the administrator. This marked the rise of the first nayak kingdom in the Tamil country.

Epigraphical sources indicate that Vaiyappa Nayak founded the nayakship in 1526 A.D. However scholars do not agree on the question whether he continued to rule or not. C.S. Srinivasachari is of the view that Vaiyappa Nayaka, after consolidating his conquests, entrusted the administration of Jinji with his associate, Tubaki Krishnappa Nayaka and returned to the imperial capital. Therefore he considers Tubaki as the real founder of the Jinji line of nayaks.[6] But A. Krishnaswami on the basis of inscriptional evidences found at

Jambai in South Arcot district and Kalavagunta in Chittoor district suggest that Vaiyappa Nayak continued to make donations to temples and to build *agraharas* for the Brahmins up to 1541 A.D. Hence it is reasonable to belive that he continued to administer the country upto this period or beyond. The successor of Vaiyappa is mentioned as Pedda Krishnappa in the inscriptions of the period, as Tubaki Krishnappa in Machenize Manuscripts and simply as Krishnappa in the ballad on the history of Jinji. The lates rulers are listed differently in different records. The Mackenzie Manuscripts give their names as Ramachandra Nayaka. Muthialu Nayaka and Venkatappa Nayak, who was also called as Krishnaappa Nayaka. These early rulers of Jinji strengthened the fortifications, improved the temples, patronised learning and consolidated their conquests, yet much of their history is not known.[7]

Krishnappa Nayaka II (1570-1601), the most powerful of the Nayaks of Jinji was a contemporary o Emperor Venkata I of Vijayanagar and of Raghunatha Nayaka of Thanjavur. A Jesuit letter dated 1606 tells of him as the most powerful of the Nayak rulers of the Tamil Country for it reads: "He of Gingee was the most powerful and he had divided his dominions among smaller Nayaks. The rulers at Vellore, Tiruvati and Devakota were his feudatories".[8] Depicted as a liberal ruler, he built towns for the settlement of people, promoted cultivation, granted toleration to all religions and maintained a powerful army. After erecting a town called Krishnapathnam on the bank of river Vellar, he invited the followers of different religions to settle there. A man of catholic views, he gave gifts to the Jesuits for building a church, permitted the Jains to erect a shrine at Sittanur and allowed the Saivites to construct a temple at Tindivanam. Father Piementa of the Jesuit Mission on his way from Cochin to San Thome visited the Nayak Country, covering the distance on foot. He found Jinji as the greatest city that he had seen in India, bigger than any in Portugal except Lisbon. Granted audience by the ruler at Chidambaram and Jinji he recorded his impressions. He Wrote: the Nayak "commanded that we should be brought to his presence. Before us 200 Brahmins went in rank to springle the house with holy water and to prevent sorcey against the king."[9]

Taking advantage of the disintegration of Vijayanagar Empire Krishnappa Nayak sought to assert his independence. Because of the aggressions committed by Bijabur and Golkonda, Venkata I was preoccupied with the defence of the northern frontiers. The Nayak chief sought to utilise the occasion to assert his independence, but was defeated in battle and imprisoned.[10] During the imprisonment of Krishnappa the Vijayanagar general Venkata administered Jinji. He dug out a large tank called Chennasagaram for promoting irrigation. It was from his descendants, Venkatappa of Vandavasi and Ayyappa of Poonamalle, that the English acquired Possession of Madraspatnam. The forces of Bijapur defeated the last ruler and occupied Jinji in 1649. The Nayakship of Thanjavur came into existence by the year 1532 A.D. The Telugu works, *Thanjavur Andhra Rajalu Charitra* and the *Thanjavuri Vari Charitra* make it clear that Sevappa Nayaka obtained Possession of this Chola Country by about 1532 A.D. as his dowry, for he married the sister of one of the queens of Emperor Achyuta Raya of Vijayanagar. Sevappa Nayak thus became the founder of the nayak line rulers of Thanjavur. His territory included Thanjavur and-part of the present day district of South Arcot. Tirichirapalli formed part of his province but he exchanged it with Madurai for gaining possession of Vallam, perhaps with imperial sanction. He assisted the Emperor in the wars against the Portuguese and the Rajah of Travancore and subsequently against the Bahmini power in the battle at Talikota.

In 1580 Achyutappa Nayaka (1560-1600) succeeded his father, Sevappa Nayaka, to the throne. Despite the defect that Vijayanagar suffered in the Battle of TAlikota in 1565, Thanjavur continued to remain loyal to the Empire and to pay tribute. The Pudukkottai place dated Saka 1505 indicates that Achyutappa supported Vijayanagar in defeating the forces of Madurai at Vallamprakara (Vallam). This led to bitter rivalry between the two nayak powers-Thanjavur and Madurai. In a war with the Portuguese he supported the ruler of Jaffna, but the latter was defeated and forced to seek refuge in Thanjavur.

After this humiliation he devoted himself to religious pursuits. At the expanse of the peasants he too founded *agraharas* and made gifts to the Brahmins. It is pointed out that he instituted free feeding to a thousand Brahmins every day. Inspite of his attempt to win the favour of delities through charitable activities, he had no peaceful reign for it was marked by repeated wars and disorders. He died in 1614, being succeeded by his son, Raghunatha Nayaka.[11]

Raghunatha Nayaka(1600-1634) a contemportsry of Krishnappa II of Jinji was the most powerful of the nayaks of Thanjavur. He distinguished himself as an able general and sagacious ruler. his early wars were fought in defence of the Empire. Due to his loyalty to Venkata I, he fought against the forces of Golkonda, which committed aggression upon Vijayanagar and against the forces of Madurai in the battle of Topur. The victories that he gained in these battles made him the most powerful feudatory under Vijayanagar. He also led an expedition against Solaga, chief the coastal area against the Portuguese in Jaffna. It is believed that Solaga was the ruler of a territory situated north of the river, Kollidam. Supported by the Nayak of Jinji, he created disturbances in Thanjavur. In consequences the forces of Raghunatha Nayak attacked the rebel stronghold and forced Solanga to surrender. After this victory, the forces of Thanjavur fought against the Portuguese in Ceylon. The ruler of Jaffna, being defeated and expelled from his kingdom by the Portuguese, sought the support of Thanjavur. Accordingly, from Devakottai Raghunatha Nayak advanced with his army along the sea coast, crossed the Gulf of Mannar by a chain of boats, attacked and defeated the Portuguese and reinstated the king of Jaffna.

However, this victory proved momentary, for the Portuguese returned in strength and re-occupied Jaffna. The forces of Thanjavur that reached again in support of Jaffna suffered defeat and retreated. Despite this reverse, the reign of Raghunatha Nayaka witnessed an expansion of overseas trade. The period was marked by a keen competition among European merchants for ascendary in the eastern market. Because of intrigues and repression the local powers sought to expel the Portuguese and often Aided with the Dutch. From Raghunatha Nayaka the Dutch acquired possession of Tegnapatam by 1610 A.D. The Danes too obtained permission to establish a settlement in his country. In 1620 they founded Danesborg at Tarangambadi. By 1622 they built a fort at this place and captured a large volume of trade. The success gained by the Danes prompted the English to seek a foot hold in the kingdom. Attracted by the good and cheap cloth painted in different colours and believing that this coast produced plenty of pepper, they wanted to open a factory at Karaikal. But by experience they found the Nayak "very covetous expecting very great presents yearly". Also pepper was not available in any large quantity. Because of these considerations and Portuguese intrigues, they abandoned their attempt. Nevertheless, it appears that Raghunatha Nayaka encouraged the different European powers to share the country's trade with a view to keeping them in mutual competition for safeguarding his interests. As the other Nayak did, Raghunatha Nayaka too made large gifts of land to the Brahmins and enabled them to possess large estates, contributing to what could be called religious feudalism.

On the death of Raghunatha Nayaka, this his son Vijayaraghava succeeded to the throne. Inspite of the preoccupation of Vijayanagar with the wars against the Deccani powers, he remained loyal to the Emperor, Venkatapati II and Sriranga III and extended support. However, he neglected the welfare of his people and spent his time in constant worship. Greatly encouraged, the forces of Bijapur and Madurai ravaged the country, as the result of which the inhabitants suffered terribly. Ultimately the Nayak himself died in a battle, fought against the Madurai army. The last ruler of the dynasty was Chengamaladas from whom the Marathas gained possession of the territory and founded their own monarchy.[12]

Another feudal estate that developed into a kingdom was Madurai. It is believed that Emperor Krishna Deva Raya in the last year of his reign,(1529-1530) organised the Nayakship of Madurai. Beginning with Visvanatha Nayaka (1529-1564)Madurai experienced the rule of numerous nayaks.

Visvanatha Nayaka fought a series of wars against the Tamil powers. Ariyanatha Mudali ably assisted his master in his wars against the Pancha Pandyas of Tiruneveli and in the reduction of the local powers to submission. In 1564 krishnappa Nayak I (1564-1572) succeeded his father Viswanatha to power. He sent an army under Ariyanatha Mudali to the aid of the Empire against the Muslim powers of the Deccan, but it fled during the battle of Talikota. There followed several other nayaks in the line. They were Virappa Nayaka (1572-1595), Krishnappa Nayaka II (1585-1601) Muthu Krishna Nayaka (1601-1609) and Mutha Virappa Nayaka I (1609-1623). As Usual their administration was marked by wars and conflicts as well as donations and gifts as a result of which it was not of any importance from the point of view of the common people, except for the troubles it heaped on them. Muthu Krishsnappa reorgainsed the administration of Ramnad with Sadaika Tevar as the Setupati in view of his failure to establish order in the Marava country. The next ruler Muthu Virappa shifted his capital from Madurai to Triuchirapalli, as he felt it essential to carry on war against Thanjavur. But the Rajah of Mysore took advantage of this conflict for advancing the frontiers of his territory to the Tamil Country.

Tirumala Nayaka (1625-1659) succeeded his younger brother, Muthu Virappa Nayaka as the ruler of Madurai. Bertrand, who edited the Jesuit letters, considers him as the most prominent of the nayak kings of Madurai. During his rule Madurai reached the zenith of its glory but at the same entered the road to eclipse.[13] When Tirumala Nayaka succeeded to the throne he found the Vijayanagar Empire as fast declining and the forces of Bijapur and Golkonda were becoming increasingly aggressive. The nayaks of Thanjavur adopted a hostile policy, while the Wodayars of Mysore threatened the northern provinces. In the east the Septuati of Ramnad and in the west the rulers of Kerala had become restless. Under these circumstances, Tirumala Nayaka found it necessary not to drain the resources of his country for paying one third to one half of his revenue as tribute to the Emperor. Also money was needed to counter the manacling odds. Therefore, he withheld payment of tribute to the Emperor and gained for Madurai an independent status. As Tirunchiapalli appeared exposed to the invaders from the north, he shifted his capital to Madurai. He constructed forts on the northern frontier and raised an army of 30,000 men. In fact the assertion of independence represented the logical culmination of the trends at work.[14] from a feudal lord, he turned into an independent ruler.

Early in the reign he had to fight a series of wars against the local powers. Chamaraja Wadayar, the ambitious ruler of Mysore, coveted possession of Salem and other territories in the north-west. His army advanced as far as Dindigul, but the nayak forces, assisted by the Poligar of Kannivadi, defeated and drove back the invaders. By 1635 the Madurai army fought against the forces of Travancore, as Unni Kerala Varma, the ruler of this state, refused payment of tribute. Tirumalanayaka invaded Nanchil Nadu and raided the villages, but it is not certain whether the tribute was collected. In the Marava country of Ramnad there broke out a civil war. On the death of Kuttan Setupati (1623-1636), his son Sadaika Tevar II became the ruler. As he withheld payment of tribute, Triumala extended support to the Setupati's brother Thambi, who contested the throne. The Nayak army led by Ramappaiyan marched to Ramnad, but the Setupati escaped to Rameswaram. The invading forces constructed a causeway, moved to the island and took Sadaika Tevar a prisoner. In this war the Portuguese supported the Nayaks, while the Dutch the Maravs. In return for their assistance Tirumala Nayaka permitted the Portuguese to propagate Christianity, in his territory to build churches and to erect a fort.[15] The balled *Ramappaiyan Ammanai* portrays the story of the expedition and the heroic exploits of the Maravas led by Vanni. However, when the rival prince was imprisoned, the people rose in rebellion. Unable to control the situation, Tirumala sent back Sadaika Tevar to his territory but before long he was killed by his rebel brother. There upon the Nayak king divided the Marava country among Thambi and his brothers, Raghunatha Tevar and Tanaka Tevar. On the death of his two brothers, Raghunatha Tevar became the Setupati of entire Ramnad.[16]

Tirumala Nayaka supported Vijayanagar against the Muslim powers. However as Emperor Sriranga III termed against Madurai because of the refusal of tribute, Tirumala won the support of Golkonda and saved his kingdom. Now, Bijapur made a settlement with Golkonda, conquered Jinji, subdued Thanjavur and threatened Madurai. Confronted with this unexpected situation, Tirumala won the support of the Kallar tribes and routed the invading forces of Bijapur. When the difficulty was overcome, he found a hostile combination of Vijayanagar and Mysore against Madurai. Kathirava Narasa Rajah of Mysore, who was allied to the Emperor invaded Satyamangalam and advanced to Madurai in 1656. The Mysore army massacred the people and cut off the noses of the captives. At the critical moment Tirumala Nayaka appealed to the Setupati for help. The combined forces of Madurai and Ramnad fought a fierce battle near Dindigul against the Mysore army and won a great victory. Each side lost about 12,000 men. the victorious army persued the retreating forces and ravaged Mysore. This decisive victory saved Madurai from the threat of total extinction.

Though he had to fight a series of wars, Tiumala Nayaka up held the independence of Madurai, gave security to his people and maintained order to his country. Art, architecture and religion received his encouragement. He built pagodas, choultries, gopuras and palaces in Madurai, but these works were undertaken frequently with forced labour. The Mahal, that he erected, remains as a monument of his rule. He extended his patronage to other religions.[17] The Jesuit letters tell of the hardships experienced by de Nibili, the Jesuit missionary, in preaching Christianity because of the hostile attitude of the officials and chieftains. In consequence he was compelled to leave Madurai for Sendamangalam. Though there was persecution, Christianity continued to spread. Foreign trade passed under the control of the European powers. Tirumala Nayaka supported the Portuguese against the Dutch in their mutal rivalry. In retaliation the Dutch captured the Temple of Tiruchendur and occupied from the portuguese the port of Tutukudi in 1658. This gave a blow to the prestige of the Nayaks.[18]

The successors of Tirumala Nayak were Muthu Virappa Nayak II. Their rule was a period of wars and disorders. Chokkanatha occupied Thanjavur but in his wars against Mysore and the Maravas, he suffered reverses. The period that followed was marked by a steady decline of the Nayaks. Chanda Sahiib deposed the last ruler, Queen Minakshi and occupied the kingdom for the Nevayets in 1736. The period of transition from the Nayaks to the Nevayets intressed the ascendancy of the feudatories.

After the battle of Talikota there emerged two trends in the political scene-the determined effort of the Bahmini powers to extend their conquests and the desperate bid of the remnant Vijayanagar to strengthen its authority over the Nayak powers. These endeavours made by the rival powers, after certain initial victories, failed ultimately. Frequently, Bijapur and Golkonda fought against each other yet they kept the goal of total extinction of Vijayanagar in their constant view. The Nayaks too fought against each other and also against the Emperor, thereby greatly contributing to their own extinction.[19]

Early in 1573 Bijabur and Golkonda entered into an agreement with each other, aimed at the partition of the Vijayanagar Empire between them. Bijapur was to have the plateau region covering the major part of Mysore and the central region of the Tamil Country, while Golkonda was to have the eastern region below the Ghats extending to Jinji.[20] Accordingly the two powers made repeated attempts at a thrust southward. Forces of Golkonda occupied Udayagiri and wrested control of the Telugu country. Thereupon Emperor Sriranga III won over Bijapur in return for a payment of fifteen lakhs of pagodas and reoccupied Udayagiri. Gaining a new confidence in his strength he decided to assert his sovereignty on the Nayak powers. The Jesuit letters indicate that Tirumala Nayaka unable to tolerate the overbearing attitude of the Emperor, formed a secret alliance with Thanjavur and Jinji against Vijayanagar. However, Vijayaraghava, the ruler of Thanjavur, betrayed his allies and revealed the plan of the confederates to the Emperor. Assisted by Thanjavur and other feudatories, Sriranga marched against Jinji in 1645.[21] A letter written in October 1645 reads: the Emperor brought all his great lords under his command which had not been so for forty years before. Supported by the feudal powers, the imperial army ravaged the country and defeated the forces of Jinji and Madurai. At the critical moment Madurai and Jinji appealed to Golkonda and Bijabur for aid.[22] This gave a welcome opportunity to these Bahmini powers to march against Vijayanagar. In response to this appeal and eager to fish in troubled waters Golkonda sent an army under Mir Jumla, while Bijapure sent an army under Mustafa Khan in support of Jinji and Maduri. In 1646 Mir Jumla advanced southwards along the coast. Pulicat held by the Dutch and Poonamallee, Kanchipuram and Chengalpattu held by different nayaks surrendered to the advancing forces. There upon Sriranga III abandoning his campaign against the nayaks turned to the north, but was defeated and forced to pay huge indemnity to Mustafa Khan . Returning to the south, he sought an alliance with Madurai, but mutual jealousies and old suspicions prevented them from forging unity. While Sriranga III fled to Mysore, Vellore passed under the control of Golkonda After this victory the forces of Golkonda threatened the Nayak kingdoms of Jinji, Thanjavur and Madurai.[23]

In 1648 Mir Jumla led the force of Golkonda against Jinji. Now Tirumala Nayaka of Madurai gained the support of Bijapur against Golkonda. The combined forces of Madurai and Bijapur led by Khan-i-Khanan marched for the rescue of Jinji. However, Mir Jumla, seeing a fellow Muslim in command of an army marching against him, made a settlement by which he left the forces of Bijapur in control of the situation and himself retired to Cuddapah. The army of Bijabur took possession of Vellore and occupied Jinji by the end of the Year 1649.[24] This marked the extniction of the Nayak kingdom of Jinji. The persian work *Basatin I Salatin* tells of Rup Nayak, the ruler of Jinji, as very proud and wealthy but because of his licentious and luxurious habits, neglected the affairs of his kingdom and invited disaster.

The fall of Jinji weakened the influence of the Nayak powers and strengthened Bijapur. The forces of Bijapur gained possession of a strategic fort and a rich territory. They looted the city and took away the accumulated riches of the ruler, which amounted to twenty crores of rupees in each and an enormous quantity of gold and jewels.[25] They carried on the work of desolation so relentlessly that they left the country in ruins. The Jesuit missionary Andrew Friere, wrote in 1666: "Nothing can equal the cruelties which the Muhammadans employed in the Government of Jinji: Expression fails me to recount the atrocities which I have seen with my own eyes". With the booty collected, the Sultan of Bijapur erected mosques and promoted conversion of the Hindus to Muslim faith. *The Basatin-i-Salatin* adds: "The country which had nothing but idol worship and infidelity for thousands of centuries are illuminated with the light of Islam through the endeavours and good wishes of the king". From Jinji the forces of Bijapur marched to the south, ravaged Thanjavur and Madurai and forced them to submit. Thevenot remarks: " the king go Golkonda siezed those dominions which lay conveniently for him, the king of Bijapur, having taken what lay next to him, pursued his conquest as far the Cape of Nagapatam".[26]

Madurai and Thanjavur were the two southern most Nayak kingdoms in Vijayanagar. Yet their mutal relation was marked by bitter rivalry. Related to the royal family of Vijayanagar the Nayak of Thanjavur wielded considerable influence in the Empire and extended their steady co-operation to the Emperors in times of war as well as in peace. Madurai on the other hand followed a policy of isolation and frequently withheld payment of tribute, seeking an independent status. Thus differences in their external policy together with territorial ambitions involved them in suicidal wars and sapped their resources. Ultimately they fell a prey to the northern powers.[27]

In 1673 the forces of Madurai stormed Thanjavur, killed Vijayaraghava, the ruler of the territory, and occupied the kingdom. Therefore Chokkanatha, the Nayak of Madurai, appointed a governor, but the latter revolted and asserted his independence. Now the Marathas took advantage of the situation and their chief Ekoji usurped the Throne for himself Madurai in the meantime had to encounter the threat from Mysore and challenges from auxiliary powers. Devaraya Wodayar (1659-1672) the ruler of Mysore, launched a policy of aggression southward. His successor Chikkadeva Raya (1672-1704) pursued this policy more vigorously. Chokkanatha Nayaka ruler of Madurai was an able soldier, but was rash and short sighted. The constant wars that he waged against the nearby powers so much weakened his authority that his kingdom appeared vulnerable. As the situation appeared fovourable Chikkadeva Raya occupied Satyamangalam and consolidated his strength with the construction of military posts. In a battle at Erode he defeated the forces of Madurai, By 1690 he conquered a major part of Baramahal and Salem and extended his territory southward. An expedition led by Kumararaja, the general of Mysore, reached Tiruchirapalli, but was defeated and forced to retreat. Yet during the regency of Mangammal (1689-1706) Chikkadeva Raya completed the conquest of Salem and Coimbatore. As a result, Madurai lost a major part of its territory.[28]

In the south west Raja Ravi Varma of Travancore and the Rani of Attingal withheld payment of tribute. The Army that was sent by Rani Mangammal for collecting the arrears marched up to Kalkulam but was routed. Thereupon in 1697 she sent an expedition under Narasappiyan. The Madurai army defeated the Raja and forced him to clear the arrears. The endeavour to collect the tribute from the Rani of Attingal failed as the Dutch took her off to safety in their ship.[29]

The Jesuit records and ballads *Ramappaiyan Ammanai and Nadar Mannarum Nayaka Mannarum,* tell of the repeated struggles made by the local Tamils to liberate the country from Telugu sway. The Paravas won the support of the Portuguese and fought against the Nayaks but were overwhelmed. The Nadars rose in a series of rebellions but were suppressed. The Maravas on the other hand despite their shattering experiences carried on a heroic resistance until they regained independence. These developments greatly weakened Madurai and reduced the extent of its possessions. In 1736 the Navayets led by

Chanda Sahib deposed Minakshi, the last ruler, and annexed Madurai with Arcot.

As the Nayaks declined and disappeared from the political scene, the order of the Poligars emerged prominent in the feudal set up. In the three tier polity of Vijasyanagar the rayas, the nayaks and the poligars presented the constituents, each in its turn supporting and sustaining the other. The rayas who were emperors declined and as they declined the nayaks emerged as independent monarchies. When these monarchies went out of the scene, the poligars came to the forefront. They were in fact lesser nayaks but were called *palayakkarars* or poligars, as they were holders of palayams or armed camps. If the nayaks held possession of large territories, the poligars held possession of different tracts of land, needed to support an armed establishment. Like the nayaks they served the nayaks and subsequently the nayaks. They had to encounter a new situation as the nayaks went out of power and external powers established their sway.

Notes and References

1. Sewell's list of Antiquities, Vol. 1, p. 379.
2. R. Sewell (1900), *Forgotten Emperor,* London, p. 373.
3. *Ibid.,* p. 281.
4. T.V. MahAlingam (1955), *Administration and Social Life under Vijayanagar,* Madras, p. 197.
5. R. Sathianathier (1934), *History of the Nayaks of Madura,* Madras, pp. 57-61.
6. C.S. Srinivasachari, *A History of Gingee and its Rulers,* p. 181.
7. A. Krishnaswami, *The Tamil Country Under Vijayanagar,* pp. 246-252 and Taylor, *Oriental Historical Manuscripts,* Vol. 2, p.109.
8. H. Heras (1927), *The Aravidu Dynasty,* Madras, p. 407.
9. A. Krishnaswami, *op.cit.,* pp. 280-283.

11. F.C. Danvers (1894), *The Portuguese in India,* London, Vol., p. 70.

10. Taylor, Oriental Historical Manuscripts, Vol. II, p.109.

12. V. Vriddhagirisan (1942), *The Nayaks of Tanjore,* Annamalainnagar, pp. 62-104.

13. Bertrand (1850), *La Misson du Madura, Paris,* Vol. II, p. 124.
14. R. Sathianathaier, *History of the Nayaks of Madurai,* p. 119.
15. F.C. Danvers, *op.cit.,* p. 268.
16. R. Sathianathaier, *op.cit.,* pp. 120-122.
17. Indian Antiquary, Bombay, 1914, Vol. 43, pp. 186 and 199.
18. F.C. Danvers, *op.cit.,* pp. 293-294.
19. A. Krishnaswami, *op.cit.,* pp. 270-272.
20. S. K. Ayyangar, *The Rise of the Maratha Powers, Journal of Indian History,* Vol. IV, p. 77.
21. W. Foster (1913), *The English Factories in India,* Oxford, p. 289.
22. A. Krishnaswamy, *op.cit.,* pp. 351-353.
23. *Ibid.,* pp. 357-358.
24. J.N. Sarker, *Hisory of Aurangzeb,* Vol. I, p. 254.
25. Bertrand, *op.cit.,* Vol. II, p. 47.
26. Thevenot, *Travels,* Part III, pp. 91-105.
27. Father Heras, *op.cit.,* p. 360.
28. R. Sathianathaier, *op.cit.,* pp. 181-182.
29. Madras Council, *Public Despatches to England,* 1694, p. 126.

CHAPTER – 2

POLIGARS AND THEIR OVERLORDS

Under the Nayak powers the country was dotted with the feudal estates of the poligars. Most them were concentrated in Tirunelveli, Madurai, Ramnad, Thanjavur, Tiruchirapalli, Dindugal and Coimbatore. The resources of the territories decided the political status of the respective poligars. The chieftains of western Tirunelveli and Ramnad were mostly of Marava community, those of Madurai, Tiruchirapalli and Thanjavur were of Kallar tribes and those of eastern Tirunelveli, Dindugal and Coimbatore were nayaks of totiens. They spoke either Tamil or Telugu or both. The number of poligars varied from time to time yet it does not appear that their strength exceeded a hundred at any time. Early in the Nayak period it is believed that there were about seventy two poligars in Madurai country alone, while a few others came into existence under the Muslim administration. By 1752 their strength was indicated at about sixty.[1] Towards the end of the eighteenth century the number of palayams in the Carnatic region was placed in treaty records at forty six.[2] Creation of new palayams and sequestration of existing ones by the rulers caused frequent fluctuations in the strength of the poligars. The annexations as well as alienation's, made by the poligars, too had contributed to this. Ramnad, Sivaganga, Sivagiri, Wadagara, Natham, Melur, Pudukkottai, Manapparai, Wodayarpalayam, Ariyalur, Turaiyur and Virupakshi represented the most important of the palayams. In the districts of Tirunelveli, Madurai and Ramnad any territory belonged to the circar.[3]

Organisation of the Poligars

In the country there were two classes of leaders: (1) the traditional chieftains, who descended from the royal houses of the post and as such they wielded considerable influence among the people and (2) the feudatories who owed their loyalty to the fallen sovereigns, yet lived in a state of independence. To the first order belonged the Pandya and Chola princes. In consequence of the absorption of Madurai within the political limits of the Delhi Sultanate, the Pandyas withdrew to Tenkasi and sphereheaded a struggle aimed at political liberation. To counter the Pandyan endeavour for gaining independence, the Afghan rulers planted Chola princes, called Mavali chiefs, at Manamadurai and other centers. Between the Pandyas and the Cholas, was shared much of the loyalty of the inhabitants.[4] Next in order came the auxiliary powers. Many of the claimed authority from divine right or by royal concession, obtained as favour or in return for signal services. In Ramnad the Setupati claimed himself as the guardian of the causeway to Rameswaram, the famous temple to which pilgrims flocked all over from India. He considered it his prerogative to afford protection to the pilgrims against the robbers, who infested the nearby jungles. According to tradition Sri Rama during exploits in South India entrusted this responsibility with the Setupati. However, the early line of the Setupatis became extinct by the sixteenth century. Yet some of the descendants, who commanded local influence, decided to reasset their authority, taking advantage of the collapse of the Second Pandya Empire[5] Marudappa Tevar of Uthumalai traced his decent from a warrior, who was stated to have sprung from the side of Goddess Minakshi with clubs in his hands to assist her in the wars against the rebels of Madurai. Because of his daring exploits during his service under Vadamalaiyappa Pillayan, The governor of Tirunelveli, under the Pandyas a rebellion in Tenkasi was suppressed. In return for this service he gained from the Pandyas the possession of Uthumalai.[6] Another chieftains name Apadhurhura Tevar at the orders of the Pandyan ruler, Ugra Pandya Rajah, routed a Kannada army that advanced to the plains. He founded the authority of his family at Singampatti, given in reward.[7]

Kumara Ettappa Nayakkar undertook an expedition to Iramil at the direction of a Pandya king. He was hit by an arrow from an unknown foe, while he was returning after defeating the enemy. In 1584 he was granted Kalaugumalai as blood money.[8] According to tradition Ketti Pommu or clever Pommu, who founded the Kattabomman line of chiefs at Panjalamkurichi, served under the Pandyas and gained from them the possession of that territory. In fact when the nayaks reached Tamil Country there had already existed a class of chieftains, who drew their influence from the possession of the territories, that they inherited or acquired.

V. Rangacharya in *Indian Antiquary* and R. Sathianathaier in his *History of the Nayaks of Madura* make references to the organisation of the poligari system by Visvanatha Nayaka. However, it is not very correct to assert that the rulers of Vijayanagar created the System. What they really did was to accept a situation that had already existed, partly because of their inability to change it and partly because of the advantages it offered and to put it into a definite form. The Nayak Chief, after assuming the administration of the Tamil territories, occupied Tiruchirapalli, strengthened its fortifications, cleared the jungles on either bank of the Kaveri and suppressed the robber gangs, who took asylum in the area. At his direction his general Ariyanatha Madali led an expedition to Tirunelveli.

However, the task of consolidation of Nayak authority faced insuperable odds. The chieftains who called themselves as 'Pancha Pandyas', believed to be the tributaries of the Pandyas, refused to accept any earthly superior. They assembled an army and entrenched themselves at a place referred to as Kayattattur, ready to fight out the issue. The local tradition of Panchalamkurichi indicates that the Pancha Pandyas took their stand at a *Kurichi* or a valley between two hills and hence the name of that place. Therefore it is likely that Kayattattur was Kayattar, situated near Panchalamkurichi. This development threatened to give the signal to the outbreak of a formidable rebellion throught the country. As Sathianathier has rightly asserted, the Pandyas, legitimate and illegitimate, frequently questioning each other's legitimacy, held their sway over different territories. It seemed certain that they would unite under a common banner to fight the common enemy. The troops of Travancore and the robbers who made jungle tracts of the west their habitat waited for opportunities for makiing irruptions into the plains. The attitude of the Portuguese, who exercised an overwhelming influence over the Paravas and independent authority over the coastal region, served as a source of constant concern. The Bahmini Sultanates, particularly Bijapur and Golkonda, concentrated their forces against the vulnerable frontiers in the north. The rulers of Kalinga too were hostile. So great was the magnitude of these perils that it appeared as nothing but impolite to provoke the chieftains of the Tamil country to raise the banner of resistance. In the meantime the generals who were serving the empire through changing fortunes clamoured for territorial rewards. Guided by these considerations, Visvanatha Nayaka saw the wisdom of effecting a settlement that would pacify the chieftains and serve the needs of the times. The result was the acceptance of the *poligari* system on a feudal pattern as in case of the *nayankara* system. As this reform was of considerable political importance, it appears that he implemented it with the approval of Achyuta Raya, Emperor of Vijayanagar.

The nayaks associated the poligars with the administration and defined their rights and duties. The chronicles indicate that Visvanatha Nayaka gave recognition to seventy two palayams and entrusted the defence of each of the seventy two bastions of the Fort of Madurai with a particular poligar. Normally the chieftains gained possession of their districts either through inheritance from the ruling houses of the past or by their military night or in recognition of their distinguished service to the state. The nayaks permitted these chieftains to retain possession of the same territories or granted them the possession of other territories. The poligars were allowed to collect the taxes and required to pay one third of the collections as tribute to the sovereign, to maintain such number of troops as could be supported with one third of the revenue, and to retain the rest for their private expanses. They were directed to render military service to the sovereign, whenever it was demanded and to administer justice to their people. This arrangement, important as it was, accorded legal sanction to the poligari system rather than creating something new and left the chieftains as masters of their territories, with fixed rights and duties. They received remissions in their payments and grant of more villages, in return for devoted service to the state. The settlement fulfilled two major objectives of the government; firstly, it provided for the administration of the remote and rugged territories and secondly, it created a second line of defence, indispensable during this period of anarchy and disorder.[9]

The period that followed witnessed the emergence of more of the poligars. The sultans of Golkonda and the nizams of Hyderabad found in the poligari system a convenient agency for tackling many of the problems that they encountered in the conquered territories in the far south. Not only did they accept the system but found it expedient to expand it. They created new *palayams* and granted them to their servants in recognition of meritorious service or in compensation for the protection of the properties of the circar, villagers, travellers and pilgrims. This accounted for the rise of several poligars in the Arcot region. The poligars held possession of their territories on a hereditary basis, with right to alienate any portion there of at any time. In subsequent times the Nawabs of Arcot created a class of chieftains with or without right to enjoy possession of estates on a hereditary basis or to alienate any part of them. However these chieftains were not treated as equal in status with the poligars.

In short what the nayaks proceeded to do was to accord recognition to a historical phenomenon, created by the vicissitudes in the fortunes of the ruling houses of the Tamil Country. The eclipse of the old royal houses with the rise of new powers left in its wake numerous chieftains in possession of territories of reduced extent. In the mean time adventurers gathered armed gangs and asserted their power in different areas taking advantage of the disorders of the times. The followers and favourites of the new aggressors obtained from their lords concessions in land in reward of their service or sacrifice. Apart from these, the rulers found it necessary to assign lands to chieftains as compensation for the services, that they continued to render.[10] Thus a four fold process, as an ultimate analysis would indicate, contributed to the rise of the poligars. They were (1) descent from royal houses (2) assertion of authority in command of armed followers-in these cases the chieftains obtained the recognition of the sovereign, (3) acknowledgment granted for a distinguished public service and (4) the need to protect public interests - in these cases they owed their existence to a deliberate act of the sovereign. However it is difficult to tell that a particular polilgar owed his existence to one particular cause or the other. While the early poligars gained more of rights through service to the rulers, the later chieftains took advantages of the turmoils of the times to attain the status of early poligars. In fact a combination of different factors contributed in one way or the other to the emergence of the poligars into a powerful institution.

With the decline of the Vijayanagar Empire, the nayaks of Madurai and Thanjavur asserted independence but their endeavour to save the country from disorders proved futile. There came more of external aggressions and internal conflicts. The later rulers of Vijayanagar upon a course of warlike action with an ambition not only to regain the lost ground but also to reassert their waning authority over the provinces. They carried the war to the Tamil Country too. Mysore, Madurai and Thanjavur in the mean time entered into a three cornered rivalry for political supremacy. To add to the embarrassments, the Decani powers the Marathas and the Mysoreans made frequent inroads into the Tamil Country. As the prospect of political establisation vanished, the nayaks looked upon the local chieftains not only for support to carry on their own administration but also for assistance to check aggressions. The family records of the poligars and other chieftains furnish numerous instances of their exploits in supported of the nayaks to check foreign invasions and to suppress the defiant powers. These developments forced the nayaks to make additions to the existing *palayams* and to create new ones either to provide for new situations or to accommodate the new chieftains.

The Marava Palayams

The number of new palayams that came into existence under the later Nayaks cannot be ascertained. However, the most significant of them were the Marava palayams. The territorial extent and economic resources of these palayams were so considerable when compared with the ordinary estates, that they were often called as states and their rulers as rajahs.[11] In fact the nayaks entrusted the administration of Ramnad with two commissioners, but found it impossible to afford effective protection to the pilgrims going to Rameswaram or to hold the Portuguese under check. Therefore Muthu Krishnappa Nayaka (1601-1609) of Madurai decided to appoint a chief acceptable to the inhabitants to carry into effect the reorganisation of the administration. The person whom he selected for the difficult task was Sadaikka Tevar, who belonged to the line of the ancient Setupatis. Appointed as deputy in 1604 Sadaikka Tevar established military posts along the road from Madurai to Rameswaram, provided escorts to the pilgrims and restored order. As the Nayaks grow into prominence in the service of the Rayas of Vijayanagar, the Setupatis gained in their power in the service of the Nayaks of Madurai.[12] Raghunatha Setupati, at the orders of Tirumala Nayaka, fought and repulsed a Muslim invasion and suppressed a rebellion orgainsed by the poligars of Tirunelveli. As reward for his service he received the villages near Mannarkovil and a share in the reverse from the pearl fishery at Tutukudi. However, when Chokkanatha Nayaka came to power, Raghunatha Setupati disregarded the central authority and refused co-operation in resisting a Muslim aggression. In retaliation the Nayak troops invaded Ramnad but could gain no decisive victory. In 1702 Rani Mangammal sent another expedition, but the Marava forces rounted the Madurai army. In the same year the old Raghunatha Setupati, who was also called Kizhavan, declared the independence of the Marava territory. Yet the independence was not accepted and hence continued to be treated as a *palayam*. The new state of Ramnad extended from the sea in the east to within six miles of Madurai in the west and from River Vypar in the south to Thanjavur kingdom in the north.[13]

A territorial grant made by Kizhavan Setupati contributed to the formation of Pudukkotai. As a young man, he fell in love with Kathali, a girl of the Kallar tribe, and married her. He granted possession of a tract of territory to Raghunatha Raya Tondaiman, the brother of the girl. Ragunatha Raya (1686-1730) built the town of Pudukkotai, annexed the neighbouring *palayams* and asserted his independence by 1711. This marked the establishment of the Tondaiman dynasty of Pudukkottai. Adjoining this state were the tribal regions of Melur and Natham. Ruled by tribal council, they were in fact commonwealths of tribes. They had no hereditary chieftains and they paid no regular tribute to any sovereign. Inhabited by the warlike and independent Kallar tribes, the three districts, Pudukkotai, Melur and Natham, constituted what was called Kallarnadu.[14]

A second territorial concession made by Kizhavan Setupati to Periya Wodaya Tevar, a local chieftain, for maintaining 300 armed men for the service of the central authority served as the nucleus of the state of Sivaganga. Sasivarna Tevar, who succeeded Periya Wodaya Tevar, married on illegitimate daughter of Kizhavan Setupati and gained possession of more of the villages from Ramnad, adequate to maintain 3000 armed men.[15] As the Setupatis grew in strength through service to the nayaks, so did the Sivaganga chiefs to the Setupatis. A young man of enterprise, Sasivarna Tevar ably assisted Setupati Kattaya Tevar (1723-1734) in repulsing an expedition, which the Marathas of Thanjavur sent to Ramnad. In acknowledgment of this important service, the Setupati divided his territory into five equal parts, retained three divisions in the south for himself and the rest in Sasivarna Tevar. This marked the rise of two estates within the bounds of Ramnad. Inhabited by the people belonging to the Marava community, the larger of the two called Greater Maravar and the smaller, lesser Maravar.[16]

The Marava powers present a striking paradox, in the history of the poligars. To begin with Ramnad was a palayam, constituted by the nayaks. It paid tribute and rendered military service to Madurai. But when the influence of Ramnad was on the ascendancy the authority of Madurai was on the decline. This enabled the Setupatis to establish their independence. Having achieved this, they created new palayams within their territory. If the break away of the territory were a factor in the decline of Madurai, the loss of Pudukkotai and Sivaganga was equally a factor in the decline of Ramnad. Despite the assertion of independence, the Nawabs of Arcot when they extended their authority to the far south, considered the Marava and Kallar powers not as states but only as palayams.

Unlike the ordinary Poligars, the Rajah of Travancore had a dual status. He was the poligar under the Nayaks of Madurai and subsequently under the Nawabs of Arcot so far his possession of Kanaykumari and Kalakkad were concerned but was a sovereign by himself in regard to his authority over territories on the west coast. Mohammad Ali claimed the Rajah of Mysore and the king of Jaffna as his poligars, but he exercised no auhtority over them. He sought to enlist British support for the enforcement of his claims but with no purpose.

Changing Masters

The Vijayanagar rayas and the Nayak powers, to whom the poligars extended their loyalty, traditionally, declined in their influence by the end of the sixteenth and seventeenth century respectively. The advent and exist of aggressive powers in quick succession together with internal dissensions among the Nayaks presented stresses and strains to the political system of the land. The poligari system too experienced the consequent vicissitudes in its fortune. Frequently assailed from different quarters, the chieftains strained their resources to defend their traditional rights. Their effort to maintain the declining Nayaks in power headed towards an inevitable fiasco. Repeatedly the foreign invaders administered upon them devastating blows and subjected them to shattering experiences. These developments threw them into a quandary-whether to surrender to alien exaction and humiliation or to resist and assert their independence. As circumstances warranted, they relied upon one course or the other, but generally the second. Not only did they survive the long chain of threats but greatly did they consolidate their strength.

As Mysore occupied Coimbatore and Salem, the north western provinces of Madurai, the poligars in this region passed under the control of the rulers of Mysore. In 1674 Ekoji the Maratha adventurer and half brother of Sivaji, occupied Thanjavur from the Nayaks. Two years later Sivaji at the command of 30,000 cavalry and 40,000 infantry undertook a campaign to the Carnatic. He occupied Jinji from Bijapur, advanced to Thanjavur and routed a combination of the poligars of Chittur and Vellore. Rustom Khan, a Muslim adventurer, sought to establish his authority at Tiruchirapalli and to expel the Nayaks. But his daring bid was thwarted by the timely intervention of the poligars. The Setupati of Ramnad and Chinna Katiri nayak of Kannivadi gained the support of the followers of the usurper, entered into a collusion with them, killed Rustom khan and re-established Chokkanatha Nayak in power. Between 1685 and 1688 Emperor Aurangazeb subdued Bijapur and Golconda, the premier Muslim powers of south India, and annexed them. In 1694 the Emperor appointed Zulficar Khan as Nawab of the Carnatic with capital at Arcot. This development posed a direct threat to the Hindu kingdoms of the far south. The Mugal forces marched to Thanjavur and Madurai and levied contributions. Rani Mangammal (1689-1706) of Madurai and Rajah Shahji (1684-1712) of Thanjavur accepted the Mughal sovereignty. However, in 1707 when Emperor Aurangzeb died, there began a period of disorders during which the Empire collapsed and provinces declared their independence. Sadat-ullah Khan organised the Carnatic into an independent kingdom under the rule of his house, the Nevayets.[17] This development placed a different power claiming authority over the chieftains.

Apart from these events of major consequence, that which a direct and adverse impact upon the poligars was the outbreak of a civil war, in the Nayak kingdom of Madurai. On the death of Vijaya Ranga Chokkanatha in 1732 wihtout leaving a direct heir to the throne, his favourite queen, Minakshi, succeeded him at Tiruchirapalli, to which place capital was shifted from Madurai in 1665. Bangaru Tirumalai, cousin of the departed ruler, challenged her claim and organised a rival government at Madurai. The glamour associated with the possession of Madurai city and the proximity of the rival government persuaded most of the poligars to transfer their loyalty from Minakshi to Bangaru and from Tiruchirapalli to Madurai.[18]

In the civil war that broke out Chanda Sahib, who commanded the navayet army and encamped on the bank of the Kaveri, saw his opportunity. He entered into an alliance with Queen Meenakshi and routed the force of Bangaru Tirumalai, who were engaged in besieging Tiruchirapalli.[19] After this victory, he advanced towards Madurai. The poligars and kallar tribes, who assembled in strength in the hilly region of Natham, intercepted his march and forced him to retreat, Rajah Tukkoji of Thanjavur in the meantime attacked Pudukkottai, but the Maravas rallied to its defence and drove out the Maratha troops. In 1736 Chanda Sahib deposed Queen Minakshi and usurped the throne of Madurai for kingdom. However, the consolidation of his authority required the liquidation of the influence of the poligars, who remainted stubbornly loyal to the Nayaks. He assembled a large army and attacked the palayams of Pudukkotai, Ariyaur and Wodayarpalayam. The Tondaiman after a futile resistance fled to Manipallam, while the chieftains of other palayams to the coast. Another Nevayet army made its way through the woods of Nathem and descended upon Madurai. Bangari Tirumalai and his son Vijayakumara, finding resistance futile, escaped to the Marava country for asylum. But the poligars of Tirunelveli assembled their irregulars at Settur to resist the Nevayet invasion. Despite their daring struggle, Budda Sahib and Sadak Sahib, the brothers of Chanda Sahib, in command of the Muslim troops routed the poligars. The Nevayets forces took several of the chieftains as prisoners and shut them in the fort of Madurai. They suppressed the poligars occupied their fords and erected new outposts with a view to keeping the country under submission.[20]

Inspite of this serious reverse, the poligars refused to accept the authority of the invading power. They appealed in the Marathas, the most prominent of the Hindu powers of the time, for intervention. The chiefs of Ramanathapuram, Sivaganga and Pudukkottai offered to furnish 5,000 horse and 40,000 foot for service with the Marathas to expel the Nevayets from the country.[21] King Sahu, guided by different considerations, decided to embrace the opportunity. He entertained an anxiety to ensure the survival of the Maratha kingdom of Thanjavur, which was repeatedly threatened by the Nevayets, to check the Mohammadan advance to South India and to extend the Maratha influence right up to Kanayakumari.[22]

In 1740 the Maratha army consisting of about 50,000 strong cavalry under the command of Reghuji Bhonsle and Fateh Singh advanced to the Carnatic. In May 1740 they defeated and killed Nawab Dost Ali in the battle at Damalcherri near Chandragiri. Defences of the Carnatic collapsed and Arcot fell to the invading forces. After this major victory early in 1741 the Marathas marched to Tiruchirapalli. The records of the period do not indicate whether the poligars joined them. Yet it was possible that because of the promise of aid already made and the identity of interests, they would have sent their troops to join the Maratha ranks. In March 1741 the invading army occupied Tiruchirapalli, took Chanda Sahib, a prisoner and appointed Murari Rao as the governor of Tiruchirapalli.[23] The Nevayets troops from Tirunelveli and Dindugal rallied to the aid of Chanda Sahib but they were intercepted at Manapparai and their generals, Budda Sahib and Sadak Sahib were killed in battle. Murari Rao sent an army under the command of Appaji Rao to the far south and established his authority at Madurai.[24]

The Martha intervention relieved the poligars from the treat of extinction and led to the re-establishment of Hindu power. The chiefs of Ariyalur and Wodayarpalayam returned to their districts. The Tondaiman regained possession of Pudukkotai. The poligars, who had been thrown into captivity at Madurai, obtained their freedom. The Marathas respected the rights of the poligars as guaranteed to them by tradition and maintained cordial relations with them. The country returned to order.[25]

However, this period of harmony with the central authority did not last for long. Determined to re-assert the mughal power in the Carnatic and when the Marathas were preoccupied with their internal conflicts, Asaf Jah, the Nizam of Hyderabad at the command of 80,000 horse and 2,00,000 foot marched unopposed to the Carnatic. After establishing his influence at Arcot, he marched to Tiruchirapalli. In March 1743 he attacked the defences of the fort. The siege continued for six months, after which the Nizam entered into a settlement with Murai rao, agreeing to give him Penukonda and gained possession of this stronghold.[26] Asaf Jah now led his army to Madurai. Undeterred by the formidable strength of the enemy, the Kallans and the poligars harassed the enemy by frequent irruptions but failed in checking his progress.[27] Asaf Jah took the city and appointed Khwaja Abdulla as Nawab at Madurai and as the guardiian of the Nevayet prince, Saadat-Ullah Khan II. Because of the worsening situation in the Deccan during his absence, the Nizam made no attempt to suppress the poligars and hurried back to Hyderabad.[28] This came as a relief to the local powers.

On the Death of Kwaja Abdulla in 1744 Asaf Jah appointed in his place his general Anwar-ud-din. In June 1744 Saddat-ullah Khan, the ten year old prince, was killed; it is believed with the collusion of Anwar-ud-din, his guardian. Yet, more interested in the preservation of his own influence than in the punishment of the perpetrators of this atrocious crime, the Nizam appointed Anwar-Ud-din himself as Nawab of the Carnatic. The new ruler founded the rule of the dynasty, the Wallajahs. The rise of another alien power in the country created again a situation of embarrassment in the poligars. Refusing to compromise with this new regime, they rallied to the Nayaks and sought to elevate their chief Vijayakumara, as the ruler at Madurai. Anwar-ud-din in 1744 sent his son Maphuz Khan on an expedition to the far south for the suppression of the poligars. The Kallans again attacked the invaders at Natham, they defeated Maphuz Khan and forced him to retreat. Mohammad Ali, the second son of Anwar-ud-din, commanded a second but more powerful expedition. He manoeuvred through the mountain passes of Natham, gained control of Madurai and advanced against the defiant chiefs. At.Tirunelveli he routed a confederacy of poligars and dismantled seventy two of their mud forts. He took several of them as prisoners, levied contributions and gained a partial control of Tirunelveli. The victorious army with considerable treasure in its possession began its return march to Tiruchirapalli. The Kallans in the meantime reassembled their irregular troops and waited on the hills of Natham. When the enemy entered their bounds, they ambushed them and looted their camp. Mohammad Ali made a narrow escape. So complete was this rout that it undid what the Nawab's army achieved with great sacrifice.[29] The poligars now made a concerted move. Let by the Marava cheiftains, they entered into a settlement with the Rajah of Mysore to expel the Wallajahs from the country and to re-establish the Nayak rule. Before this plan could be translated into practice there came unexpected developments which thwarted their venture. Nasir Jang and Muzaffar Jong son and grandson respectively of contested for authority in the Deccan. Sayaji and Pratap Singh the Marva princes came into conflict with each other in Thanjavur. The Wallajahs and the Nevayets entered into a bitter struggle for the possession of the Carnatic. The Mysoreeans in alliance with Murai Rao made a determined bid for the acquisition of Madurai. The English and the French embarked upon a prolonged war for supremacy in south India. All these powers, far and near, conspired together in converting the Tamil Country into their area of conflict, with the fort of Tiruchirapalli as the centre of concentrated attack. Overwhelmed by these unforces developments of major magnitude and left with different powers claiming control authority, the poligars found it to their advantage not to extend their authority to one power or other but to retire into isolation and concentrate upon matters of local interest. The period was marked by an expansion and consolidation of their influence.[30]

Notes and References

1. Miltary Country Correspondence, Fort St. George, 20 January 1752, Vol. 1, p. 74.
2. Revenue Consultations, Madras, 23 July 1802, Vol. 118, pp. 2463-2464.
3. B. S. Ward, Geographical and Statistical Memoir of Madura and Dindigul, Vol. 3, p. 61.
4. R. Sathianathaier, *op.cit.*, pp. 5-7.
5. *Ibid.*, p. 212.
6. Memoir showing the Origin of the Caste and Family of the Zamindari of the Estate of Uthumalai, Para 2, 5.
7. History of the Singampatti Zamindari (Trents from a Telugu Record), pp. 9-10.
8. Family History of Ettaiyapuram (Tamil), (mss), p. 1.
9. R. Sathianathaier, *op.cit.*, p. 58.
10. Chandrasekhara Reddi, *Vikramasimhapuri Mandalasaraswamu*, (Printed) pp. 85-88.
11. William Taylor (1857), *Oriental Historical Manuscripts*, pp. 161-163.
12. R. Sathianthaier, *op.cit.*, pp. 90-91.
13. *Ibid.*, p. 212.
14. S. Radhakrishna Ayyar (1916), *History of Pudukkottai*, pp. 125-127.
15. K. Annaswamy Ayyar (1899), *The Sivaganga Zamindary*, pp. 1-3.
16. Militaray Consultations, 3 February 1771,
17. Hussain Nainar, (ed.), *Tuzak-i-Walajahi*, Part I, pp. 58-64., Vol. 41, p. 108.
18. Besse, *Father Beschi*, p. 125.
19. Indian Antiquary, Vol. 46, pp. 218-219.
20. Madura Mission, Annual Letter, 14 July, 1736.
21. Public Country Correspondence, Fort St. George, 5 December 1740, p. 63.
22. S. Radhakrishna Ayyar, *op.cit.*, p. 182.
23. Ananda Ranga Pillai, Diary, Vol. 1, p. 118.
24. Public Country Correspondence, Fort St. George, Vol. 1, p. 89.

25. Indian Antiquary, Vol. 46, p. 243.
26. Ananda Ranga Pillai, Diary (trans), Vol. 1. p. 243.
27. Venkatarama Ayyar, Pudukkottai, Manual, Part 1, p. 276.
28. Madras Council, Military Consultations, 29 July 1765, Vol. 23, pp. 715-716.
29. Military Country Correspondence, Fort St. Gergo, 12 June 1767, Vol. 15, p. 139.
30. Ananda Ranga Pillai, Diary (trans.), Vol. 5, p. 177.

CHAPTER – 3

FEUDAL ORDER OF THE POLIGARS

The poligars represented the feudal order in the Tamil Country. The responsibilities and functions of these chieftains appeared similar in many respects to those of the feudal barons of medieval Europe and the jagirdars and zamindars of medieval India. In fact the possession of estates and protection of their subjects usually formed the basis of their authority and fluence. The poligars, as the medieval barons did, held possession of tracts of land, as their estates on a military tenure. They maintained their own armed retinue or armed establishment yet unlike the nobles in medieval Europe, the poligars of the Tamil Country claimed no proprietory rights on the lands of the inhabitants and never considered the cultivators as their serfs. The jagirdars of Moghul India rendered military and at times civil service too, to the sovereign in return for the right to possess estates, while the zamindars paid rents to the ruler. On the other hand the poligar chief combined in himself the powers and functions of the jagirdars of the zamindars. As local chiefs they held possession of their own territory, maintained establishment of army, police and revenue and undertook social and cultural activity. They were the administrators of their respective estates, renters to their sovereign commanders of their own forces, guardians of public welfare and ryots among the peasants. In fact poligar combined in himself the authority of a ruler as well as the status of a subject in the local community. Accordingly, his functions included maintenance of bodies of troops continually equipped for military service protection of their own communities, suppression of criminals, punishment of offenders against person and property and payment of compensation in the event of their failure to restore property lost through theft .[1] In return for the due fulfillment of these duties, the poligar was treated as the proprietor of the rent from his estate.[2] A concentration of rights and responsibilities, arising from a combination of these obligations and functions accounted for the influence of the poligars of the Tamil Country.

Poligari Estate

The territorial extent of the feudal estate called *palayam* varied from each other. Ramnad and Sivaganga were the largest, while Maniachi and Ezhayirampannai were among the smallest. Each *palayam* consisted of villages, personal lands of the chieftain, public lands and temple lands. The jurisdiction of the poligar extended beyond the borders of his territory, if he exercised the right of protecting the inhabitants of the circar villages.

As the feudal baron did, the poligar kept a part of his district, usually the best land, for his own cultivation. He kept heads of bullocks and several ploughs and employed workers for cultivation. The British records indicate an instance that a chieftain of Anamalai kept 120 ploughs for the cultivation of his personal lands and levied upon his people no taxes for his private expanses.[3] The rest of the personal estate of the poligar was distributed among his servants called, *sherogars* who were both solidiers and peasants. The *sherogars* and their followers cultivated the fields in times of peace and rallied to their chieftains for military service, whenever there were hostilities. This arrangement enabled the poligars to assemble a considerable number of troops at short notice. The Setupati of Ramnad for instance, found it no difficult a task to assemble 30,000 to 40,000 armed men on a week's notice. However it cannot be denied that the two fold nature of the service made them at the most irregulars, more useful for guerrilla war than for pitched battles.

The people, who were related to or associated with the poligar, either because of common identity or because of loyal service held a privileged status in the villages. They entrusted the actual cultivation of land with a community of workers, called the Pullers, who were the counterparts of serfs in a baronial estate in Europe. The workers, who tilled the fields belonging to the poligar, received as compensation a quantity of dry grain but those, who tilled the fields of the *sherogars* as military chieftains under a poligar received a fixed share of the harvest. Status of the employers and preference of the farm workers perhaps accounted for different practices. At no time did the field workers of the estates receive wages needed to live a life above marginal subsistence. This was particularly so in the case of the Pullers in poligar lands. Thought they were not tied to the estate as in medieval Russia, their poverty was of such dimension that they were forced to sell their services for long terms. In that case, it is pointed out, the local custom gave their master the right to extract every kind from them-to mortgage them to another master for the money borrowed, to hire them out to others for daily labour and even to transfer them to another person, by whom they were held in the same bondage. Yet it cannot be concluded that the status of such a field worker was not different from that of a black slave; for they were not subjected to it compulsorily and were permitted to go free on the fulfillment of the agreed conditions. The want of employment opportunities and prevalence of appalling poverty accounted for this tragic situation. This was the feature not only in the poligar estates but also in the circar territories too. Despite their scanty means of subsistence, the Pullers eager to obtain relief from affliction in bondage, usually contracted their wants to the were preservation of their lives, with an expectation that the accumulation of their savings might enable them to purchase their freedom at not a distant future. This would happen with no difficulty, when their master consented to release them on receipt of an amount or when he was involved in some distress. On obtaining their freedom from bondage these workers usually mobilised all their resources to improve their lot as could be expected from liberated people.[4]

Many of the palayams were situated in the hilly regions of the country and were covered with jungles to a large extent.

The poligars cleared the forests, formed villages, constructed reservoirs and promoted cultivation.[5] Also they took interest in cultural activities like temple festivals, constructed *agraharms* for the Brahmins and participated in horse race, buffaloe race and the like. In fact the poligars in general identified their interests with those of the people of their territory[6], yet maintaining a life style of their own.

Administration of the Estate

Irrespective of the extent and resources of his territory the poligar maintained a government of his own and observed those forms and ceremonies, which were usually associated with the royal houses. In his palayam he was the absolute ruler, exercising both civil and military authority. He collected taxes and customs, enforced law and order, maintained his own armed establishment and administered justice. Though he was not allowed to construct forts without the consent of the sovereign, in practice he did not observe this restriction upon his authority. In fact the function at style of the poligar resembled those of a virtual king.[7]

Among the public officials of the palayam the principal minister was called the *pradhan* or *dalawai*. He assisted the poligar in the transaction of public affairs and exercised more powers or less, depending upon the character and calibre of his master. The poligar was the commander of his army and was assisted by the military officers called *sherogars*. He had his acredited minister, called *stanapati*, at the court of the ruler. It was through this representative that he carried on official correspondence with the central government. Such a practice continued for long. However when the Wallajahs their authority over the Tamil Country they at the instance of the English dispensed with the ministers of the poligars.

As a rule the chieftains gave considerable importance to their dignified and elegant appearance in public. The paraphernalia, needed for appearance, included among other things turban, turban band, laurel for the head, war bracelets, gold chains, bangles, golden bells to be tied around the waist, white fleece, sticks, flags, umbrella, torch and parasoles.

Because of a complex of status and dignity and determined to leave an impression with the people all around, each chieftain wasted much of his time to equip himself with sophisticated items and reduced himself to self imposed ordeal in this warm country. More than these on important occasions the poligar adorned himself like a peacock and held grand durbars. Extravagance marked the celebration of all marriages in his family. He rode on horse, camel or elephant or travelled in palanquins. Accompanied usually by a large retinue, his movements were attended with considerable pomp and spelendour.[8]

Village communities functioned in the territories of the poligars. Except in cases of internal feuds the poligars did not normally interfere with their working. The village had a local council. In the democratically constituted councils all land holders were members,[9] while in other bodies only the representatives of different communities.[10] The village council on the poligar appointed the village headman and the village accountant, normally on a hereditary basis. The headman called *maccadam* or *patel,* as the intermediary between the poligar and the villagers, commanded considerable influence. He served as the collector of taxes, magistrate and judge. The village accountant called *karnam* assisted the village headman in the performance of his functions. He kept a *rosham* or register, which furnished details of all land holdings in the village. The subordinate establishment consisted of the *kavalkars* or watchmen and the *totiens* or scavengers. No uniform system of remunerating the local servants remained in force. They were compensated for their service either in the form land, grain or cash.[11]

The administration of justice received no serious attention as in any other part of the country during the period. Nevertheless the local panchayat and the poligar settled the cases. The panchayat tried the parties, who were involved in cases and gave its verdict. If it found it difficult to ascertain and decide the matter of dispute the trial by boiled ghee was resorted to and it was performed with great solemnity.[12] However the working of the panchayat was not free from irregularities, for influence and bribery had their baneful effect upon the jury. Yet it served as a corrective to the prevailing system, for if the litigants had no such body, they received no settlement at all. When the people relied upon verbal promises and entered into transactions without proper documentation, the panchayat familiar with the day to day developments came to their rescue. If the parties felt that they received no justice, they were free to appeal to the chieftain, who served as a higher court.[13] Still the poligar could award no death penalty or mutilation without the consent of the sovereign. Approval of capital punishment was not found possible, when there was no sovereign or when his authority was weak during periods uncertainly and it was found anachronistic, when the sovereign himself allowed killing in return for payment of money.[14]

Income and Expenditure

The sources of revenue of the poligar were principally the rent from the lands, income from the personal possession, customs and *kaval* dues. His share of the produce was known as *potuchilavu,* which literally meant common- expanse. It was estimated at fifty per cent of the yield, the assessment being made on the basis of soil conditions of the fields.

The share of the chieftain was regulated by 'mamool' or custom, but it being an undefined term, was used in reality as a plea for committing every kind of abuse. The fluctuations of taxes, the want of an established standard in the assessment of dry-grain fields and the intricate details of ready-money collections were real evils in the revenue administration of the poligar territories. The peasants, on their part, relied upon evasive tactics against the irregularities in the administration of revenue. It was a common practice that a ryot managed to possess greater extent of land than what was found on the records, either by keeping the actual extent unnoticed by the officials or by bribing the surveyors. The additional area for which the peasant paid no tax varied from 50 to 100 per cent of the extent of the land, for which he actually paid. Thus the system rested upon a state of conflict between oppressive exaction and fraudulent evasion.[15]

For the purpose of taxation the cultivated lands were classified into four categories, based upon productivity, as decided by ascertaining the nature of the soil. They were (1) *kirsul* or black cotton soil, free from stones and sand, (2) *shevul* or land containing a mixture of red soil, gravel stones and sand, (3) *pottul* or land with a mixure of black and white soil with stones and (4) *veppul* or land with a mixture of brown earth, clay and sand. This classification was applied only on wet lands, while the dry lands were dealt with differently. This indicates that a scientific analysis of lands was attempted for deciding the criterion for levies.[16] The ryots in the poligar territory were not completely free from exaction and oppression, which were in fact the order of the day. Yet they were not of the proportions as in the circar country. In the *palayam,* the inhabitants had to pay tax or rent only to the chieftain and the village committee while in the circar territory to the central authority, local administrators, village committees and the invading maraudars. Not unfrequently the poligars too collected contributions from circar territories. There were instances when the peasants unable to bear the Nawab's oppression took shelter in the *palayams.* Indirectly this alternative that was open to the inhabitants had a mitigating effect upon the central administration. In the opinion of the British administrators the economy of Ramnad appeared prosperous when the Setupatis were in power, but it collapsed by 1765 when the Nawab assumed the direct administration.[17] In 1765 when the Nawab annexed the *palayams* of Ariyalur and Wodayarpalayam, his amuldars found the taxes so low that they increased them by four times.[18] These instances indicate that the inhabitants of the poligar territories were required to shoulder much less burden of levies than their counterparts in other areas. This situation, however, had changed drastically as the eighteenth century advanced towards its end. This was because the Nawab handicapped by mismanagement and harassed by the British for presents and contributions, oppressed the chieftains and the latter in their turn enhanced the taxes that were levied upon the people. The Nawab and the British were responsible to a large extent if the poligars were set against the inhabitants of their own territories.

The poligar spent the money collected from his subjects under different items of expenditure. He paid tribute to the sovereign in normal times and used the rent for supporting his civil and armed establishments and his household. The tribute called *peishcush* was divided into installments called *kists.* Every year the chieftains sent their representatives to a specified place, generally the taluq headquarters, for verification of accounts by the officials.[19] The armed servants were not always paid in cash. Lands at concessional rent were left in the possession of military servants. Every year the chieftains spent large sums as charitable endowments particularly for religious purposes and for promoting cultivation and armament.

The chieftains defrayed the remuneration to their servants in the civil and military establishments in the form of money or grain or land. Money payments were either nominal or actual. During those days of unemployment and uncertainly many people took up service without pay, just for gaining experience and in anticipation of securing a job in some distant future. In regard to actual payments, the servants as a rule, were not paid the full amount, for which their services were engaged. The importance that the inhabitants attached to the glamour of high pay contributed to his anomaly, though they were certain of receiving only a third to half of the stipulated wages. If they felt themselves aggrieved, they were at liberty to quit the service. But this was difficult because the payments for several months were generally kept in arrears. If they left the service. the possibility of recovering the arrears seemed dim. Added to these the avenues of employment were seldom. During the period of non-payment servants managed to survive on the pittance, that they derived either through loan or charity, for which the importance that they attached as the servants of the poligar, gave an adequate sanction. The money payments were extremely rare. The method most generally resorted to and considered equivalent to a money payment was to give a *tuncaw* or order to a group of eight to ten peons for collecting the amount from a renter or ryot, who had defaulted remittance for years or from a criminal, who had to pay a large fine. To secure such *tuncaws* on persons who seemed capable of paying the amount, the peons had to bribe the officers of the feudal establishment. When the *tuncaw* was issued, their demands were considered as adjusted, whether they succeeded or not in recovering the amount. If they were in urgent need of money or found the chances of recovery limited, they sold their *tuncaws* at a discount of fifty to sixty per cent, which were sometimes circulated in this manner from one person to another, its relative value being regulated as the circumstances of the person in question were considered thriving or otherwise until the amount was collected or lost. At times the peons received a batta from the person concerned and if it were refused they usually plundered his effects. Normally, however, a compromise was effected with the assistance of friends and relatives, who sold his ploughs and cattle, and with their own contributions rid him of the importunities by paying the peons a half or two thirds of their demands.

The servants engaged partly for nominal money wages and partly for grain, invariably received the particular quantity of grain in advance at a price much above the market rate. A *tuncaw* issued in lieu of money payments on amuldars, renters and ryots for any quantity of grain was considered equivalent to a money payment. This practice of issuing grain *tuncaw* was not so common in the palayams of Tamil Country as in the palayams of Coastal Andhra-Venkatagiri, Kalahasti and Bommarajapalayam.

Lands assigned in lieu of remuneration were of *amarum* tenure or *cuttabudi* tenure. *Amarum* implied ease, and rent for this category of land was fixed on a confessional basis. A village, placed under *amarum* tenure, was made over to eight to ten peons, who as *mirasdars* collected the amount and paid a rent as originally stipulated. It was in the interest of these servants to encourage the ryots under them to promote cultivation by giving them the proper share of the produce; for otherwise they deserted their villages and settled in other places, where their claims were better respected. It was not the practice with the poligars to bestow upon his servants in this manner the possession of productive and rich villages. On the contrary they selected those lands in a state of ruin and decay, which for the first two or three years the peons would enjoy free from any imposition beyond the stipulated rent fixed in earlier periods. ·But when the tanks were repaired, water courses were opened and cultivation was stabilished, they were gradually required to pay *cutnums* or presents until at last they paid nearly equal to the full value of the villages. Thus the assignment of this kind served three fold purpose-to provide remuneration, to promote cultivation and to yield additional revenue to the chief. Under the *cuttabudi* tenure the peons, who were also ryots, were assigned jungle or waste lands for cultivation in lieu of stipulated money payment. The tenure implied a gift with some obligation. The peons received loans from the poligars for the first two or three years of cultivation of the barren lands and repaid the amount in installments in the years to come. As the lands turned productive, the poligars required them to pay *cutnums,* which were considered as rent of their lands. The amount first levied was the *mamoll cutnum* or customary present and was collected every year there after. As the peons carried out improvements yield more of income the poligars collected additional presents. These ryots paid additional rent if they found it not oppressive; otherwise they settled in other places. On occasions like a marriage in the family of the poligar or the consecration of a pagoda, the servants were called upon to pay special contributions. Such a practice affected the interests of tenants though it contributed to poligar's revenue.

In respect of inheritance the possession of *amarum* as well as *cuttabudi* lands descended from father to son and so on to other degrees of affinity in the male line. On default of heirs, the land escheated to the chieftain. The obligations associated with the *cuttabudi* tenure were similar to those of *amarum* with the distinction that the peons were bound to serve either with pikes or match locks, as might be stipulated at their own expense. When they were called for other duties, or were required to attend on the poligar, the two descriptions of peons received the same rates of batta. The two groups of servants rendered identical duties in defense of the interests of the poligar and in preventing occurrences of theft. If they distinguished themselves in battles or in the detection of thefts, they received handsome rewards from their master. While the *cuttabudi* peons were more of ryots than what the *amarum* peons were, the differences in the nature of their service didn't appear very clear cut.[20]

Police and Justice

During those days of turmoil and disorder *kaval* or watch represented a basic duty of the poligars. The servants, who actually performed this work, were

called the *kavalkaras* or the *talayaris*. The *kaval* system that was widely prevalent in India represented a counterpart of the 'hue and cry' in Anglo-Saxon England. From time immemorial every village had its kaval establishment, controlled by the village councils or the central government. Until the Mughal invasion of Tamil County the poligari and the kaval systems existed as two separate and parallel organistions. The early poligars had nothing to do with the *kaval* establishment of the circar villages. However in subsequent periods when the rulers failed in affording protection to the villages and when the local communities sought protection from the chieftains, the two systems got themselves integrated, adding to the prestige of the chieftains.

In the substance the *kaval* system was based upon the principle of 'set a thief to catch a thief'. Accordingly, the responsibility of apprehending a thief was usually entrusted with those inhabitants, who were considered as traditional and professional robbers. The assignment of this duty upon a habitual thief created in him a sense of responsibility.[21] Thus the system sought to rectify a social evil by the application of a self corrective remedy.

The *kavalkars* belonged to four groups: the *arasu kavalkars* the *nadu kavalkars* the *desai kavlkars* means government, *nadu*-district, desai or desam direction or region and stalam place or village. A *kavalkara* protected the grain, cattle, and other domestic property of the inhabitants and guarded the public places like the roads and markets. If any robbery occurred, the concerned *kavalkara* was held responsible for the recovery of the stolen property, failing which to pay damages.[22] The services of the *kavalkaras* were rewarded by a fee called *desha kaval* which consisted of a portion of the crop, which they protected or a monitary payment in lieu thereof.

The two systems, the poligari and the kaval, complemented each other. The poligars rendered military service to the king and gave security to the country against external invasions. The *kavalkaras,* on the other hand, discharged police duties and preserved internal order. The poligars were for the poligar territories, while the kavalkaras were largely for the circar lands, doing complementary duties. Both the establishments were supported by the inhabitants. The duty of the sovereign was to see them functioning side by side properly without interfering with each other. The distinct existence of the two establishments appeared essential to prevent the overgrowth of their influence and to safeguard the interests of the sovereign as well as the subjects. However, the turmoil which attended the Mughal invasions and the subsequent rebellions created circumstances favourable for the integration of the two systems. The collapse of law and order exposed the inhabitants to the dangers of universal conflagration. The central administration, distracted by foreign aggressions and internal rebellions, could no more extend protection to the *kavalkaras* in the discharge of their duties. As they neglected their duties and as the forces of anarchy threatened the villages, the village communities sought and secured the protection of the chieftains and gave them a fee called *deshakaval.*[23] This development added in the resources and influence of the chieftains.

The *kavalkaras,* appointed by the poligar, kept watch at night, noted the arrivals and departures, observed the movements of the strangers and reported the suspicious characters to the chief. If a theft occurred, the kavalkara tracked the thief by tracing the foot prints. If it were established that the thief went out of the limits of the village, then it was the duty of his counterpart in the next village to take up the work in pursuit. The last village, to which the thief was clearly traced, was made answerable for the stolen property, which would otherwise fall on the village, where the robbery was committed. The *kavalkara* was required to restore the stolen property to the owner. If he failed to do it, the poligar forced him to make good for the loss to the extent of his means and levied the remainder upon the entire village.[24] This indicated that the protection of property was the individual responsibility of the *kavalkaras* and the collective responsibility of the village community.

Feudal Warfare

The poligars, as they were entitled to do, maintained their own armed establishments. In this respect, they were guided by three consideration: the duty to perform military service to the sovereign, the necessity to afford protection to the *kavalkars* in the discharge of their functions and a complex of comparative status and superiority. Frequently, they neglected their duties to the ruler, yet generally constantly they attached importance to the attendance of large bodies of armed men for their appearance in public and the assertion of their claims. The armed establishments naturally consumed a large part of their resources. Their military dependents consisted of three descriptions the *amarum* peons the *cattubudi* peons and the mercenary peons; the first two groups were paid chiefly inland and the third entirely in money and grain. The *amarum* peons were granted lands on hereditary basis. Assessed at a very favourable rate, paying only a quit rent, they were jointly bound to pay the levies as were decided for their village. These peons, placed under the command of a sardar or officer in bodies of twenty or thirty, were required to take a pledge to yield their best services to their master. Their obligations were not only to attend to the summas of the poligar but to prevent theft within their villages. They forfeited their service and land, if they were found not capable to discharge their duties. The *cuttabudi* peons were also given lands. Their tenure was hereditary, but it was less by right than by sufferance. In fact they were ryots, rendering military service and paid by assignments of waste lands in lieu of pecuniary wages. They werved their master with pikes or matchlocks at their own expense and made restitution of any properly, plundered within the villages, that were entrusted to their care. The mercenary peons were recruited only in times of emergency. During active service all the groups of armed men received subsistence in money and grain, exclusive of other privileges granted to them.

The poligars trained a considerable body of men in the profession of arms. The interests of the peons were identified with the preservation of the authority of their master. The peons regard the rights of their chief as paramount and his orders as their only law. When the poligar commanded them, they executed his orders so implicily that on such occasion, they considered murder and robbery as mere matters of duty, for which he alone was responsible.[25] In fact these practices intimately corresponded with the principles on which the poligars themselves owed their military service to their sovereign whether he was an internal power like the Nayakar an external power like the Nawab.

The chieftains excelled themselves in irregular warfare. The weapons which they used were typical of their method of war. In order to assemble their troops they fired sarabogies, a kind of park-guns.[26] The weapons in common use included the bow and arrow, cannon, muskets, wall pierces, shields, swords, pikes and match lock.[27] The pike was nothing but the bamboo spear, eighteen feet long. Target, spear, dagger, sling bow and arrow too were in use. Clay pellets, prepared by mixing the white of the egg with clay, served the purpose of bullets. Rockets were fired into the camps of the enemies. A peculiar weapon used by the poligars especially the kaller tribes was the 'valaithadi' or boomerang. It was a crescent shaped weapon, one end left heavy, while the other edge sharp. Made of some hard grained wood or iron, the 'valaithadi' measured about twenty four inches along the outer curve and eighteen along the chord arc. A solider, who wielded it, held it by the lighter-end and hurled it with tremendous force against the enemy. A whirling motion was soon imparted to the weapon, which brought it back to the spot from where it was thrown, unless it got struck on its vicitm.[28] Nevertheless these arms were of short range. The poligars constructed forts of mud or of stone either on deep cotton plain or on the hills for the convenience of defence. They enclosed the forts with barriers and woods, but appeared vulnerable to heavy cannonade.

Money, bullocks and spies were the sinews of war during this period. Money and bullocks played no considerable role with the auxiliary powers as they did with the major powers. However, the chieftains attached much importance to the gathering of intelligence from the camps of hostile powers. The *hircarrahs* or spies, generally Brahmins-for they were preferred as their religious status ensured for them security and enabled them to move freely and unmolested-went in disguise and gathered secrets of the enemy. They marked the information in small characters on a slip of paper or palm leaf called *chit.* secured it in a quill or a hallow stick or inside the turban or in some other place. When the *hircarrah* suspected any imminent threat, he swallowed it or threw it away. However, if the enemy doubted that the spy swallowed up the chit, he administered a strong purgative to the spy or kept him confined.[29] Haider Ali and Tipu Sultan of Mysore frequently resorted to such methods.

In times of conflict the opposing parties as a rule, called upon their magacians to excercise all the resources of the black art for ensuring victoroy. The competing sorcerers sought to excel each other by issuing one charm or a counter charm. The process ultimately ended in restoring the *status-quoante* of the two sides, because the opposing charms nullified each other. Ultimately military superiority and strategy decided the issue on the field. Still the magicians of the victorious party shared in a large part of the glory. This practice was not confined to the wars of the chieftains but was followed in wars of other powers too.[30]

Usually the poligars never risked a pitched battle. When a superior force threatened them, they assumed defensive positions in their thick jungles. Lying in ambush, they boldly attacked the invading army and wrought havoc.[31] If the Muslim invaders dreaded the kallans much more than the regular forces. "Uniting skill and agility to courage, they (the Kallans) went out of their woods in small bands, dispersed in the country in disguise, and were always ready to reunite at the first signal. The Kallan requires only an instant to run like lightning, rush on the horse and carry of his prey...Soon, surrounded by a hundred adversaries who rush on him he dashes like thunder across their ranks and disappears in the midst of a cloud of dust". (Letter of Proenza, 1665, quoted in *Tamilaham in the Seventeenth Century,* p. 82.) A letter of the Madura Mission gives instances of the daring of the Kallans. In 1734 a Mugal army, annoyed at the irruptions made into its camp decided to destroy the kallar village of Cunampetti. The Kallans relying on their thick woods and palisades received the enemy with such holdness that after an engagement the Mughals retreated after leaving many dead. The letter tells in admiration of the Kallans, whose number was put at fifty, for holding 10,000 Mughals in check. Joseph Vieyara, Annual Letter of Madura Mission, 14 July 1735. The ballads on the poligars are full of anecedotes describing the heroism of these chiefs.

Cavalry of the enemy launched a surprise attack, the pike-men of the poligars formed themselves into a close ring encircling the match-lock men, pointing the pikes against the attacking cavalry. They then sat down in the same order and fixed the mother end of the pike into a hole on the ground betwixt their legs, while the match-lock men kept up an irregular fire above their heads against the pressing enemy in this manner they resisted even the violent charges of the cavalry and sometimes even of the infantry; though they were helpless against artillery fire. Added to these, the poligar constructed the forts in such a way as to guarantee their easy defence. When the enemy besieged their stronghold, their troops threw themselves behind the barries for convenience of counter-attack. The match-lock-men, taking their position on the elevated spot of the fort, fired at the approaching enemy, while the troops stationed at the bastions called out gallantly. The pike-men, meanwhile wielded the sharp pikes from their sheltered enclaves in the walls. The assailants advancing towards a breach on the wall could never reach the pike-men and could seldom tell from whence the blow was struck.[32] In fact the poligars despite the limited resources at their command put up formidable resistance against the aggressive powers. The chronicle of these feudal chieftains was marked by chivalry and heroism and ballads composed by local leads commemorated their exploits.

Consolidation of Influence

The trend of the times enabled the feudal chieftains to acquire rights and concessions either at the expense of the central authority, usually that of the Nawab or that of the village communities. The rewards and grants made by the Nawabs-whether they were the Nevayets or of the Wallajahs-or their amuldars added to the resources of the poligars. The rival rulers sought the military support of the chieftains not only to sustain their claims but also to defend their authority against external enemies as well as rebel powers. The poligars considered the Nawab as usurper of the rights of the Nayaks, Yet assisted him with their armed men not in view of any obligation to their overlord but in consideration of rewards, that they expected. As the Nawab found himself threatened by a combination of hostile powers-the pathans, the kaller tribes and local rebels, he made it a policy to grant more of authority and more of revenue to the feudal interests. At the same time the local officials called the *amuldars* entered into collusion with the poligars and permitted them not only to add more of villages with their estates but also to acquire more of the revenues.[33] As a result, the poligars gained in strength and allowed the circar only such proportion of the revenue, as they pleased. In order to warrant proceedings they spared a part of the spoil to the *amuldars*. This practice was nothing more than a division of the public revenue. Repine and violence were not merely connived at but openly assisted and most of the usurpations committed by the chieftains received either public sanction or secret encouragement of the persons in authority.[34]

More factors worked in favour of the poligars. Neglect of responsibilities and pepetration of enormilies by the central administration left the village communities with no alternative but to seek the protection of the chieftains. Pre-occupied with his own problems, the ruler found it impossible to enforce law and order or to protect his subjects. Inspite of this serious failure, his public servants harassed the inhabitants with oppressive taxation and arbitrary exaction. The circar not only did not safeguard life and property, but did enter into collusion with the criminals in consideration of money. It is recorded in the ballads that if a person paid one thousand gold coins to the government, he was given the freedom to kill any person, whom he wanted to do away with. At Ervadi in Tirunelveli district a person gave an advance of 700 coins, obtained his permission and murdered a villages to the local amuldar. However, as he defaulted in clearing the balance in a week, as agree upon, he was arrested and thrown into prison at Palayamkottai.

Because of such obnoxious practices of the circar administration, the villages appealed to the poligars for protection, Readily, the chieftains responded, for they reappointed the old *kavalkars* or appointed their own servants and directed them to safeguard the interests of the inhabitants. In return for this service they received from the villages a voluntary contribution called *deshakaval*.[35] In this respect the growth of the poligari system to a limited extent, resembled the commendation in feudalism of medieval Europe. In the process of commendation, the individual land owner, to ensure his safety, commented himself to a lord, gave his land to him and received it back as a fief in return for service on his part, or the promise of protection by the over lord. The beneficium meant that the lord granted lands to the vasal in return for certain specific services to be rendered. However, in the eighteenth century Tamil Country the question of security did not demand the surrender of holdings to the poligars, but only the acceptance of his protection and the payment of fees.

In subsequent periods in their attempt to escape from the terrors wrought by the interminable conflicts more and more villages sought the protection of the chieftains.[36] Meanwhile the villages which had already accepted their protection in the past enhanced rates usually in proportion to the increased responsibility, undertaken by the poligars for holding the disorders as pay. Thus the twofold processes-more villages seeking their protection and the *kaval* villages paying increased rates-vastly extended the jurisdiction and resources of the auxiliary powers. Nevertheless, the consent of the inhabitants in enhancing the status of the chieftains served as the motivating force, through it was always the practice.

Apart from these, the poligars employed other methods to extend their authority over circar lands. One instance was to supersede the local authority. In this case, the chieftain subjected, instead of removing, the circar *kavalkars* into a complete submission to his will and levied an annual contribution upon them as a badge of their dependence upon him. A second method was to include the inhabitants of the circar villages to settle in the poligar's estate. This practice which appeared as resorted to with the approval of the inhabitants was generally encouraged by the poligar and was usually brought about by his own endeavour. When the managers of the circar asked for the return of the inhabitants, the poligar on his part demanded, as a condition, the recognition of his right to protect the villages against exactions. Threatened with the loss of revenue, the circar had no alternative but to recognise the chief as the protector of the village. This gave him a definite right to interfere in the internal affairs of the circar country and extended his influence. A third practice was to plough on the *kaval* lands and there by to encroach from one point to another. Whenever this was done to the poligar could not cancel his real intentions, for at that time he would have had abundance of uncultivated land in his own estate. Nevertheless, he undermined the authority of the central government and brought more of the villages under his direct jurisdiction.[37] Added to these, the chieftains used to diverted the trade from the circar country to his territory for obtaining the benefits, it carried. The first three of these methods were solely directed against the circar interests and the last two against the ruler as well as the inhabitants of the circar villages. In fact widespread disorders, weakness of the central authority and arbitrary proceedings of the local administration enabled and emboldened the feudal powers to take over the rights of the sovereign. This was carried into effect often with the consent of rulers or local officials yet frequently without it. The consequent extension of feudal authority eroded the resources as well as influence of the central government.

Notes and References

1. Madras Council, Revenue Consultations, 4 Sept. 1799, Vol. 97, p. 2246.
2. A.C. Borwell, *Nellore District Manual,* p. 262.
3. Board of Revenue, Proceedings, Madras, 22 May 1797, Vol. 178, p. 2921.
4. S.R. Lusington, 29 December 1800, Report to Board of Revenue, pp. 9-14.
5. T.V. MahAlingam, Administration and Social Life Under Vijayanagar, Madras, pp. 200-301.
6. Rajagopal, Uthumalai Palayapeetu, (mss.) pp. 1-3.
7. Military Country Correspondence, Fort St. George, 30 March 1795, Vol. 46, p. 36.
8. Rev. Pandyan, *The Ancient Heroes of South Indian Peninsula,* p. 17.
9. Village Organisation in Madras Presidency, pp. 1-2.
10. Sewell's List, Copper Plate No. 65A.
11. Correspondence relating to the Revision of Village Revenue Establishments of the Madras Presidency, Fort St. George, 1866, p. 6-8.
12. B.S. Ward, *Geographical and Statistical Memoir of Madura and Dindugal,* Vol. 3, p. 61.
13. Selections from the Records of Fort St. George, 1816, No. 11.
14. Military Country Correspondence, Fort St. George, 20 March 1795, Vol. 46,
15. Lusington's Report to the Board of Revenue, 29 December 1800, pp. 9-14, 32.

16. *Ibid.*, pp. 10-14.
17. Madras Council, Military Consultations, 15 June 1772, Vol. 42, p. 488.
18. Military Sundry Book, Fort St. George, Vol. 40, A letter dated 17 January 1769.
19. Rajagopal, *Uthumalai Palayapettu* (mss), p. 13.
20. K. Rajayyan (1966), *Aadministration and Society in the Carnatic*, Tirupati, pp. 69-72.
21. In Rajputana the Minas performed the function of the Kallans, entrused with village watch. If adequately paid and properly managed they excelled others, encaged as police men. They did not suffer theft of robbery to be committed. On the other hand when they were out of service the Minas, like the kallans, distinguished themselves as the worst thieves and cattle lifters.
22. Madras Council, Revenue Consultations, Vol. 97, p. 2246. In the Vijayanagar Empire the police officers belonged two categories-one maintained by the state and the other by the people, the first responsible to the government and the second answerable to the local bodies. In the provinces where the *nayankara* system was in vogue, the nayaks were made responsible for the preservation of peace in their respective areas. They themselves did not attend to the police duties but appointed subordinate persons for the work. The *kavalkaras* themselves appointed talayaris for each village under them. (Dr. T.V. MahAlingam, *Administration and Social Life Under Vijayanagar,* 1940, pp. 130-131.)
23. Madras Council, Revenue Consultations, 28 November 1800, Vol. 16, pp. 3198-3201.
24. Village Communities in Southern India, p. 55.
25. Madras Council, Revenue Consultations, Vol. 118, pp. 2688-2694.
26. Madras Council, Military Consultations, Vol. 288,p. 6934, 20 October 1801.
27. Madras Council, Military Country Correspondence, Fort St. George, Vol. 15, p. 139, Translation of a letter from Nawab Mohammad Ali 12 June 1767 to Col. Compbell.
28. Thurston, *Ethnological Notes in Southern India,* pp. 556-557.
29. K. Rajayyan, *Administration and Society in the Carnatic,* p. 29.
30. Dubois, *Hindu Mannners, Customs and Ceremonies,* Part III, Ch. 9, p. 688.

31. The Maravas and the Kallans played a conspicuous part in the poligar wars. In the Tamil classic *Kalittokai* the Maravas are described as a people with strong limbs and hardy frames. These warriors, fierce looking as tigers and wearing long locks of hair, shot their arrows at poor and helpless travellers and compelled the king at the head of large armies to turn back and fly. (quoted in *A General History of the Pudukkottai State,* p. 62).
32. J. Welsh, *Military Reminiscences,* Vol. I, p. 6776.
33. Madras Council, Revenue Consultations, 28 November 1800, Vol. 106, pp. 3197-3202.
34. Madras Council, Military Consultations, 30 October 1792, Vol. 168, p. 5485.
35. Ayyapparastalaivar, *Tirumalauvazhpuram Varalaru,* (mss.) pp. 1-2.
36. Madras Council, Military Consultations, 28 November 1800, Vol. 106, pp. 3198-3201.
37. Lushington's Report, 1799-1800, pp. 2-4 and K. Rajayyan, *op.cit.,* pp. 21-37.

CHAPTER - 4

CONFLICT OF INTERESTS

The advent of the Muslim powers-the Nevayets and subsequently the Wallajahs in the place of the Rayas and the Nayaks as the rulers of the land created an embarrassing situation for the feudal powers. The new masters owed their authority to the strength of arms and as such any moral support from the local powers was not of much relevance. While the Navayets occupied Madurai from the Nayaks, the Wallajahs took Arcot from the Nevayets. In 1749 on the death of Anwar-ud-din, founder of the Wallajah dynasty, in the battle against the Nevayets at Ambur, his son Mohammad Ali escaped to the rock fort at Tiruchirapalli. He won the alliance of the English, the Marathas of Thanjavur and Nanja Raja of Mysore and defeated the rival powers, the Nevayets and the French, during the Second Carnatic War (1749-1754). Because of the support extended by his allies Mohammed Ali could consolidate his authority. At the same time he added to the debt that he owed to the English East India Company. He claimed that he was to collect arrears of tribute from the poligars for the settlement of his debts. Accordingly, he entered into the venture, but the task appeared formidable. There followed repeated attempts made by the Nawab to collect tribute by force and the determined resistance made by the poligars. In the process the two sides weakened each other and the resultant situation invited British intervention.

The conflict of interests and the clash of arms came as a result of factors, bequeathed by internal contradictions. By tradition the chieftains extended their loyalty to the Nayak powers. Many of them shared with the Nayaks the cultural identity, for they were Hindu by religion, Telugu by language and Nayakkar by community. As the poligars owed their status to the Nayaks, a mutal obligation strengthened their ties. However, the rise of the Wallajahs as the ruling house created a new situation. On the one hand it released the chieftains from that obligation and allegiance that they owed by tradition to the Nayaks without developing anything of that kind as a parallel in relation to the Wallajahs.

Also the frequent political changes and the shifting fortunes of combatants, which marked the period from 1737 to 1754, saddled the chieftains in a peculiar dilemma. To render assistance to one party was an offence from the view point of the rival party and to remain neutral was offence from the view point of both parties. The period was full of risks. The poligars supported the Nayaks and then changed sides between the more prospective contestants like the Nevayets, the Mysore ans or the Wallajahs. By this process, many of the Poligars cultivated the animosity of the successful Wallajahs and invited trouble in the changed situation.

The collection of tribute otherwise called *peishcush* served as a potential source of embarrassment. The Nawab's demands for tribute varied year after year. Exactions had at times been carried to the highest pitch and remissions were never obtained except through resistance. The Nawab's managers made it a procative to exact whatever they could from the chiefs by diverse means-hinding internal conflicts, bogus promises and mock assignments of land.[1] There by ultimately they taught the Poligars to consider tribute not as a just payment to their sovereign but as a price paid to purchase the forbearance to oppression. Bishop Caldwell ignored the ordeals to which the Poligars were subjected to repeatedly, when he observed: "It can hardly be said that the idea of governing the country by means of an order of rude, rapacious, feudal nobles, such as Poligars generally were, turned out to be a happy one, for down to the period of their final subjection and submission to English authority 1801, Whenever they were not at war with the central authority, they were at war with one another, and it was rarely possible to collect tribute from them on revenue due to the central authority without display of military force which added greatly both to the unpopularity and expense of the collection.[2] On the other hand Caillaud, who had a better knowledge of the situation, in his letter to Orme in 1775 gives an insight into the magnitude of oppression. He wrote: "that the Nawab, if his has power in his hands, will squece these people (the Poligars) unmercifully, and we should (that is ought to) see nothing but justice done. My dear Mr. Orme, our rigid northern notion of justice will make us at last the dupes and fools to the more pliant politics of these southern climates". The letter further states: If we the Company support the Nawab let us it, and not prescribe to him in such cases as these. And after all, what have we more to do with their needs (of) government than their modes of faith. The Nawab acts justly as an eastern prince; let him not then as he please. We have the power still in out hands. You know the fable of the cat, the money and the roasted chestnuts".[3] What is disearmibale is that while throwing light on the Nawab's attitude towards the Poligars the letter indicates clearly the scope of intervention by the English East India Company for taking advantage of the state of conflict in the relation of the central authority with auxillary powers. Further, as S.C. Hill has observed, the spirit of independence and turbulence which many of the Poligars cherished in common, led them into conflict with the Nawab. The absence of any definition of their privileges, their ignorance and the state set up by them frequently misled them to uphold them selves against the circar by force of arms. With forts a few old guns and a little equipment of stores, they cared little for the central authority, Those who could not manage their own affairs, usually put themselves under the influence of adventurers, whose only interest it was to entice themselves. The jargon of these self-seekers inflated the military sprit of their masters in opposition to the Nawab's administration and guided the Poligars to a state of confrontation.

These stresses and the strains reflected upon the attitude of the Poligars towards the Nawab. Expecting no justice from the administration and holding aloft a spirit of freedom, they built up their armed strength in remote citadels and increased their resources, confident of their strength and having an easy road open to the hills for escape, whenever they were overpowered, they asserted that spirit of independence, which their situation so well quAlified them to maintain. In consequence a series of military exploits arising from the hostile concentrations of the Poligars and the repeated efforts of the Nawab to assert his authority fill the pages of local chronicle. The Nawab destroyed as many of their strongholds as he could at different times, but the more he destroyed, the more the Poligars erected. In fact construction and destruction of forts formed one of the major occupations of the inhabitant masters.

The Poligar further waited for opportunities to withhold payment of their tributes to the Nawab. Whenever they found themselves unable to resist the demands of the Nawab, they paid as much as they could, failing which they procrastinated. The Poligars, when they appeared helpless before a formidable enemy, begged pardon for their fault and offered to pay tribute. This practice was in consonance with the maxim asserted to the *Panchatantra*. the book of apologues in India, probably the oldest of its kind in the world. This book suggests the sound wisdom of procrastination, whether was with or without a reasonable hobe in critical times. The reason given for this is that by gaining time one gains the chances of success, though it cannot be considered the case always. If they found it possible to resist, they refused payments. In that case the Nawab contended himself with their gratuittious offerings, however small they were and waited for a favourable occasion to bring forward all his past demands, which always consisted of a large accumulation of the arrears of peishcush, charges of the troops sent against them and the claims of compensation for the losses suffered by the circar on account of their depredations. The result was that a state of perpetual distrust took the place of mutual confidence which might have made the feudal powers good subjects in times of peace and useful auxiliaries in times of war.[4]

The political and military environment in which the Poligars lived had a powerful impact upon their character. Exposed to arbitrary and underfined demands, they frequently practised the same injustice by force of fraud upon each other. Corrupt amuldars taking advantage of their internal disputes generally interfered not as mediators, but as fomenters of these quarrels for gaining benefits to their own advantage. Disputes among the Poligars were occasioned by the unsettled boundaries and a variety of other claims.[5] Their manner of general behaviour was such that they maintained an animosity against each other. If one Poligar joined one side, the rival Poligar went over to the opposite side. The Nawab and his amuldars instead of enforcing order, exploited their mutual rivalry for the advancement of their own interest.[6] At times, when they encountered serious threats to their common interests they forged unity. In that case they allowed their private animosities to subside and furnished their quota of peons for the defence of the besieged palayam without appearing themselves in the contest.[7] Also, they did not hesitate to join any rebellion, for they believed that no change whatever could render them worse than what they under the Nawab's administration.[8] The Poligars, thus, acting under the stress of an interplay of common as well as individuAlistic motives, followed no clear cut policy. They fought against the Nawab and at times against each other, thereby fell victims to the intrigues of external powers.

Attempt at Nayak Restoration

The Poligars felt themselves insecure so long as the Moghuls or their deputies exercised their sway over the land. Therefore they made repeated attempts peaceful as well as violent to reinstate the Nayaks in power. In 1750 when Nizam Nasir Jang marched to pondicherry in support of Mohammad Ali in the war against Chanda Sahib, the Poligars sent a mission and sought his intervention on behalf of the Nayak. However nothing came out of their representation, for after sustaining a night assault by the French, he made a hasty retreat in the course of which he was assassinated. In 1752 Nanja Raja of Mysore sent an army to the south, Khub Sahib, who led the expedition, expelled the Nevayets from Madurai and gained possession of the territory for Mysore. However, the slaughter of cows and destruction of coconut trees by the Muslims Alienated the Sympathy of the Hindu inhabitants.[9] Setupati Vijaya Raghunatha (1748-1760) of Ramnad and Rajah Uddaya Tevar (1750-1779) of sivaganga, supported by other Poligars, orgainsed a rebellion and drove off the Mysoreans. They crowded Vijayakumara, son of Bangaru Tirumalai of the nayak dynasty of Madurai as the ruler of Madurai. However this victory proved momentary, for immediately after the Poligars withdrew their forces, Miana, the Navayet general, gained control of Madurai. Vijayakumara fled to Sivaganga.[10] Marking the failure of a combained Venture.

Since then the Poligars made an appeal for British aid. On the 20th January 1754 they represented to Governor Thomas Saundars (1750-1755): "As we have had no king from these twenty Years past to rule this country it was in a distressed condition and as we the Poligars are 50 or 60 in number, We are in a very bad circumstance having no ruler to command us. If his Honour settle the country and appoint a Ruler over us it will be a means to require him (the Governor) a good name reputation. We shall pay the tribute to the Nawab according as it was customary to the Subah of Arcot and agreeable to him and will eneavour to deserve his honour's favour, this will settle the country.[11] This representation was indicative of the recognition that the chieftains gave to the growing influence of the English East India Company and their willingness to accept the Wallajah sovereignty, subject to the elevation of a prince at Madurai for maintaining order in the country. The Madras council took interest in the suggestion but Mohammad Ali refused his concurrence. It appears that the Poligars demanded the restoration of Vijayaakumara to power, for in 1757 too they sought the elevation of this prince to authority.[12] But an error of judgment led Mohammad Ali reject the appeal. Had he restored the Nayaks to power, nominally no doubt, he could have gained an effective control of the country without any serious difficulty and could have won the allegiance of the Hindu powers.

The attitude of Mohammad Ali left the Poligars without any acceptable leadership and in a state of hostility with the Wallajahs. In the meantime the Nawab, hard pressed for money because of his prolonged wars against the rival powers-Chanda Sahip and the French-and the frequent demands made by the English East India company as his ally for money decided on military option. There followed a series of expeditions. Nawab Mohammad Ali claimed overlordship over the feudal chieftains but for long he found it impossible to assert his rights because of his prolonged wars against the Nevayets, the French and the Mysoreans. However, early in 1755 he found himself retrieved from threats to his survival and felt free to proceed against the rebel powers, Yet what added to the urgency was his financial predicament. When he was pressed for payment, the company was made to belive that he was to collect the arrears of tribute from the auxiliary powers but the Nawab had no adequate strength. Therefore the company extended its support to the Nawab in his wars against the feudal powers.

Expedition of 1755

In January 1755 the Nawab assembled an army at Tiruchirapalli in preparation of a campaign against the Poligars. It consisted of the Wallajah troops commanded by Maphuz Khan, the native troops of the Company by Khan Sahib and the European troops by Alexander Heron. Maphuz Khan was the elder brother of Nawab Mohammad Ali but lacked will power and martial talents, needed to make him an able general. Khan Sahib and Heron on the other hand were noted for their ability in the conduct of military campaigns. Yet mutal suspicions hampered the developments of proper understanding about the leaders. Nevertheless, considering the importance of the expedition for the suppression of the feudal forces and consolidation of his authority, the Nawab accompanied it in the southward march.

Leaving Tiruchirapalli on 4th February 1755, the army reached Manaparai on the 10 th and established contacts with the chieftains. However, the demands made by the Nawab were so exorbitant that the Poligars led by Lakshmi Nayak decided to resist. Thereupon the forces of Khan Sahib attacked the barriers and occupied two palayams.[13] The chiefs now submitted to the authority of the Nawab and paid a part of the tribute. Mohammad Ali saw enough of bloodshed and returned to Tiruchirapalli. The army, resuming the march, made its way through Melur and Natham in Kallarnadu and occupied Madurai. The defiant chiefs entrenched themselves at kovilkudi but were attacked and dispersed. In the course of the conflict the invading forces seized the brass images, which the Kallana worshipped. The massacre of the Vanquished and spoliation of the temples drove the kallans of frenzy.[14] In the course of the struggle for idols they fell upon troops but their atrocities were countered by equally severe reprisals. Heron offered to restore the idols in return for a payment of 5,000 rupees but as the Kallans had no money he carried them off in a tumbril.[15]

The combined forces of the Nawab and the company advanced to TirunelvAli by the end of March 1755. The Poligars were not only allied with the Nayaks but appeared remiss to pay the arrears of tribute. Maphuz Khan hesitated to resort to coercion for fear that the chieftains would seek the protection of the French or asylum in the jungles. Yet as no other alternative seemed open, he decided on offensive operations. To begin with, the forces stormed Nattakottai, a rebel stronghold near Tirunelveli, and wrought havoc with indiscriminate slaughter. The atrocities spread such a terror in the region that several Poligars submitted, cleared part of the arrears and gave security for the rest.[16] Raja Marthanda Varma of Travancore withdrew his troops from the occupied territory of Kalakkad and Papnagudi. Still many of the principal Poligars, particularly Kattabomman of Panjalamkurichi and Puli Tevar of Nelcatansevval refused to yield and clear the arrears, as demanded.[17]

On the 30th of April the detachments stormed Panjalamkurichi. Now Kattabomman, the Poligar, agreed to pay tribute and gave security. After this victory the troops infested Kovilpatti and forced the Poligar of Ettayapuram to accept terms. Maphuz Khan and Heron made settlements for a total amount of 4,50,000 rupees but the real collections came to 1,10,000 rupees only against as expenditure of 70,000. As the expectation of collecting huge amount proved a sheer reverie and as the threat of a French invasion of Tiruchirapalli seemed real, Governor Pigot became disenchanted with the operations. In compliance with his repeated orders the army in May began its return March from Tirunelveli.[18] As the forces advanced a few miles, Maphuz Khan prevailed upon Heron for undertaking an expedition against Puli Tevar, the most formidable and talented of the chieftains of the western region of Tirunelveli. Accordingly, the troops marched to Vasudevanallur, one of the strongholds of the Poligar, and directed him, to make an immediate payment of Rs. 20,000 under threat of coercion. An indomitable chief as he was, Puli Tevar contemptuously ignored the demand. Thereupon the assailants launched a vigorous attack upon the fort. However, for want of heavy cannon all attempts to make a practicable breach failed. By gallant sorties the troops of the rebel chief repulsed the attack. Humbled and humiliated, the forces abandoned the siege and made a retreat.[19] To add to their predicament while they were passing through the defiles of Natham, the Kallans fell upon the exhausted troops and regained possession of their brass gods. In fact the expedition ended in an anti-climax.[20]

Much was expected from expedition but it yielded no benefit, either to the Nawab or to the company. Neither from the military nor political nor financial point of view did the campaign prove fruitful. Not only did the army fail in the suppression of the chieftains but also did suffer serious reverses at the hands of Puli Tevar and the Kallans. Settlements were made with several Poligars but they could not be enforced. In accordance with the prevailing tendency the generals of the Nawab and the company gave more attention to the receipt of presents that to the collection of tribute. The chieftains, subtle as they were, united against the common enemy for taking advantage of the corrupt system. They administered bribes to the avarice of their enemy and procrastination to its passion for command but retained their military strength and political independence almost unassailed. In consequence, the results were negative. Because of hostilities the inhabitants abandoned cultivation and manufacture. The Poligars learned how to deal with the troops of the Nawab and the company. The conflict between the two generals, Maphuz Khan and Khan Sahib opportunities to the rebel powers to re-assert their influence.

Appointed as Governor, Maphuz Khan assumed the administration of Madurai in April 1755. As Governor, he was required to pay fifteen lakhs of rupees as the annual rent for Madurai and Tirunelveli. Subject to this condition, he was left in absolute control of the administration. In a bid to restore order in the land, he made a strenuous effort to suppress the Poligars, but the problems which faced him appeared formidable. The local powers, among whom the most conscious were the Patan chiefs, the Kallans, the Maravas, Kattabomman, Puli Tevar, and the Rajah of Travancore, defied the Wallajah authority. The patan chiefs in CO-operation with the Kallans re-established themselves in Madurai.[21] The rulers of the Marava states of Ramnad and Sivaganga allied themselves with the Dutch. Kattabomman occupied the villages adjoining Panjalamkkurichi, while the Rajah of Travancore took possession of Kalakkad. The western Poligars of Tirunelveli in the mean time extended their sway over Nadumandulam.[22] Varaguna, the Poligar of Wadagara, was the most powerful of the western Poligars, but Puli Tevar by his ability and subtility of his character gained an ascendancy in the councils of the chiefs. Puli Tevar proposed a union of the western and the eastern Poligars against Maphuz Khan, but the chieftains of Panjalamkurichi and Ettayapuram appeared reluctant, as they had given hostages to the Nawab during campaign in 1755. Yet most of the chieftains made a common cause against the wallajahs and decided to resist the Nawab's claims.[23]

Against this hostile combination Maphuz Khan found his resources to surmount it limited. He was the commander of the forces, but his army was neither well disciplined nor properly equipped.[24] Nor was he assisted by any able deputy. Danishmund khan, otherwise Known as Barkatoula, was in control of Madurai, but he was more interested in diversion with the dancing girls than in safeguarding the interests of the Wallajahs.[25] Still Maphuz Khan had two advantages; the control of the principal forts of Madurai and Palayamkottai and the absence of any binding unity among the rebel chiefs. Some of the Poligars even appeared inclined to change sides in consideration of rewards.

Maphuz Khan sought to take advantage of the differences among the Poligars. His attempt was to detach the eastern Poligars from their attachment with the western. This appeared not very difficult as there was not much of affinity between the two groups, for the eastern was Telugu by descent while the western Tamil. He called a few villages and granted concessions in tributes to the Poligars of Panjalamkurichi and Ettayapuram in return for their alliance. Reinforced by the troops furnished by them, he expelled the forces of Travancore from Kalakkad. In March 1756 the rebels numbering about 20,000 assembled near Tirunelveli but on the 21st in a hard fought battle Maphuz Khan defeated them and killed their chief, Miana. Despite this victory the ravages by the Poligars continued so unabated that no collection could be made. Convinced of the necessity of taking more vigorous steps, the Nawab appealed to the Madras council for military support. Accordingly, at the inistructions,of lord Pigot (1755-1763) the governor of fort St.George, an expedition advanced to Tirunelveli. Khan Sahib,[26] who commanded the army, faced the situation firmly. He stormed the forts of the Poligars and mercilessly massacred the fleeing population. The fury with which he connected the operations threw the chieftains into panic. The rebels begged for guarters, paid tribute and evacuated the circar villages. Among the chieftains who surrendered were Puli Tevar and Varaguna of Sivagiri. The coercive means of Khan Sahib proved markedly successful but the settlement which he made in disregard to Maphuz Khan's authority led him into a conflict with the latter.[27]

Maphuz Khan Vs. Khan Sahib

Maphuz Khan looked upon the proceedings of Khan Sahib especially the admission of the company's troops into the fort of Madurai and the collection of tribute from the Poligars in disregard to civil authority as a direct challenge to his administration. Despite his inability to settle the country or to pay the rent, the jealousy with which he decided to retain his powers in opposition to the independent attitude of Khan sahib led the Two leaders into conflict. Maphuz Khan proceeded to Madurai, Expelled the company's troops from the fort and entered into an understanding with the rebel chiefs to further his interests.

The defiant proceedings of Maphuz Khan began as a move against Khan Sahib but they assumed the proportions of a rebellion against the Nawab and his ally, the English, as the feudal powers were drawn into it. It would have been possible to nip the trouble in its bud had Nawab Mohammad Ali and Governor Pigot had taken timely action to ally the suspicions of Maphuz Khan but they did not, as their own political interests came into clash. The Nawab in accordance with his favourtie policy of dispensing with an ally on the realization of his purpose, urged Lord Pigot to recall Khan from Tirunelveli. He complained that Khan Sahib had interfered in his administration, collected taxes and admitted troops into the fort of Madurai without his authority. Also he asserted that the presence of Khan Sahib in Tirunelveli was no longer required and that his brother had no money to pay the expenses of the forces of the company.[28] Despite the complaint, Lord Pigot anxious to preserve the influence of the company in Madurai, defended what Khan Sahib did. He point out that Khan sahib collected the revenue as per the agreement, which provided for the sharing of the rent between the Nawab and the Company and that he garrisoned the fort of Madurai for the security of the country, Not only did he refuse to recall the Company's forces but also did inform the Nawab that Maphuz Khan to rejoice at what Khan Sahib did. In this apparent conflict between Maphuz Khan and Khan Sahib, there was involved in reality the rivalry between the Nawab and the Company for political influence. Therefore the issue raised by Maphuz Khan's operation to Khan Sahib offered no immediate solution. It became evident that unless a governor acceptable to both the Nawab and the Company were appointed, it would be difficult to enforce a co-ordinated policy for the suppression of the feudal rebels and settlement of the country.

Accordingly, Lord Pigot and Mohammad Ali decided to appoint Tatarapa Mudali, a wealthy financier, as renter of Tirunelveli with effect from the 1st of July 1756. Barkatoula, appointed by Maphuz Khan, retained control of Madurai country while Khan Sahib the Madurai fort. Tatarapa Mudali Made settlements with the village heads and Poligars for the payment of taxes. But the rivalry between Tatarapa Mudali and Khan Sahib for supremacy again created complications. Khan Sahib expelled the Poligars from the cutchery of Tatarapa Mudali and executed five men sent by Puli Tevar for the payment of tribute. These high handed proceedings held the authority of the renter in ridicule, drove the Poligars again in hostility and helped Maphuz Khan to organize resistance with the support of the chieftains.[29]

In August 1756 Maphuz Khan went through a ceremony of receiving a firman or order of appointment to governorship from the Nawab. He went out of his camp with great pomp, saluted a person mounted on an elephant and received a rolled paper. After proclaiming himself as governor of Madurai, he issued orders appointing Baraktoula as his deputy for Nadumandalam and Mr. Jaffar and Tirunelveli.[30]

Yet the rebellion could not be sustained without the support of the Poligars, against whom he fought on several occasions. Eager to gain their alliance, he granted concessions in territories, which were not his own, to the chieftains. Accordingly, he ceded Wallachinattam, Taravedi and Terembur situated near Madurai to the Patan Chiefs in return for their military and financial aid.[31] He permitted Kattabomman to occupy the Nawab's villages adjoining Panjalamkurichi and the Rajah of Travancore to annex Kalakkad. The Poligars, angered at the imperious behaviour of Khan Sahib, on seeing the prospect of gaining more territories, joined the ranks of the rebels. In January 1757 after posting the Kallans for safeguarding the northern borders of Madurai, Maphuz Khan proceeded to Nelcatansevval, granted the districts of Alwarkurichi, Ambasamuram, Papankulam and Tengasamudram to Puli Tevar and won his alliance. The rebels made Nelcatansevval the principal base of operations in Tirunelveli. In a bid to win the support of the Hindu powers he promised the restoration of the country to the Nayaks and sent his deputies to the Marva states and Mysore for seeking aid.[32] However, the confederacy suffered from glaring anomalies. Some of the principal Poligars especially of Sivagiri and Ettayaypuram gave no support to Maphuz Khan. Many of the allies were half hearted, for they were guided more by their own interests than by any common objective. Obviously the rebellion assumed the proportions of an unorgainsed struggle aimed at the realisation of no common goal. While Maphuz Khan promised the restoration of the Nayaks to their former dignity, he did not define the satatus which he himself aimed at. The Poligars, on the other hand, decided to annex as many villages as possible, without giving any regard to the jurisdiction of their leader or of the Nawab. In short, the pursuit of common policy was not there.

Yet rebellion broke out in January 1757 causing considerable alarm. Rebel forces consisting of 1000 horse and 10,000 armed men made incursions into circar territories in Tirunelveli. Spreading desolation everywhere, they moved to Panjalamkurichi, where the troops of Kattabomman numbering 4000 joined them. Tatarapa Mudali's irregulars fled and his administration collapsed.[33] Maphuz Khan Puli Tevar summoned the Poligar of Ettayapuram to join their ranks, but the latter refused. Thereupon they ravaged his palayam and sent the spoils of plunder to Nelcatansevval. Khan Sahib advanced from Srivilliputtur to intercept the convey of the rebels, but did not succeed.[34] The Poligar of Wadagarai occupied Kadayanallur,Tangachi and Sankaranainarkovil, While the Rajah of Travancore took valliyur. With the spread of the rebellion, the major part of the province of Tirunelveli passed under the control of Maphuz Khan and his associates.

The troops of the Nawab and the Company retained control of a few strong posts, yet their render could collect no taxes from the villages except in competition with the rebel chiefs. Khan Sahib, aided by the Poligars of Sivagiri and Settur, repulsed rebel attacks on his post at Alwarurichi.[35] In these battles Puli Tevar lost two of his generals. The Poligar of Wadagarai one of his legs.[36] With no side gaining any significant victory, disorders descended upon the land on a large scale.

Expedition of 1757

In an attempt to regain control of territories, governor Lord Pigot sent an army in support of Khan Sahib. John Caillaud in command of the expedition marched to Ramnad as the Kallans closed the direct route through Natham and reached Tirunelveli early in March 1757. Still the forces found it difficult to launch offensive Operations. The shortage of provisions and the onset of the monsoon presented difficulties. Puli Tevar and Barkatoula appealed to Haider Ali of Mysore for aid. As the Third Carnatic War broke out, it appeared that the French would send an expedition to Tiruchirapalli in support of the rebels. Because of these considerations, Caillaud and Khan sahib began their return march on the 11th of April for fear of an assault on Madurai which was in rebel occupation the rebels led by barkatoula, trekked in pursuit, in skirting along the hills. For the night they helped on the borders of Sivagiri. Taking them as intruders, the troops of Sivagiri. Taking them as intruders, the troops of Sivagiri fell upon their camp and dispersed them. In the early morning the rebels reassembled and resumed their march to Madurai.[37]

Khan Sahib and Caillaud on their return march made on attempt on Madurai. The fort of Madurai was large and had two surrounding walls with square towers at intervals. The inner wall was twenty two feet in height but was neither well maintained nor properly manned. Yet, what added greatly to its strength was that the space between the two walls was so over grown with thick bushes of thorny plants that it appeared insurmountable at most of the places. However Caillaud discovered a small open space near a gate, not well guarded, on the wastern part of the ramparts. He decided to escalate the walls through this vulnerable spot. In the night of the 29th of April the troops approached the foot of the walls undiscovered, fixed up the ladders and got over the first wall. The assault progressed according to plan and the assailants moved steadily forward to the inner wall. Now a cur dog, which silently followed one of the sepoys, frustrated the bold venture. Overwhelmed by its helplessness to reach its master into the fausse-bray it gently barred; instantaneously its counterpart in the fort answered it.

The rebels took up the alarm, hung out blue lights of sulphar and started a shower of arrows, stones, lances and fire arms on the intruders. In the resultant confusion, the troops of Caillaud retreated, but without suffering any serious loss.[38] With the task unaccomplished, Cailaud led his forces back to Tiruchirapalli as he had to protect this fort against the French.

In the meantime the depredations by the Poligars of Tirunelveli and the military operations against the rebels of Madurai confined. Maphuz Khan Tevar recovered possession of the lost posts, but their attempts to storm the fort of Tirunelveli failed. However, when a body of troops left the fort on its way to Madurai, Maphuz Khan captured it, After this victory the rebels attacked Palayamkottai but Tatarapa Mudali won over the Poligars of Panjalamkurachi and Ettayapuram to his side, and rescued the besieged garrison. Still the rebels retained control of most of the Country in the far South.[39]

At Madurai the siege continued. On the 9th of July the rebels sallied out in great strength, but were beaten. After the return of Caillaud from Tiruchirapalli the attempt was renewed and on the 10th of July a part of the wall was battered down. At 2 o' in the afternoon, the forces advanced to the breach. The rebel garrison taking the signal, flanked the towers and stubbornly resisted the assaults.

They set fire to bags filled with powder as they tossed them down over the besiegers, Ultimately, unable to storm the fort and suffering considerable loss, Cailaud withdraw from the walls.[40] Now the assailments relied upon intrigues. Caillud and

Khan sahib persuaded several chiefs, including the rajahs of the Marava states, Mudemiah and the Poligars of Panjalalkurichi, sivagiri, Ettayapuram and Settur to join their camp. Either their conviction that the struggle was futile or their desire to win the favour of the Nawab forced them to change sides. Kattabomman furnished 1000 troops for service with Khan Sahib, while Mudemiah brought with him the Kallans of Natham. These defections considerably weakened the rebels. Still Puli Tevar, BarkatoulaNabi Khan Kattack remained firmly in their alliance with Maphuz Khan.[41]

As reinforcements either from Tirunelveli of from Mysore were expected Barkatoula continued the defence of Madurai against a concentration of the hostile columns. He appealed to Maphuz Khan for support but was of no purpose. Haider Ali too did not send any relieving expedition. Greatly disappointed, Barkatoula consented to surrender the fort if the Nawab paid twelve lakhs of rupees.[42] After prolonged negotiations, Caillaud made a settlement with Bharkataula agreeing to pay an amount of Rs. 170,000. On the 8th of September 1757 the rebels evacuated Madurai and Cailaud took possession of the fort. The acquisition of Madurai deprived the rebels of the control of a province and interrupted their communications with kallarnadu. Maphuz Khan withdrew from the siege of Palayamkottai and retreated to the hills of Nelcatansevval.[43]

Occupation of Madurai fort was a major victory, Yet Caillaud could not follow it up on account of the outbreak of the war with the French- the Third Carnatic War. In October he returned to Madras after entrusting the command of the defences of Madurai with Khan Sahib.[44] The withdrawal of the forces and the rebellion of the Poligars encourged Haider Ali to advance to the far south. In October 1757 championing the cause of the Poligars, he marched to Madurai and occupied sholavadan. However, khan Sahib attacked Haidar Ali at Nathamand forced him to retreat to Dindugal.[45]

After his return from Natham, Khan Sahib sought to settle the war torn country. He strengthened the defences of Madurai and Sholavandan and posted the Kallans to guard against

Mysorean incursions. Eager to promote the settlement of the country he impressed upon the Madras Council the necessity of persuading Maphuz Khan to leave Madurai. He stated categorically that unless Maphuz Khan withdrew from his alliance with the Poligars, the disturbance would never cease and that the Nawab could never all the revenue. Accordingly, Lord Pigot advised the Nawab to persuade his brother to evacuate Madurai by promising to make a decent provision for his support.[46] In compliance with this suggestion Mohammad Ali sent his deputies to Nelacatansevval. The deputies saw Maphuz Khan residing in a hut made of straw and living a life upon what Puli Tevar parted with. Still, he demanded the recall of Khan Sahib from Madurai and his grant of a district yielding two lakhs of rupees as the condition for his withdrawal from the alliance with the Poligars. But the Nawab rejected the terms. By the end of 1738 Khan Sahib himself marched to the north for the defence of Madras which was then besieged by the French led by the Count de Lally.[47] As a result the rebel chieftains reasserted their influence. However in 1758 the Nawab established his say over Turaiyur, an important Palayam in Tiruchirapalli, taking advantage of a succession dispute. The ruling chief was Varadaraja Reddi but his claims were contested by his cousin Venkatachala Reddi. In September 1758 at the request of Venkatachala Reddi for military aid, the Company's forces led by Khan Sahib and Joseph Smith marched to Turaiyur. As the forces captured the barriers, the Poligar fled to the borders of Mysore. A large section of the population joined the chief in exile. Venkatachala Reddi now assumed management of the palayam and it seemed that the expedition was a success.[48] However, in March 1759, soon after the withdrawal of the forces, the expelled chief descended upon the district. Now the rival Poligar fled and a body of troops which had been stationed by Khan Sahib surrendered. Yet Varadaraja Reddi, offered terms, which the Nawab accpted for fear of the Poligar joining the French. Mohammad Ali recognised the title of Varadaraja Reddi and received tribute.[49] This settlement contributed to the extension of Nawab's influence in the Kaveri basin.

The Madras council with the approval of the Nawab appointed Khan Sahib Governor of Madurai in May 1759. On his arrival at Madurai he found all the territories extending from Natham near Madurai to the walls of Travancore again occupid by the Poligars, belonging to the camp of Maphuz Khan. In his bid to weaken the rebel ranks, he decided on a policy of divide and rule. Accoringly, he won over the rulers of Ramnad, Sivaganga and Pudukkottai and at the same time dealt woth the defiant chiefs firmly. The kallans refused payment of tribute and treated the demands for payment with contempt. Whenever they were required to pay *peishcush* they used to remark: 'the heavens give rain to the land, our cattle plough the fiels and we cultivate, why should we pay tribute to an equal.[50] But khan Sahib refused to compromise with his autority. He attacked the villages of Kallarnadu and continued his policy of desolation during the entire month of June. As resistance failed, the Kallans submitted and paid tribute. After effecting this settlement, the forces began a simultaneous offensive against the eastern and western Poligars of Tirunelveli. In the east he ravaged Ettayapuram and Kolarpatti and forced the chieftains to clear, the arrears.[51] In the west he stormed Kalkondan, held by the troops of Maphuz Khan and Puli Tevar. The Poligars entrenched themselves at Kanguntram but were routed and the Palayams of Sorandai and Uthumalai were occupied. In September 1759 Khan Sahib with the support of Travancore attacked Vadagarai. On the approach of the forces the Poligar fled to Nelcatensevval. Confronted by a difficult situation, Puli Tevar requested the ruler of Trvancore to withdraw from the alliance but without success. In return for military aid Khan Sahib ceded Kalakkad to Trvancore without the Nawab's consent. In November the combined forces attacked Vasudevanallur. On the 27th when the assault was in progress Puli Tevar with 3000 men gallantly fell upon the assailants. The Poligar lost 350 of his men against Khan Sahib's 200. At the critical hour a heavy cannon of the Company burst. Puli Tevar wrested victory and the enemy was put to fight. This gave a serious blow to the authority of the Nawab.

However, in July 1759 when the military operations were still in progress, Maphuz Khan sent messages to Lord Pigot conveying for his support and the cession of Ambasumudaram and Rangasamudram to Puli Tevar.[52] In response the Nawab wrote letters promising to make adequate provisions for his support, but indicating no concessions to the Poligars.[53] In March 1760 the rebel chief left the camp of Puli Tevar and returned to the court of the Nawab.

Thus the rebellion of Maphuz Khan ended, but it did not settle the relation of the Nawab with the rebel Poligars.[54]

Alliance System of Poligars

The significant victory of Puli Tevar over a combination of powers in December 1759 bolstered the hopes of the rebels and set in motion fresh wave of disturbance. The Dutch whose commercial interests were threatened in consequence of the growing influence of the English, drew closer to the Poligars. The prospect of getting aid from Haider Ali and the French appeared bright. These factors contributed to the rise of the eastern and the Western coalitions against the Nawab. Kattabomman and other Poligars of the eastern region of Tirunelveli organised themselves into a coalition.[55] While Puli Tevar and other Poligars of the western region formed another coalition.

Maphuz Khan remanded at peace with the Nawab for the next few years. In 1765 he expressed a desire to go on pilgrimage to Mecca and requested his brother to give him a loan. Mohammad Ali paid Rs. 1,03,000 after taking a bond and furnished him with an arcort, a few camels and tents. A few days later, Maphuz Khan represented that he spent away the money in liquidating his depts and requested the Nawab to advance Rs. 5,000 more; upon which Mohammad Ali paid him Rs. 10,000. Maphuz Khan took leave of his brother and started for Mecca, but after proceeding upto Chittur, a few miles north of Arcot, he returned. The Nawab, now remarked that Maphuz Khan was always guided by his women. (Military country Correspondence, Vol. 13, pp. 299-304 Nawab to Madras council, 17 September 1763).

The eastern poligars received the support of the Dutch. The western poligars, on the other hand, organised their resistance in close association with Haidar Ali and the French.[56] The rebels received further encouragement when Haidar Ali and the French entered into an alliance against the Nawab and the English. By a settlement made in April 1760 the two Powers decided to conquer the Carnatic and to divide it between themselves; Haider Ali was to get the southern Carnatic and the western part of the central Carnatic while the French the rest of the Carnatic.[57]

To begin with Kattobomman occupied Ottapidaram, while the Dutch invaded Alwar Tirunagari and Nanapad.[58] But Khan Sahib encountered these aggressions with vigour. Gaining the support of the rulers of Ramnad and Sivaganga, he expelled the Dutch from the circar country and recaptured Ottapidaram.[58]

On the 4th of June Haidar Ali's forces consisting of 1500 horse and 2000 sepoys arrived at Tyagadurg on the southern borders of Mysore, expecting the arrival of a French army for operations in support of the Poligars. But Lally failed in sending his forces because of the desperate state of his finances. The English occupied Karur and forced Haidar Ali to withdraw his troops sent to Natham.[59]

In December 1760 Khan Sahib began his compaign against the Western coalition. On the 19th he entrenched himself within three miles of Nelcatansevval. The following day Puli Tevar charged the hostile columns but withdraw after he lost 100 of his men. The siege continued for about four months. In Split 1761 on the arrival of reinforcements, khan Sahib captured a hill, which commanded the view of the fort. Erecting batteries on the hill, he kept up an uninterrupted cannonade and cut off the rebel communications. Unable to withstand the ordeal or to obtain supplies, Puli Tevar surrendered on the 16th of May 1761.[60] After this discomfiture the rebels evacuated their strongholds at Panagur and Vasudevanallur. Khan Sahib magnanimously permitted his enemy to escape to Ramnad. He followed up this victory with the suppression of other rebel chiefs and demolished twenty nine mud forts.

The success which attended these operations assisted the establishment of Nawab's authority.[61]

Retreat of Travancore Forces

In 1762 when Khan Sahib was engaged in the settlement of Madurai, the chiefs of Travancore, Sivagiri, Wadakarai and Panjalamkurichi united together into a confederacy. Dharma Rajah of Tranvancore (1758-1798) who had 16,000 troops, trained by de Lannoy, a Dutch general and numerous irregulars, headed the confederacy. This development represented a reaction against the growing influence of Khan Sahib. The Rajah in particular, after extending his Kingdom upto Cochin, displayed an ambition to gain territories on the east coast.[62] In November 1792 the troops of Travancore assembled at Tovala, on the south-eastern border of the kingdom. Reinforced by the troops of the Poligars of Panjalamkurichi and Pittapuram, the rebels occupied Panagudi, Ervadi and Tirukkurangudi. Another column assembled at Aryankavu on the Western Chats and made a junction with the troops of Wadakarai and Sivagiri.

The combined forces numbering about 30,000 captured Shenkkottai and raided the circar villages.[63]

On hearing this ominous development Khan Sahib at the command of 1000 horse and 6000 sepoys advanced by forced marches to the southern borders. He greatly increased his strength by obtaining the assistance of the Madras and allied Poligars. After sending one army to the far south, he himself took the field in the west. He attacked the invading columns at Wadakarai and dispersed them. The forces of Travancore and the Poligars evacuated Shenkottai and Puliyara and retired to the hills. After stationing two columns on the western border, he with the remaining detachments moved to Kalakkad. Before he could reach to the rescue of the columns, the Poligars won a victory over them.[64] Yet on the 14th November he pressed upon the forces of Tranvancore, but the assault failed. Between the 14th of November and the 22nd of January 1763, he engaged the enemy in ten bloody actions but all of them proved indecisive. In February he received reinforcements from different quarters, in consequence of which he embarked upon another drive against the enemy. Inflicting heavy losses, he forced the rebel forces to evacuate all their posts and to retreat to the walls a forward step by carrying the war into Travancore.

Accordingly, he captured Aramboly, advanced upto Neyyattinkarai, and even cut off the nooses of the prisoners of war. It appeared that Travancore would fall. The Rajah was so alarmed that he made entreaties to the Nawab for protection.[65] Finding them of no avail, he submitted to the terms dictated by the triumphant invader. By the terms of the settlement signed on 21st February 1765 both the chiefs agreed to their territories.[66] The rebel powers suffered a set back, but they found more of opportunities when Khan Sahib himself turned against the Nawab.

Expedition of 1766

In 1763 Khan Sahib organised a rebellion against the Nawab and sought to establish the independence of Madurai. The Poligars utilised the situation to regain their lost ground. Many of the chieftains extended their support to Khan Sahib in his rebellion, withheld payments and occupied circar villages. However in 1764 the Nawab defeated and executed Khan Sahib. There upon he decided to chastise the feudal powers for their defiant proceedings and enforce collection of tribute. Accordingly, he won the support of the company and waged more of compaigus in 1765 Colonel Rumley led two expeditions to Kallarnadu. He attacked the villages and killed 5000 of these rebels. The Kallans submitted and paid part of their tribute.[67] In the meantime Umdut ul Umara, son of Mohammad Ali, assisted by Donald Campbell, led the forces to Ariyallur and Wodayarpalayam. The two palayams with their well preserved tanks and rich fields appeared flourishing because of the benevolent administration of the chieftains. On the appearance of the forces the Poligar of Ariyalur fled to Wodayarpalayam. In a battle at Wodayarpalayam the Poligars were defeated and their territories were occupied. After this defeat the two chieftains escaped to the Danish settlement at Tarangambadi.[68]

This victory represented a major for the Nawab against the feudal powers in Tiruchirapalli.

In December 1766 Major William Flint led the forces to Tirunelveli, attempts to capture Kollankondan in Sivagiri and Ettayapuram failed it. However, in February 1767 the troops occupied Panjalamkurichi.[69] In April 1767 the Wallajah and British forces launched a second campaign. Donald Compbell in command of the operations occupied Kollankondan and Settur. In May the forces marched to Sivagiri, a well fortified town with 20,000 inhabitants. The Varaguna, as the ruling chief was called, with his followers evacuated the town and took his position in the inaccessible woods. The invaders occupied Sivagiri and stormed Vasudevanallur and Singampatti.[70] Early in June they moved to the hills of Sivagiri but finding the task hazardous, withdrew.[71] The Poligars now sought a peaceful settlement. On an examination of the accounts Campbell was convinced that the Nawab's policy of oppression and exaction drove them to rebellion. Whereas Khan Sahib during the seven years of his administration collected from Sivagiri total amount of 18,000 chakrams, the Nawab levied 33,000 for 1765 alone. Added to this, because of Haidar Ali's incursions to the Carnatic the forces were to be sent to the northern frontiers. Considerations of justice and expediency required a peaceful settlement. Campbell accordingly restored Sivagiri, Settur and Wadakarai to the Poligars and accepted what they paid.[72]

Conquest of Marava Palayams

In 1763 when a civil war broke out in the Marava principalities, the Nawab decided to take advantage of the situation. The conflict began as the result of a struggle for power that followed the death of Setupati Sella Tevar (1748-1760). Muthuramalinga, an infant, was elevated to the throne while Muthu Viaja Raghunathta assumed the office of the regent and Damodara Pillai continued as minister. The struggle for power drove the regent and the minister to hostile camps. Damodara Pillai with the support of Tandavaraya Pillai, the minister of Sivaganga, occupied most of Ramnad, but his attempt to capture the capital failed. In December 1763 the two ministers paid a visit to Colonel Preston, while he was engaged in the military operations for the suppression of the rebellion organised by Khan Sahib. The Nawab advised Preston to make use of the opportunity for securing support of the ministers against the rebel powers without placing much confidence in their alliance. Accordingly, the English general asked for their military support against Khan Sahib as a condition of his extending any support for the occupation of the fort of Ramnad. The ministers accepted the proposal and assisted the British troops for the reduction of Madurai, held by Khan Sahib, to submission.

But after the fall of Madurai, as per the design neither did Mohammad Ali nor did Preston show any inclination to help the ministers. Meanwhile, the regent for fear of the machinations of Damodara Pillai, sought the protection of Mohammad Ali. Thus the rival parties applied for the Nawab's intervention. The deceitful Mohammad Ali promised to support the regent too. On his part the regent agreed to admit two companies of the Carnatic troops, as was suggested by the Nawab, into the fort of Ramnad, apparently for its defence.

Had this settlement been implemented, the Nawab could have perhaps easily occupied the fort, but this was rendered impossible because of the sudden death of the regent by small pox.[73]

On hearing the death of the regent, the ministers struck off to Ramnad, without taking leave of the Nawab or Preston and pretending as if they were apprehensive of the security of their persons but really because of the fear that the Nawab would demand the payment of tribute. Considering the services rendered by the ministers and fearing that the method of their departure would create an unfavourable impression upon the other allies of the Nawab, Donald Campbell who commanded the forces at Madurai, sent messages with assurances that they might return in safety after taking leave of Mohammad Ali, Yet they persisted in their pretended apprehension.[74] Damodara Pillai gained the control of Ramnad town and restored order in the estate. The Nawab on his part did not pursue his attempt either for the collection of tribute or for annexation, but waited for a better opportunity.

In 1771 Mohammad Ali gained the support of the English for the annexation of the Marava states. He represented to the Madras Council that the Marava chiefs occupied circar villages, harboured the most, notorious robbers in their woods and they permitted the Dutch to establish factories without his consent. He also pointed out that despite their state of subjection, they paid no tribute, rendered no service for an expedition to Thanjavur[75] and that the ruling Setupati Muthuramalinga Tevar obtained from him no permission for his ascension. The Madras council in consideration of the Company's alliance with the Nawab but without examining merit of the case, decided to extend military assistance for the expedition. In justification of this decision the English dubbed the Marava rulers as dangerous delinquents and declared that unless they were suppressed there was no safety to the government of the Carnatic.[76] Thus excuses were formulated for military operations.

However, the contentions of the Nawab and the Madras Council were just allegations calculated to justify what they decided to do. The Nawab did not specify the villages if they were occupied by the Marava chiefs. The robbers infested those jungles, where they found shelter without anybody's asking. The Maravas granted commercial facilities to the Dutch only after the English rejected a similar offer, made to Colonel Heron. Further, there existed no state of real subjection as to oblige the rulers of Ramnad and Sivaganga to serve the Nawab or to pay tribute to him or to dissuade them from establishing relations with foreign powers like the Dutch.

In January 1772 the Nawab's forces entered Sivaganga and occupied Tondi, the important sea port. The Marva troops led by Semialinga Pillai sought to expel the invaders, but were dispersed. Yet, the Nawab suspended the operations because of the possibility of a Maratha invasion of the Carnatic. In May 1772 the campaign being resumed, the combined forces of the Nawab and the Company led by Joseph Smith advanced to Ramnad. The fort, equipped with a heavy cannon and fifty light guns and surrounded by an open space had forty four bastions and a ditch. On the 28th the army moved to the fort before the queen regent knew that there was a complaint against her. Another army led by Benjour advanced from Madurai to the eastern borders of Sivaganga and captured Tiruppuvanam, thereby preventing the troops of Sivaganga form marching to the aid of the Setupati. The military operations were thus effectively coordinated for the suppression of the two principalities.[77]

Undut ul Umara, son of Mohammad Ali, exercised general control of the operations. He opened negotiations with the queen regent for a peaceful occupation of the palayam, but it proved unfruitful. On the 1st of June Smith ordered a general siege and the next day made a breach on the walls. At 5 p.m. on the 2nd a party of grenadiers led by Major Braithwaite carried the fort by assault. A large part of the 3000 strong Marava garrison died fighting, while the rest fled. The invaders plundered the flourishing town and imprisoned the royal family including the queen-regent, he r son Setupati and her two young daughters. On the fall of the fort, Smith wrote to the Madras Council :The fort of Ramnad is old, but the palace is one of the best buildings, I ever saw in the country and the inhabitants lived in truly Eastern Luxury which I am afraid they will never experience again. Young Maravar is about 12 years of age but the Rani has been invisible at least to Europeans. She has two daughters, both fit for matrimony. I have felt very much for the distress of these miserable people. Though there were 3000 armed men they did know what to do or how to act being attacked in sudden.[78] The royal prisoners were sent to Tiruchirapalli.

A two pronged offensive decided the fate of the principality of Sivaganga. Joseph Smith from the east and Benjour from the west invaded the palayam in June 1772. The country was very busy of cocksure thorn, though there were villages and open spaces here and there. Raja Udaya Tevar in anticipation of the invasion, erected barriers on the roads, dug trenches and established posts in the woods of Kalayarkoil. Undut ul Umara directed the rajah to pay one lakh of rupees but the latter evaded, abandoned his capital town of Sivaganga and established himself in the woods. On the 21st of June the detachment of Smith and Benjour effected a junction and occupied the town of Sivaganga. The next day, the forces marched to Kalayarkoil, and captured the posts of Keeranoor and Sholaveram. Now Tandavaraya Pillai, the minister of Sivaganga, sent messages to Undut ul Umara expressing his readiness for an accommodation. Therefore, smith wrote a letter in English directing Benjour to halt his advance until the result of negotiations was made known. But the troops of Sivaganga intercepted the letter and detained it without understanding the contents. Benjour, continuting the operations, came into conflict with the main body of the troops of Sivaganga on the 15th June. The Raja with many of his followers fell dead in the battle. His widow and daughter fled to Virupakshi in Dindugal. The invading forces plundered the town, collected jewels worth 50,000 pagodas and established the circar authority.[79] Thus the Nawab suppressed two of the powerful poligars and greatly weakened the hold of feudalism.

In fact the epilogs under the rule of the Wallajahs encountered a complicated situation, created by conflicting interests. They were required to deal with the administration of the Nawab the English East India Company as an ally of the Nawab and the rival powers. Assisted by the English, the Nawab sent expeditions against the chieftains and made a limited advance towards the consolidation of his authority. But this trend could not be sustained because of the opposition organised by the rival powers like the Nayaks and the Nevayets and the rebel powers, particularly Maphuz Khan and Khan Sahib. The consequent wars spread terror and termoil yet the feudal foures found it possible to take advantage of the disorders to expand the influence. For a time Nawab instead of pursuing his policy of coercion, resorted to a policy of conciliation with a view to gaining their alliance and granted them more of rights. The rival and rebel powers sought their aid and gave them concessions. More of the circar villages accepted their protection and paid taxes. However this situation did not last long. The auxiliary followed no uniform or common policy in relation with the new developments. Mohammad Ali on the otherhand was supported by his British ally. This led to the suppression of several of the poligars and the annexation of the palayams of Turiayur, Ariyalur, Wodayarpalayam, Sivaganga and Ramanathapuram. These gains were significant, but the Nawab found himself more and more indebted tc the English.

Notes and References

1. Madras Council, Military Consultations, Vol. 168, pp. 5465-5466.
2. Bishop Caldwell, *History of Tinnevelly,* p. 58.
3. S.C. Hill, *Ysuf Khan,* p. 45.
4. Board-of Assigned Revenue, Proceedings, 31 December 1785, Vol. 8, pp. 612 616.
5. Madras Council, Political Despatches to England, 5 October 1792 Vol. 2, p. 110.
6. Military Country Correspondence, Fort St. Geroge, 21 August 1763, Vol. 11, p. 227.
7. Military Consultations, 10 July 1792, Vol. 163, p. 2938.
8. *Ibid.*, 1 July 1775, Vol. 52, p. 943.
9. Military Country Correspondence, Fort St. Geroge, Madras, 11 January 1754, Vol. 2, p. 56.
10. Rajaram Row, T., (ed.) (1933), *Ramnad District Manual,* p. 236.
11. Rama Nayak, 20 January 1754, letter to Governor Saunders, Military Country Correspondence, Vol. 1, pp. 74-77.
12. Madras Council, Military Consultations, Madras, 4 February 1754, Vol. 3, pp. 36-37.
13. *Ibid.*, 13 February 1755, Vol. 4, pp. 24-44.
14. *Ibid.*, 6 March 1755, Vol. 3, p. 19.
15. *Ibid.*, 17 September 1755, Vol. 4, p. 159.
16. H.C. Hi!l, *op.cit,* pp. 37-38.
17. Military Country Correspondance, Fort St. George, 21 June 1757, Vol. 5, pp. 127-129.
18. Madras Council, Publlic Consultations, Madras, 29 September 1755, Vol. 84, p. 381.

19. Madras Council, Military Country Correspondence, Madras, 4 June 1755, Vol. 4, pp. 88-91.
20. *Ibid.*, 19 June 1755, Vol. 4, pp. 206-207.
21. Military Country Correspondance, Fort St. George, 10 April 1756, Vol. 4, pp. 43-44.
22. *Ibid.*, 8 November 1755, Vol. 5, p. 80.
23. Bishop Caldwell, *op.cit*, p. 98.

    Ranga Pillai, the diarist, says that Maphuz Khan was incapable of mking himself respected; was black and ugly, manners were unknown to him, he did not know how to treat visitors, and that the peons were orderly, decent and wore clean clothes, and turbans, but he was worse than them. (The Diary, Vol. 1, p. 308)
24. Military Country Correspondence, Fort St. George, 10 April 1756, Vol. 4, pp. 43-44.
25. *Ibid.*, 4 March, 17 July 1756, Vol. 4, pp. 29, 43, 44 and 107.
26. Khan Sahib was born of Hindu parents in Ramansthapuram, but early in his life he ran away from his house and coverted to Islam. After serving the French and the Nawab he entered the seervice of the Company with the rank of subedar. His fidelity, intelligence and martial talents won for him the admiration of the Enlish.
27. Military Country Correspondence, Fort St. George, 23 August, 1756, Vol. 4, pp. 69 and 129.
28. *Ibid.*, 15 May 1756, Vol. 4, p. 57.
29. *Ibid.*, 19 May 1756, Vol. 4, p. 59.
30. Madras Council, Military Consultations, 7 September 1756, Vol. 6, p. 733.
31. Military Country Correspondence, Fort St. George, 15 August 1756, Vol. 4, pp. 125.
32. *Indian Antiquary*, Vol. 46, p. 274.
33. The observation of the historian Mr. Orme that Kattabomman, dreading the consequences of his refusal to co-operate with the rebel, joined Maphuz Khan and Puli Tevar *(History of Indostan*, Vol. II, pp. 199-200). is untenable. The official records of Fort St.George state that Kattabomman was reluctant but subsequently entered into an alliance with Maphuz Khan sent his troops to the rebel camp. (Military Country correspondence, Vol. II, PP.180-181).

34. Robert Orme, *History of Indostan,* Vol. II, pp. 199-201.
35. Military Country Correspondence, Fort St. George, February 1757, Vol. 5, pp. 25 and 53.
36. Madras Council, Military Consultations, 12 March 1757, Vol. 7, pp. 226-227.
37. Robert Orme, *op.cit.,* Vol. 2, p. 200.
38. Madras Council, Military Consultations, 16 May 1757, Vol. 7, p. 427.
39. Robert Orme, *op.cit.,* Vol. 2, pp. 235-239.
40. Madras Council, Military Consultations, 9 July 1757, Vol. 8, p. 641.
41. Military Country Correspondence, Fort St. George, 15 August 1757, Vol. 5, pp. 159-160.
42. Madras Council, Military Consultations, 11 June 1757, Vol. 7, p. 583 and Vol. 8, p. 704.
43. Military Country Correspondence, Fort St. George, 8th September 1757, Vol. 5, p. 174.
44. Radhakrishna Aiyar, *A General History of the Pudukkottai State,* p. 216.
45. Madras Council, Military Consultations, 20 October 1757, Vol. 8, p. 926.
46. Robert Orme, *op.cit.,* Vol. 2, p. 252.
47. Military Country Correspondence, Fort St. George, 8th March 1757, Vol. 6, p. 31.
48. Madras Council, Military Consultations, 12 and 27 March 1759, Vol. 10, pp. 56, 92.
49. Robert Orme, *op.cit.,* Vol. 2, pp. 336-340 and 365.
50. B.S. Ward, *Geographical and Statistical Memoir of Madura and Dindigul,* Vol. 3, p. 7.
51. Military Country Correspondence, Fort St. George, 12 July 1759, Vol. 7, p. 150 and pp. 363-365.
52. *Ibid.,* Vol. 8, p. 114 for 1760. Copy of a letter from Maphuz Khan to the Nawab (no date).
53. Military Country Correspondence, Fort St. George, 17 September 1759, Vol. 7, p. 263.

54. *Ibid.*, 10 May 1760, Vol. 8, p. 165.
55. Military Country Correspondence, Fort St. George, 15 June 1760, Vol. 8, pp. 194-195.
56. The principal Poligars of the eastern Coalition were those of Panjalamkurichi, Ettayapuram, Kulattur, Mailamandai, Maniachi, Kadalgudi, Nagalapuram, Ezhayirampannai, settur and Kolarpatti. The important western Poligars were the chiefs of Vadakarai, sivagiri, Nelcatensevval, singampatti, utamalai and Surandi.
57. According to the terms lally agrees to cancel the bond for Rs. 25 lakhs which Naja rajah had given to the French during the struggle for Tiruchirapalli. (Military consultations, 9 June 1760, Vol. 12, p. 516).
58. Military Country Correspondence, Fort St. George, 5 June 1760, Vol. 6, pp. 194-195 and Vol. 8, pp. 205-213).
59. Madras Council, Military Consultations, 9 and 27 June 1760, Vol. 12, p. 580 and Vol. 15, p. 614.
60. Robert Orme, *op.cit.*, Vol. 2, p. 707.
61. Military Country Correspondence, Fort St. George, 25 May 1761, Vol. 9, p. 58 and Vol. 58, Vol. 10, p. 40.
62. *Ibid.*, 6 February 1763, Vol. 11, pp. 41-43.
63. *Ibid.*, 1763, Vol. 11, pp. 135.
64. *Ibid.*, 22 January 1763, Vol. 11, pp. 46.
65. *Ibid.*, 18 October 1764, Vol. 12, pp. 356-367.

    The Trivandrum district gazetter (1962) does not mention about this humiliation of Dharma Rajah by Khan sahib. but it gives a misleading statement that Yusuf Khan invaded Travancore as the Maharajah refused asssistance to the rebellion organized by the former. (Trivandrum District Gazetteer, pp. 205-206).
66. Military Country Correspondence, Fort St. George, 16 February 1765, Vol. 19, p. 369.
67. B.S. Ward, *op.cit.*, Vol. 3, pp. 6-7.
68. Military Council, Military Consultations, 10 January 1765, Vol. 22, p. 31.
69. H.R. Pate (ed.), Tinnevely district Gazetteer, 1917, Vol. 1, p. 76.
70. Military Council, Military Consultations, 8 May 1767, Vol. 26, pp. 385 and 318.

71. *Ibid.*, 15 June 1767, Vol. 26, p. 477 and 574.
72. *Ibid.*, 1 November 1763, Vol. 19, pp. 644-645.
73. *Ibid.*, 16 January 1764, Vol. 20, p. 32.
74. *Ibid.*, 22 December 1764, Vol. 21, p. 906.
75. In September 1771 the Nawab, assisted by the English invaded Thanjavur. Rajah Tujaji was defeated ans forced to cede a part of his territory and agree to pay eight lakhs of rupees as annual tribute.
76. Military Country Correspondence, Fort St.George, 3 November 1771, Vol. 19, p. 247 and Madras Council Military Despatches to England, Vol. 7-9, pp. 125-127.
77. Military Country Correspondence, Fort St. George, 1772, Vol. 21, p. 159.
78. Joseph Smith of June 1772 lellei to Madras Council, Military Consultations, Vol. 42, p. 488.
79. Military Council, Military Consultations, 26 June 1772, Vol. 42, p. 533-536.

CHAPTER – 5

BRITISH INTERVENTION

The military operations that were undertaken by the Nawab against the feudal powers were marked by ups and downs. A limited success was won, for part of the arrears of tribute was collected and certain palayams were brought under the direct authority of the circar. But most of the poligars continued to retain their influence. At the same time any external intervention appeared to afford opportunities to the chieftains for regaining their last ground. The Madras Council felt that the Nawab would collect the arrears of rent that the poligars owed to him and that he would clear his dept[1] to the English east India Company's and offer rewards. With this end in view it extended support to military operations. But it was disappointed, for nothing much could be collected and what was collected was not adequate to meet the expenses of the expeditions. In this situation the Company's found it necessary to mobilise resources for the conduct of major wars against Mysore. This required the intervention of the Company's not only in the internal administration of the country but also in Nawab's relations with the feudal powers.

The second Mysore War broke out in 1780 and it continued up to 1784.[2] In the course of war Haidar Ali , the ruler of Mysore, invaded the Tamil country. As a result of a brilliant campaign be occupied Srirangam and Thanjavur on the Kaveri delta. Advancing southward Tirunelveli, Palayamkottai and Vasudevanallur from the forces of the Nawab.[3] In an attempt to win over the support of the poligars he crowned a Nayak prince referred to as *Kattu Raja* as the king at Madurai.[4] After occupying the southern provinces the Mysoreans moved to the north and gained possession of more of territories -Vellore and Kanchipuram.

The outbreak of wars offered an opportunity to the restive chiefs to throw off the mask of loyalty to the Nawab. In a bid to regain the support of the poligars and to dissuade them from joining the camp of the invader, Nawab Mohammad Ali adopted a conciliatory policy. He waived the *peishkush* for two years, released the imprisoned chiefs from confinement and assured them that his circar would respect, their rights. Yet this was of no avail, for these concessions were taken as opportunistic. They were on the other hand guided by their own experiences- loss of their estates and imprisonment of their agents and more than these, their affinity with the Nayaks and the influence of Haidar Ali's emissaries.[5] In the wake of the troubles, caused by the Mysorean invasion, the poligars returned from exile to their districts. Thereupon they orgainsed disturbances on a large scale. Confronted with the challenges presented by external threat and internal disorder, the Nawab's administration collapsed and the Madras council found it impossible to raise the resources needed for the conduct of war. These negative trends invited British intervention in the administration.

Taking advantage of the war against Mysore the chiefs of Wodayarpalayam and Ariyalur returned to their palayams while the chieftains of Sivagiri and Panjalamkurichi joined the camp of the Nayak prince. In Wodayarpalayam and Ariyalur during the period of Nawab's rule the circar *amuldars* increased the taxes four times of what the inhabitants paid to the poligars in former times and tortured or killed those who did not yield to exactions. The inhabitants therefore rose in rebellion and demanded the restoration of the poligar system.[6] Haidar Ali, understanding the favourable situation, sent bodies of his troops in support of the poligars. Supported by the inhabitants, the chiefs expelled the Nawab's troops and re-established their authority.[7] In the meantime the kallar tribes after taking possession of Melur, Vellaloor and Serugudi in kallar nadu made inroads to the vicinity of Madurai.[8] Kattabomman of Panjalamkurichi entered into a close alliance with the Dutch and hoisted their colours on his fort.[9] On the other hand, Varaguna, the poligar of Sivagiri, assisted by the western poligars occupied Srivilliputtur.[10] These disturbances were so widespread that Christian Swartz of the Danish Lutheran Mission observed, "it seemed as if all the country people wished for a change, Worriarpaliam, Maravar, Tinnevelly country, Madura were all up in arms".[11]

After more than two years of turmoil, the country saw the prospect of the return of peace. In December 1782 Haidar Ali passed away. In February 1783 the Marathas withdrew form their alliance with Mysore and made peace with the Company. The British forces, released from the war against the Marathas, invaded the western region of Mysore in 1783, in consequence of which, Tipu Sultan withdrew his forces from the Carnatic.[12] The destructive war was brought to an end by the Treaty of Mangalore, signed on the 7th of March 1784. Tipu Sultan and the Company agreed to effect mutual restitution of conquered territories and return of prisoners.[13] In the end neither party gained anything, but the fury of war spelled disaster to the country and enabled the poligars to regain their hold.

Assignment Expedition Against the Poligars

The exigencies of conflict caused a serious strain on the finances of the Madras Government. As the burden of war fell upon the Company, the Council of Fort St.George applied to the Nawab for financial support. Mohammad Ali promised to pay a considerable amount, but even after eight months of war he extended no relief.[14] His servants, on the other hand unconcerned at the destructive war, exacted money from the inhabitants and wasted it. At the same time the Nawab by his oppressive exactions alienated the poligars and it was found imperative to establish a degree of order by a policy of conciliation, so that they could be persuaded to make their customary contributions to the circar.[15]

Accordingly the Madras Council requested Nawab Mohammad Ali to transfer the revenues of the provinces of Tiruchirapalli and Tirunelveli to the Company for the duration of war. The Nawab agreed: he gave consent either because he did not derive any substantial income from these provinces due to the disorders or he did not grasp the implications of the Company's proposed intervention. Nevertheless, by an agreement made in February 1781 the Company appointed receivers in these provinces for the collection of the net revenue from the Nawab's *amuldars*. These receivers were not granted any right to interfere in the internal administration, but were to be consulted in regard to the disbursement of the charges of collection by the revenue servants.[16] In effect the receivers were entitled to exercise supervision over collection, but had no powers. That appeared essential for control. As a result the system did not work. The Nawab's servants disregarded the orders of the receivers, did not furnish the accounts of collection, and continued to harass the poligars and the peasants.[17] Added to these, there came disputes between the receivers and the *amuldars* and the Nawab's interference in the working of the arrangement.

Thereupon the Madras Council suggested to the Nawab to make an unconditional assignment of all the provinces of the Carnatic to the Company during the war period. Mohammad Ali more sensitive of his rights than formerly what he was, opposed the demand and quoted a treaty that he settled with the Bengal Government in 1781. It exempted him from all financial demands beyond the expances of ten battalians of the troops of the Company and affirmed his sovereignty over the Carnatic. Yet the Madras Government was not prepared to retreat from its demand. By a compromise it was agreed that the revenues of the Carnatic should be transferred to the Company for a period of five years and one-sixth of the annual collections should be assigned for private expenses of the Nawab. A settlement that was signed accordingly on 2nd December 1781 granted to the Company the right to nominate the renters to be appointed by the Nawab to fix the rent for the districts with the renters and *peishcush* for the feudal estates with the poligars. These rates were not to fall below those settled by the Nawab under similar circumstances.[18] While the Company agreed to pay one-sixth of the settled rent to the Nawab, it consented to give account for the rest to his credit. This agreement covered all the provinces of the Carnatic, conferred much discretion to the Company for the settlement of rent and ensured for it direct control over the renters and poligars. Thus the Company gained jurisdiction over the feudal system together with revenue for a collection period of five years.

The Madras Council constituted a committee of Assigned Revenue for administration of the assignment. The Committee consisting of a Senior Member and five Members functioned through native officers called Company's Collectors who resided at the taluq or district headquarters.

The committee of Assigned Revenue made an earnest attempt to improve the system. It kept the collectors closely to their duty, watched the conduct of revenue servants, sought to check fraud and embezzlement and attended to the progress of cultivation as well as collection.[19] In an attempt to conciliate the poligars, it appointed the former poligars of Wodayarpalayam and Ariyalur as renters of their respective districts. These chiefs in consequence abandoned their alliance with Tipu Sultan of Mysore and joined the side of the Company. The rents of the two districts were fixed at what appeared as reasonable amounts 35,000 pagodas for Wodayarpalayam and 8000 for Ariyalur. Further, the Committee restored Palamaneri occupied by the Nawab, to the possession of Ramnad and Tiruppuvanam to Sivaganga. In an endeavour to win the confidence of the chieftains, it relieved them from the renter's jurisdiction, which occasioned oppressive exactions and placed them under its direct authority.

Thereby, the poligars for the first time experienced the direct administration of the English.[20] Yet, the success of the Company's administration was limited. The Committee was handicapped because of the limited. It found it essential to rent extensive districts to the highest bidders and to entrust unrestricted authority with the renters for the strict enforcement of collections. Due to the short duration of the assignment and the necessity to raise the maximum amount possible for the conduct of war; it could not pay much attention to the proceedings of the local servants. In addition, the transfer of administration from an establishment authority to an alien power created a general district among the poligars.[21] Consequently, its conciliatory policy failed, oppression continued and the Company had to resort to force for keeping the feudal powers in subordination.

In July 1783 the situation appeared favourable to proceed against the poligars and to curb their influence, the Mysore War ended most of the forces returned to the Presidency. Several of the chieftains who were in alliance with Haidar Ali defaulted in their payments and were not prepared to clear the arrears. At the same time the Company was in need of money to settle the war torn country. Because of these considerations Lord Macartney, Governor of Madras (1781-1785) decided on the employment of forces.

Colonel William Fullarton commended the operations. In July 1784 the forces threatened the kallar tribes with fire and sword and forced them to pay tribute.[22] The military posts established in Kallarnadu kept the population in awe and prevented it form going to the aid of the rebel poligars. On the 4th of August the army entered Sivaganga. Fullarton directed the Marudus, the ministers of Sivaganga, to clear the arrears of tribute, but the latter withdrew to the woods of Kaliarkoil and assembled about 10,000 armed men. However, as a result of negotiation a settlement was made. The Marudhus paid 40,000 rupees in clearance of a part of the arrears and settled terms.

Kattabomman of Panjalamkurichi in the mean time invaded the poligar estate of Chokkampatti and with 14,000 irregulars he lay in wait for the appearance of the Company's forces. But Fullarton taking a circuitous route through Palamaneri and Nagalapuram, descended upon Panjalamkurichi, He ordered the suprised garrison to surrender, but the latter refused. As it was essential to capture the fort before Kattabomman hurried back from Chokkampatti for its defence, the army commenced a siege with expedition. The rebels kept up a well directed and constant fire. The besieging forces destroyed a strong hedge which surrounded the fort, battered down a part of the wall and in a bright moon shine advanced steadily to the breach. Yet, they found it impossible to reach the summit of the walls, as the rebels continued their resistance with determination. After considerable slaughter on both sides, the British troops withdrew from the venture. As the fort appeared insecure, the troops of the poligar sallied out and fled. On the 14th of august 1783 Fullarton occupied the fort. He sought to bring the poligar to an equitable settlement, but did not succeed. On the other hand the rebel chief with his troops joined Varaguna, the poligar of Sivagiri.[23]

In alliance with Kattabomman, Varaguna, refused payment of tribute and made preparations for resistance in his woods. Therefore, the British troops took possession of the town of Sivagiri and carried the operations to the hills. The rebels disputed every step, but unable to hold the ground before superior fire power, retreated to the recesses of the mountains. Fullarton captured a strong post, manned by the poligars' troops and employed pioneers to cut a road through the inaccessible wood. A road three miles long having been completed, the forces reached the foot of the hills occupied by the poligar. The rebels thereupon climbed up the lofty heights of the perpendicular cliffs and took their stand. Because of insurmountable obstacles, the British forces saw their task unattainable. At this juncture, the poligar of Chokkampatti, taking service with the Company's troops, discovered a secret path, reached the summit of the hills and surprised the rebel-posts.

The rebels fled in panic to different directions.[24] The dispersal of the rebels of Sivagiri completed the victory won at Panjalamkurichi, for the two principal palayams fell under the control of the Company.

After establishing a few posts in Sivagiri, Fullarton encamped at Srivilliputtur, ready to make an accommodation with the poligars. The rebels procrastinated, but offered no terms for a peaceful settlement. However, threatened with a renewal of hostilities, Kattabomman and Varaguna paid 30, 000 chakrams each in lieu of all the previous claims that the Company had and gave bonds for 15,000 pagodas each as condition for the restitution of their forts.[25] In the province of Tiruchirapalli Eyles Irwin, the Superintendent of Revenue, strengthened the Company's administration. As the chiefs of Wodayarpalayam and Ariyalur did not pay the rent, he imprisoned the chiefs and established the direct administration of the Company.[26] Despite these, no attempt was made either to disarm the poligars or to curtail their rights. The Company in fact sought to combine its policy of coercion with that of conciliation.[27]

The Carnatic Treaty of 1787

Concerned at the attempts made by the Company to occupy the feudal estates and to strengthen its influence, the Nawab set himself vigorously at work for the revovation of the assignment. In January 1783 he obtained an order from Governor General Warren Hastings for the restoration of the revenue administration. The Board of control, which was constituted under the Pitt's India Act of 1784, too decided in favour of the Nawab's demand. It directed the Madras Council to make a settlement with the Nawab providing for the liquidation of his debts, which he owed to the Company or guaranteed by it and to surrender the assignment. Accordingly in June 1785 the Nawab entered into a settlement, regaining control of this revenues.[28] Thus he regained his rights before the lapse of the full term of five years for which he made the assignment.

As a condition for the restoration of the revenue administration, the Nawab was required to enter into a settlement in 1785 and it was formed into a regular treaty in 1787. This treaty signed by Mohammad Ali and Governor Sir Archibald Campbell (1786-1789) on the 24th February 1787, consisted of Articles. The Treaty of 1787 formulated the principle of joint defence for the Coast and increased the Nawab's contribution for the same from four lakhs of pagodas to nine lakhs of star pagodas. In effect the Carnatic was reduced to the status of a protectorate under the guise of a joint system of defence. The Company gained the right to garrison the forts and to demolish them if so deemed essential. The English presided over the defence system and undertook to support the stability of the Nawab's administration as in Lord Wellesley's Subsidiary System.[29] Nothing in the treaty prevented the Nawab from maintaining an army, but the crushing financial burden that was imposed upon him by way of contribution rendered it impossible.[30] In the event of war the Nawab was forced to apply four-fifths of his revenues for the conduct of war and to meet 25/51 parts of the total war expenditure, but the treaty made no provision for the division of the spoils. If the enemy won the conflict he might lose his rights over his territory and if he won, the Company might appropriate all the gains for itself. The guarantee of military support to the Nawab's government served as an inducement to depend upon the English for the coercion of the feudal forces and to neglect the administration. The steady deterioration in the administration, which was already corrupt, started a chain process in the decline of the revenue and increase of debt. This in turn created a vicious circle in which the Wallajahs played into the hands of the Company. There followed more of British intervention in Nawab's administration.

Assumption and Treaty of 1792

In 1790 the English East India Company assumed the revenue administration of the Carnatic and Thanjavur, despite the opposition of the rulers. In April 1790 Tipu Sultan attacked the lines of Travancore, an ally of the Company, and there followed the outbreak of the Third Mysore War(1790-1792). In consequence Lord Cornwallis, the Governor General (1786-1793) formed a triple alliance with the Marathas and the Nizam against Mysore and mobilised forces. Tipu Sultan advanced along the bamk of the river Kaveri, laid waste Srirangam and marched to Thanjavur. However, as the forces of the coalition threatened Mysore, he withdrew from the Carnatic. Since then the war was confined largely to the territories of Mysore, yet the Company used it as an opportunity to invoke the emergency clauses, included in the Treaty of 1787. Further, the resources of the Company, though supplemented by payment of four-fifths of the revenue of the Carnatic and Thanjavur appeared inadequate to support the expensive military operations.[31]

There were other causes too. Lulled into a state of security, granted by the Treaty of 1787, the Nawab attempted no improvement of his administration. The tyranny of his *amuldars* assumed region and the ryots groaning under the cruel oppression, neglected cultivation, leading to the fall of revenue and default in the payments to the English. Such a trend needed to be corrected. In the mean time no good relations existed between the Company and Amir Singh the Rajah of Tanjore. The Rajah pleaded his inability to pay his contributions, as required under the Treaty of 1787 and three lakhs of pagodas accumulated as arreares. The Madras Council was not prepared to compromise with any default in payment during the war time.[32]

Mohammad Ali and Amir Singh opposed the assumption of their revenues. Yet the Company disregarded their opposition and proceeded to issue a proclamation, assuming the revenue of the Carnatic in August and that of Thanjavur in September 1790 by a proclamation. The Madras Council guaranteed the right of the rulers to inspect revenue accounts. At the same time it promised payment of one to the respective rulers as provided in the treaties.[33]

On an assessment of this development it cannot be denied that the Company exceeded the authority acquired by it under the treaties of 1787, for they conferred upon it no such rights for assumption. Considering its own financial embarrassment, caused by the war with Mysore, it proceeded ahead with wholesale assumption without establishing that the rulers diverted or secreted four-fifths of their revenue for purposes other than war. It was true that their contributions fell in arrears, but the remedy prescribed by the treaties was the assumption of the revenue of such districts as were needed for the realisation of the arrears. The Madras council charged the Nawab and the Rajah of oppression; but by refusing financial relief, it failed to do what it could do to correct such a situation. In fact, the shortage of time for the recovery of the country from the devastating blow inflicted by the Second Mysore War, and the failure of rulers to reorganise the administration threw the public finances into disorder.[34]

The Madras Council created the board of Assumed Revenue for the management of revenue and to exercise supervision over collections. It entertained in its service the revenue-servants of the Nawab and of the Rajah and appointed collectors for the enforcement of the collections.[35] The Board divided the districts into allotments and farmed them out for one year period with the object of minimising the risk of rensactions and avasion. At the same time it sought to take precaution against entrusting the estates with over grown renters,who had for long excelled themselves in the art of exaction.[36] In Thanjavur the Company's two Collectors setup a court of justice and functioned jointly in deciding cases of property. In an attempt to win over the attachment of the auxiliary powers to its side, it reduced the tribute fixed for Ramnad from 3,00,000 rupees to 2,20,000 and that settled for Sivaganga from a similar sum to Rs. 1,75,000.[37]

During the war, when the English withdraw their forces from the far south for moving them against Mysore, the poligars withheld payments and make incursions into the circar territories. Still Lord Cornwallis felt that seldom the poligars would commit acts of violence without provocation. At his instructions Benjamin Torin, the Company's Collector of Assumed Revenue, made an enquiry to ascertain whether the poligars has any just cause of complaint. The Collector attributed the disturbance to their turbulent disposition. Still, the Madras Council decided to treat them with forbearance, as the forces in the mean time were employed against Mysore. Infact unfamiliarity with local situation made Torin to depend upon the views of officials for giving a report about the poligars.[38]

The Board Assumed Revenue experienced serious difficulties in the administration. At the orders of Mohammad Ali, his *amuldars* made a show of disobedience to the

Company's authority by denying access to revenue-accounts. The temporary nature of the management, the pressing necessity of raising revenue and the absence of the detailed knowledge of local customs prevented the Board from reorganising the method of collection, separating revenue from the other branches of public activity, protecting the ryots against oppression, improving irrigation facilities and establishing direct contact with the inhabitants. In consequence it had to adjust with the prevailing system, improving where it could do without encountering complications.[39] Besides, while it had to content itself with the exercise of general supervision, it was compelled to grant vast discreation to the persons on the field.[40]

Nevertheless, supported by the resources of the Tamil Country the British found it possible to win the war. The forces marched on Mysore from different directions. They occupied Dindigul, Erode and Satyamangalam-the key posts of Mysore. In February 1792 Lord Cornwallis assumed the command of the operations supported by the Marathas and the Nizam's army, he captured Bangalore and threatened Srirangapatinam, the capital. Tipu Sultan used for peace and on the 19th of March 1792, he signed a treaty surrendering half of his territories to the victorious powers. The English, as their share of the spoils of war, acquired possession of Dindigul, Baramahal, Coorg and Malabar, while the Nizam and the Marathas annexed the territory extending from river Krishna to beyond river Pennar and that between the Krishna and the Wardha respectively. These gains gave a defensible barrier to the British territories on the east coast, besides the possession of an extensive region. But neither did the Nawab nor did the Rajah, inspite of their contributions to military expenses and operations gain anything. Infact, the resources of the Carnatic and of Thanjavur contributed to the expansion of the British Empire.

The English gave up the administration of assumed revenues of the Carnatic and of Thanjavur in 1792, but occupied a recognised position of authority under the treaties signed in 1792. The Carnatic Treaty of 1792 combined in itself the fundamental principles enshrined in a preliininary settlement and the lessons gained by the English through the assumption, less to the advantage of the Nawab and more to that of the Company. The quantum of the Nawab's annual payments was reduced from 21 lakhs of pagodas to 15,21,105 star pagodas.[41]

This gave a limited relief to the over burdened resources of the Carnatic. But the new treaty made the punctuality of payments rigorous, for in case of a second default the assumed territories would remain in the permanent possession of the Company while not provision was made to grant any concession during a calamity, Besides, the treaty placed restrictions upon assignment of lands to private creditors. In consequence exaction was continued. If exaction excited reaction, the Nawab could obtain military aid, but his apparent gains would be neutralised by the requirement to pay expenses of military campaigns. On the other hand, if the English refused support to the collection of revenue, the income would sink and the helpless sovereign could invoke no clause of the treaty for his support, as there was no provision to deal with the Company's refusal of support. In fact of military aid could strain the Nawab's finances and refusal could impede collection. Thus the treaty was a double-edged weapon, which could be adroitly wielded in either direction, in consequence of which the Nawab might lose his territory. The English gained other advantages too. While the Treaty of 1787 required the Company to furnish to the Nawab an annual report on military establishments, the Treaty of 1792 granted to it exclusive military authority. The Treaty of 1787 provided for the appointment of receivers, in times of war for the collection of four-fifths of the revenue from the Nawab's servants, if such revenue were diverted for purposes other than war. But the Treaty of 1792 confirmed the procedure adopted during the Third Mysore War, for the Company could assume the revenue while the sovereign was to get one-fifth of it. In addition the Nawab lost his control over his foreign policy and his right to collect revenue from the poligars.[42] These factors helped the English to suppress the feudal powers in the name of the Nawab.

The Madras Council signed a treaty running largely along the lines of the Carnatic Treaty of 1792 with Thanjavur in 1793. In September 1792 Sir Charles Oakeley (1792-1794) the Governor of Fort St.George, announced the Company's decision to abolish the Tanjore Treaty of 1787 and to settle another. The Madras Council, without consulting the Rajah, prepared a draft-treaty and sent it to Rajah Amir Singh for his signature. As the proposed settlement envisaged no substantial relief to his finances, Amir Singh conveyed his anxiety that it would make the country bankrupt. The Madras Council, on the other hand, refused to make any concession and asserted that the Rajah could fulfil the conditions entered into the draft treaty by a prudent management of public affairs.[43] Thereupon the Rajah requested Lord Cornwallis to restore the country to him on the ground that the Mysore War ended. But Lord Cornwalllis directed him to comply with the proposed terms before the surrender of assumption could be made.

In consequence, the helpless Amir Singh anxious to regain possession of his country, gave his assent.[44] Still, the Madras Council, annoyed at the hesitation of the Rajah, declared that until his temper and conduct had changed to such an extent as to afford a reasonable ground of hope that "the interests of the English and the property of the people" would not suffer by a restoration, he could not expect to regain the control of the country.[45] The state therefore, continued under British administration for six months after the Rajah gave his assent to the treaty. On the 12th of July 1793 the Madras Council restored administration of the country to the Rajah, on the suggestion of the Bengal Council that, "it would be more suitable to our national character to hazard an error on the side of lenity than to expose ourselves to the imputation of having treated him (Amir Singh) with excessive rigour".[46] The Country thus utilised the surrender of 'assumption' for the enforcement of an unilaterally formulated treaty on the state. Despite the dissatisfaction of Amir Singh with the terms of the Treaty of 1792, the new settlement granted him a limited relief. The total annual payment to the Company was brought down from seven lakhs of pagodas to 5,13,333 pagodas, though this was subject to change as years passed by. Besides, in times of war when the state was in the possession of the Company, he was allowed to have one lakh of star pagodas in addition to one-fifth of the net revenue. However, the Company, as in the Carnatic Treaty of 1792, made the terms rigorous, obtained sole military control and the right to assume the revenues in times of war.

The two treaties were of significance as they imparted legal sanction to the encroachments made by the Company on the rights of the rulers since 1787. In fact they represented an acknowledgment of the superior status of the Company. The 'assignment' and the 'assumption' were two landmarks in the history of the British ascendancy in the Tamil Country. The settlement were of considerable advantage to the Company when it was engaged in major conflicts with other South Indian powers, especially Mysore and the Marathas. The apparently common defence system of the region as envisaged in the treaties served as an instrument to force the Nawab and the Rajah to furnish their resources for the support of large-scale military operations of the English, as and when they were required.

Notes and References

1. The Nawab owed large amounts to the Company's for its wars in defense of his rights against the French and the Nevayets.
2. The support extended by the English East India Company's to the Nizam of Hyderabed and the Nawab of Arcot against Mysore served as the major cause of conflict between the Company's and Mysore.
3. Madras Council, 26 January 1782, Military Despatches to England, Vol. 15, pp. 50-55.
4. Military Consultations, Fort St. George, 4 February 1781, Vol. 73, p. 273. *Kattu Raja* means king of the forest. It is to be noted that after losing the country, the Nayaks took asylum in the Wilderness of Sivaganga.
5. Military Country Correspondence, Fort St. George, 18 November 1781, Vol. 30, pp. 156-172.
6. Madras Council, Military Consultations, 4 February 1781, Vol. 73, pp. 273.

7. Collector's Report on the Deposed Poligars of Udaiyarpalayam, Ariyalur and Turaiyur, 1816, pp. 1-2.
8. *Memoir of Madura and Dindigul,* Vol. 3, p. 8.
9. Madras Council, Military Consultations, 30 August 1781, Vol. 76, pp. 2374.
10. Military Country Correspondence, Fort St. George, 18 April 1781, Vol. 30, pp. 155-170.
11. A letter of Rev. Swartz, 19 December 1780 quoted in *A History of Pudukkottai,* p.261.
12. M. Wilks, *History of Mysore,* Part II, Madras, 1869, p. 9.
13. Montgomory Martin, *The Indian Empire,* Vol. 1, pp. 350-359.
14. Madras Council, Military Consultations, 13 May 1787, p. 1187.
15. Board of Assigned Revenue, Proceedings, 27 May 1782, Vol. 2, p. 243.
16. Military Country Correspondence, Fort St. George, 5 March, Vol. 30, pp. 89-92.
17. Board of Assigned Revenue, Proceedings, 27 May 1782, Vol. 2, pp. 243-4.
18. Aitchison, *A Collection of Treaties,* Vol. 5, p. 181.
19. Board of Assigned Revenue, Proceedings, 20 October 1781, Vol. 1, pp. 2-4. The members of the committee as appointed in 1781 were Paul Benfield (Senior Member), Charles Oakeley, Eyles Irwin, George Proctor, william Fallofield and Paul Plumber.
20. *Ibid.*, 27 April 1784, Vol. 5, pp. 210-214.
21. Military Sundries, Fort St. George, 13 August 1784, Vol. 66, p. 218.
22. *Memoir of Madura and Dindigul,* Vol. 3, p. 9.
23. Tinnevelly Book, September 1783, Letter No. 41.
24. Madras Council, Military Consultations, 10 July 1792, Vol. 163, p. 2938.
25. Military Sundries, Fort St. George, 13 August 1784, Vol. 66, p. 71. A Pagoda was exchanged for 3 rupees and a rupee for 88 Chakrams.
26. Mohammad Ali, 14 October 1790, letter to Madras Council, Military Country Correspondence, Vol. 40, pp. 132-133.
27. Board of Assigned Revenue, Proceedings, 22 June 1785, Vol. 9, p. 494.

28. Aitchison, *A Collection of Treadies,* Vol. 5, pp. 181-182.
29. *Ibid.,* Vol. V, No. XLI.
30. According to the terms of the Treaty, the Nawab contributed every Year 12 lakhs of pagodas towards the liguidation of his dept. and 9 lakhs of star pagodas as his contribution to "current charges" while his total revenue was calculated according to Rajah Amir Singh's estimate-which does not appear very accurate-at 23 lakhs of star pagodas. Military Country Correspondence, Fort St. George, 17 September 1792, Vol. 43, pp. 264-267.
31. William Medows and Council, 16 November 1791, Military Consultations, Vol. 154, p. 5812 and 9 July 1790, Vol. 136, p. 2066.
32. Amir Singh, 28 May 1790, Letter to Madras Council, Military Country Correspondence, Vol. 41, pp. 334-335.
33. Madras Council, Military Consultations, 7 August and 24 September 1790, Vol. 139, pp. 2607-3346.
34. Military Country Correspondence, Fort St. George, 3 February 1793, Vol. 44, pp. 67-68.
35. Madras Council, Military Consultations, 7 August 1790, Vol. 137, p. 2607.
36. *Ibid.,* 8 November 1791, Vol. 154, p. 5678.
37. Madras Council,16 January 1792, Political Despatches to England, Vol. 2, p. 32.
38. *Ibid.,* p. 4.
39. Madras Council, Military Consultations, 8 November, 1791, Vol. 154, p. 5678.
40. *Ibid.,* 28 January 1791, Vol. 144, p. 465.
41. While a Pagoda, a Gold Coin, was exchanged for Three rupees, a Star Pagoda for Three and a Half rupees.
42. Military Country Correspondence, Fort St. George, 17 September 1792, Vol. 43, pp. 265-267.
43. *Ibid.,* 11 October 1792, Vol. 43, p. 315.
44. *Ibid.,* 7 October 1795, Vol. 46, p. 125.
45. *Ibid.,* 15 January 1793, Vol. 44, p. 15.
46. Madras Council, 20 September 1793, Political Despatches to England, Vol. 2, p. 243.

CHAPTER – 6

DUAL SYSTEM STRESSES AND STRAINS

The treaties of 1787 and 1792 formulated and established a dual system of administration in the Tamil Country. The English exercised military authority and controlled foreign relations. The Nawab of the Carnatic and the Rajah of Thanjavur, on the otherhand, administered revenue and justice in their respective territories. However, in times of war, this form of dual government was liable to be replaced by the sole jurisdiction of the English. The dual form of control was extended to the poligar system too. The Nawab retained his sovereign authority over these feudal powers, while the English collected tribute. The Fifth Article of the Carnatic Treaty of 1792 provided that the Company would have right to collect the customary tribute from the poligars and to enhance the demand on them, if on enquiry there appeared that they had to pay an amount larger than what they usually paid, by virtue of any lawful engagements . At the same time the Sixth Article laid down that the Company, desirous of preserving the Nawab's rights of sovereignty over the poligars, would engage to the utmost of their power and consistent with the realisation of tribute to enforce the allegiance and submission of these chieftains to the Nawab in regard to customary ceremonies and established practice of furnishing their services for the protection of the inhabitants property. The poligars were thus required to serve two matters. Their duties to the Nawab were to attend to customary ceremonies in the Nawab's court, to render military service and to perform village-watch. On the otherhand, their responsibility to the Company required them to pay tribute. The first category of service entitled them to maintain their armed strength and the second category expected them to hold possession of their territories. In consequence the poligars at least in theory retained their influence intact. At the same time, the Nawab and the Company restricted each other in the exercise of definite authority over these chieftains.

However, the terms under which the poligars were transferred to the British authority proved incompatible with the objects of the policy on which they were founded. The chieftains retained as it was natural for them to do, a strong desire to exercise military and independent power. They engaged in mutal conflicts and defied the Company's authority whenever they found it possible to do so.[1] To add to the trouble, the Nawab's *amuldars* misled the poligars to believe that the settlement of 1792 was a temporary arrangement and that they would be brought back to the circar administration. Such a manouver encouraged the poligars to defy the British authority and to neglect payment of tribute.[2] These factors embarrassed the Company's administration. The English found it impossible to interfere in the disputes not connected with professed object of collecting tribute, for fear that any other conduct would expose them to strained relations with the sovereign.[3] In an attempt to remove the anomaly created by the Treaty of 1792 and to introduce for its object an entire control of the tributaries, the Madras Council made repeated representations to Mohammad Ali, requesting him for his consent for a modification of the settlement of 1792, but the latter refused to accept any such erosion of his rights.[4]

The dual system infused ill-feeling in the relations of the poligars with the English. As under the feudal set up, the Nawab collected presents from the chieftains on different occasions. After 1787 the *amuldars*, denied of the right to collect the customary tribute, lost no opportunity in exacting presents under different pretexts. Their exactions and armed interventions proved a potential source of trouble. As the poligars paid tribute to the company, they looked upon it for protection; 'but the English refused to defend the poligar's interests as the rights of the Nawab as sovereign came in the way. At the same time the poligars could not appeal to arms, as the English undertook to enforce the obedience of the chiefs to the circar. This anomaly kept the poligars denied of the shield of protection as well as the right of self-defence.[5] The poligars felt that the English were responsible for their predicament and as such their subsequent resistance to authority assumed anti-British overtones.

Dispute over Sivagiri and Ramnad

The rights of the Nawab as sovereign and the policy of the Company as collector of tribute from the poligars came into conflict with each other over the possession of occupied palayams. The forces of the Company moved onto Sivagiri, a principal palayam in the province of Tirunelveli, in 1792 and occupied Ramnad, the Marva palayam, in 1795. But the Nawab, despite his waning influence sought to assert his authority over them in an attempt to Thwart the design of the English.

Chinna Tambi Varaguna, the chief of Sivagiri, in his bid to expand his estate annexed the former palayams of Tomachi Nayak and Puli Tevar. Further in May 1792 he invaded the palayam of Settur and killed the young poligar.[6] Collector Torin summoned Varaguna to his presence to explain his conduct, but the poligar did not comply with. Thereupon Col. Maxwell, taking the command of a force, advanced to Sivagiri in July 1792. The rebels evacuated the Town and took their position on the height of rolling hills. The troops cut their way up the terrain through the declivity of the mountains but the poligar's party was seen climbing up the steep ranges.[7] As the task appeared hazardous Col.Maxwell sent searching parties and himself withdrew to the plains. On 28th of August one of their parties captured Varaguna a prisoner.

The Company held an enquiry into the conduct of the poligar, but acquitted him of the charge of his personal responsibility for the murder of the chief of Settur. Still, the Madras Council, considering that the violent attack on Settur by his men and the total disregard shown to the Collector's order for attendance at his office constituted an outrage committed in contempt of the established authority, decided to deprive him of the possession of the palayam. The Nawab, on the other hand, called upon the Madras Council to hand over the possession of the palayam to his circar. In support of his demand he cited his sovereignty over the poligars. This requisition considerably embarrassed the Madras Council, for it wanted to take over the poisson of the estate and to establish its direct administration over the territory. Still obliged by the Treaty of 1792, the Madras Council promised to comply with the Nawab's demand after the restoration of order in Sivagiri. Subsequently, it referred the issue to Bengal for the decision of the Supreme Government.[8] Lord Cornwallis, the governor general decided against sequestration, alleging that Varaguna was not so much involved in the murder of the poligar of Settur, as it was believed and that it was essential to avoid giving an impression that the English were carrying on a traffic of making and unmaking rulers for the advancement of their interests. Accordingly, the palayam was restored to Varaguna, thereby defeating the Nawab's bid. Varaguna paid his allegiance to the English and restored Vasudevanallur and Settur to the possession of their former ruling houses.[9]

There emerged another dispute over the possession of palayam. It was the case of Ramnad after its conquest in 1795. The factors that led to the reduction of Ramnad to submission were centered on a conflict between that palayam with Sivaganga. After his failure to incorporate Sivaganga with Ramnad through a matrimonial alliance, the ruling Setupati Mutturamalinga Tevar closed a road leading from Tirunelveli to Tondi, in consequence of which Sivaganga lost the customs collected at Partibanur. In retaliation Chinna Marudu, the minister of Sivaganga, diverted a stream flowing form his territory to Ramnad. Now both the states armed against each other and entered into hostilities, marked by incursions, freebooting and killing. The conflict spread, when several poligars openly or clandestinely aided one side or the other. The Madras Council restricted by the Nawab's sovereignty over the poligars, took no action to nip the trouble in its bud. In consequence, the war continued, culminating in battles at Vesianoor, Paramagudi, Arandoo and Anundoor with neither side gaining any decisive victory.[10]

Concerned at the magnitude of atrocities, the Madras Council and the Nawab decided to intervene. London, the Company's Collector of poligar-peishcush, directed the warring camps to stop the war and suggested to the Setupati to reopen the road and to Mardu to let the water to the stream. Chinna Mardu complied with the instruction, but Muthuramalinga Tevar trifled with it. Thereupon, the Nawab warned the Setupati that his conduct would involve him in lasting ruin, in consequence of which the troops of Ramnad too withdrew from the war. George Powney, the successor of London, directed the Setupati to attend on him for an explanation of his conduct, but the latter refused.[11] In May 1794 the Nawab himself represented to Sir Charles Oakelay (1792-1794), the governor that Muthuramalinga Tevar was a man of such savage disposition that he felt no remorse in taking away the lives of his people and that he gave no consideration to the circar. Anxious to get possession of Ramnad, he sought British aid for the overthrew of the Setupati, from power. In consequence, the Madras Council decided to take military action against Ramnad.[12]

Accordingly in February 1795 the Company's forces led by Major Stevenson marched to Ramnad. The unexpected appearance of the army took the Setupati by surprise. Encountering no opposition, the forces occupied the fort on the 8th of May. The Company deposed the Setupati, sent him as prisoner to Tiruchirapalli and established its rule over the territory. The Madras Council granted a monthly allowance of 1,000 rupees for the support of Muthuramalinga Tevar. In an attempt to pacify the inhabitants it issued a proclamation promising then peace and security.[13] The Madras Council entrusted the administration of Ramnad with the Collector of the Poligar peishcush and introduced certain reforms. It organised the troops of all descriptions into a disciplined force, controlled and paid by the company, abolished the collection of customs which checked the progress of trade and introduced a village settlement for the strict collection of revenue.

The Madras Council looked upon these measures as the foundation upon which an extensive and permanent system might be formed for the efficient administration of all poligar territories.

However, the Nawab Umdut ul Umra, the son and successor of Mohammad Ali, annoyed at these proceedings, which were enforced without any reference to his authority, directed the Madras Council to hand over the territory to his circar. There upon the Company informed him that it would give him credit for the met revenue of the province, but refused to comply with his demand. In an attempt to thwart the Nawab's endeavour and to conciliate the inhabitants of Ramnad, the Company decided the succession the inhabitants of Ramnad, the Company decided the succession in favour of Mangaleswari Nachiyar.[14] Thereupon the Nawab questioned the right of the English to determine the issue of succession, declaring that it legally belonged to him. Still, the Company's will prevailed. Thus the Nawab's rights suffered a set back in another round of struggle with the Company.[15]

Reaction of the Poligars

The policy that was adopted by the English towards the feudal powers had its own reaction. It was aimed at the extension of its authority over the poligars through treaty settlements with the Nawab as well as refusal to respect his authority and armed intervention as in the case of Sivagiri and Ramnad. In the defensive strategy of the poligars Sivagiri was of particular significance. Situated on the eastern slopes of the Western Ghats and surrounded by barriers, it was not easily accessible and was eminently suited both for defensive and offensive operations.[16] The British intervention in Ramnad, one of the principal palayams, added to the apprehension of the chieftains and the inhabitants, for the Setupati, as the ruler of the principality and guardian of the causeway to the shrine at Rameswaram, commanded the veneration of the people. Lilkewise in 1795 the Poligar of Palani, the guardian of the

Muruga Temple, was imprisoned at Dindigul and the palayam was placed under the Company's control.[17] What aggravated the situation was the humiliation of the Poligar of Panjalamkurichi. As tribute fell in arrears, collector Jackson in August 1798 summoned Vira Pandya the young poligar of the estate to his office at Ramnad. After sending the order, the Collector left Ramnad on a tour of the feudal estates of Tirunelveli. Thereupon the Poligar proceeded to Tirukuttalam where the collector encamped but was told that he could see Jackson at his next halt at Chocumpatti, then at Sivagiri, then at Settur and then at Srivilliputtur. Kattabomman waited at all these places but was finally told that Jackson would grant him interview only at Ramnad. While the poligar followed the Collector for 23 days on a journey of 400 miles, the letter allowed even lesser poligars to meet him and remit the tribute. On 20th September 1795 at Ramnad the Poligar was permitted an interview. On an examination of accounts it was found that Kattabomman remitted most of the arrears, leaving a balance of 1080 pagodas.[18] Yet he was required to stand before Jackson for three hours and subsequently to wait inside the fort. Now a few sepoys appeared and Kattabomman escaped. At the gate of the fort there occurred a clash, in which a few sepoys including an English man died. On hearing this development Governor Edward Clive (1798-1803) ordered a public enquiry, found Jackson quality and suspended him from service.[19] The policy of the Madras Council appeared conciliatory, yet the Poligar found himself insulted. Accordingly he proceeded to organise a league of the poligars against the British. The employment of the forces of the Company against Mysore during the Fourth Mysore War(1798-1799) and widespread unrest against the Company's administration presented the needed opportunity.[20]

By this time the poligars of Nagalapuram, Mannarkottai Powalli, Kolarpatti and Chennalgudi in Tirunelveli had organised an alliance system for the assertion of their kaval rights in Ramnad. Kattabommon joined this combination and assumed its leadership by virtue of his personality and armed strength. In this bid to strengthen the league, he persuaded the poligars of Kadalgudi, Kulattur and Yezhayirampannai to join it. As a next step he drew the chiefs of Saptore and the Kallar tribes of Elavarasanur to join his camp.[21] In August 1799 the League sought to establish its influence in Sivagiri. The fort of Panjalamkurichi being situated in an open plain, appeared vulnerable to the attacking forces. Sivagiri on the other hand, was not so. It was reported that Kattabomman's design "in marching peons against Sivagiri is to get possession either by force or treachery of that fort and a narrow Pass which leads to it, difficult of passage, where he hopes to stand his ground against the forcewhich his fears naturally suggest to him will be sent to punish him".[22] Kattabomman sought the alliance of the chief of Sivagiri, but as this bid was not successful, he won the support of the son of the chief and sent his armed men to that estate. As the poligar of Sivagiri was a tributary to the Company, the Madras Council took it as a direct challenge to its authority.[23]

In the meantime in the court of Directors of the English East India Company, London, decided that "all subordinate military establishments should be annihilated within the limits now subject to our dominion" and accordingly sent instructions to Fort St. George.[24] The trend of the times too appeared favourable to enforce this directive. The Mysore war (1798-1799) ended and the forces were free to move against the southern poligars. In May 1799 Lord Mornington, Governor General, who was at Madras, issued orders for the movement of troops from Tiruchirapalli, Thanjavur and Madurai to Tirunelveli. The forces of Travancore joined the expedition. Major Bannerman armed with extensive powers was directed to take the command of the expedition. The order that was issued to him read: "The rebellious conduct of Catabomanaiq (Kattabomma Nayak), Poligar of Pandalamcourchy (Panjalamkurichi) having rendered it necessary to equip a military force for the purpose of suppressing the commotions excited by him, the Right Honourable Governor General (Lord Mornington) has resolved to avail himself of this opportunity to carry into effect, the orders of the Honourable Court of Directors for disarming the whole of the Southern Poligars and for reducing those irregular chieftains to the authority of the Civil Government". In fact the object of the expedition was not merely to suppress resistance but to carry out an already formulated policy, aimed at the destruction of the armed establishments of the feudal order.[25]

Accordingly, in May 1799 Major Bannerman commenced his military operations from Ramnad. He engaged the armed men of the rebel poligars in a decisive battle at Palamaneri. The rebels lost many of their armed men including their chieftain Chingum Chitty. Those who fell into the hands of the English suffered execution. Bannerman stuck up the heads of the executed insurgents in the villages of Ramnad. Many of the inhabitants fled in terror to remote areas. However, a restlessness continued to reign over the country. Though the insurrection in Ramnad broke out chiefly because of the suffering of the masses due to oppression and famine, Bannerman took no step to apply remedies to lessen the hardship of the people or to concentrate them.[26]

After suppressing the insurrection in Ramnad, the forces marched against the rebel poligars of Tirunelveli. On 1st September 1799 Bannerman issued an ultimatum to Kattabomman, directing him to a attend on him at Palayamkottai on the 4th, but the Poligar informed him that as the specified date was unlucky, he could not obey the order. The reply being evasive, Bannerman ordered the troops to take the field. As the rebels were seriously alarmed at the advance of the British troops, he lost no time in appearing by surprise before their stronghold. Meanwhile, he sent express orders to the forces stationed at Kayattar and Koilpatti to advance to Panjalamkurichi. On the 5th September by day break, all the forces assembled before the rebel stronghold ready for assault. The Fort of Panjalamkkurichi, an irregular parallelogram of 800 feet by 300 feet with walls constructed entirely of mud, had small square bastions and short curtains. The armed rebels, though were not well equipped with arms, had taken their positions for defense.[27]

On their arrival at Panjalamkurichi, the troops cut off the communications of the rebels with the countryside. The armed men of the Poligar, moving from the country side, sought to enter the fort, but were intercepted and repulsed with heavy loss. Now Bannerman debuted Rama Lingam Mudali to the fort to demand the unconditional surrender of the Poligar and to collect military secrets. Kattabomman refused to surrender, but Rama Lingam Mudali to obtained valuable information. Rama Lingam disclosed to the assailants that he observed a wide breach in the bastion east of the main gate of the citadel and that no preparations had been made to barricade the inner part of that gate and the gate itself was weak.[28] On the basis of this vital information the assailants formulated the military strategy.

Accordingly, Bannerman ordered the assault of the fort. On the 5th of September 1799 a six pounder broke the gate and the troops advanced with order and resolution to the breach. However the insurgents retaliated with determination and threw the attacking columns into disorder. A second attempt was made but it too failed. The rebels under the leadership of Umathurai, the brother of Kattabomman, put a stubborn resistance and frustrated the repeated efforts of the forces with heavy loss.[29] Bannerman feelingly wrote to the Madras Council about the discomfiture. He Stated: "The attempt was persevered in so long as there was a shadow of success and never was European energy more gallantly displayed than by the officers on this unfortunate occasion.."[30] In this battle the native troops of the Company displayed no definate enthusiasm perhaps because of their sympathy for the rebels. The failure of the English was, therefore, due to the indifference of the native troops and the determined resistance of the insurgents.

After this reverse, Bannerman, sent orders for more of reinforcements from Palayamkottai. On the 6th evening fresh troops arrived; but could not re-commence the assault before dark. However, as the fort seemed indefensible against a second assault, the rebels evacuated their stronghold in the night. On the 7th morning the *vakeels* of Kattabomman waited upon Bannerman with a proposition that he might be permitted to proceed to Fort St. George with his usual retinue to represent his case to the Madras Council. After much discussion on the subject, Bannerman communicated to the Poligar his resolution that he would permit the latter to proceed to the Presidency only after surrender. But Kattabomman declaring that it was no assurance, broke off the conference and directed his course to Kadalkudi. Subsequently, a clash occurred at Kolarpatti. The forces with the support of the troops of Ettayapuram killed many of the rebels and took Sivasubramonia Pillai as captive. Bannerman followed up his victory by his march against other rebel poligars. On 9th September he occupied Nagalapuram and forced the associates of kattabomman to surrender. To spread terror among the chiefs, the army marched to Kayattar through Koilpatti. The Poligars of the western range assured their loyalty and submission to the Company. Thus the army suppressed the rebel poligars and established its authority in the eastern region of Tirunelveli.[31]

The ring leaders of the rebellion suffered capital punishment. Bannerman brought the rebel chiefs to an assembly of the poligars at Nagalapuram. He charged the leaders quality of defiance to British authority. On 15th September he executed the rebel chiefs Soundarapandyan at Gopalapuram and Sivasubramonia Pillai, at Negalapuram. He paraded the dead body of Sivasubramonia Pillai through the streets of Panjalamkurichi and piked his head on the bastion of the citadel.[32] In the meantime Vijayaraghunatha Tondaiman, Poligar of Pudukkottai, caught Kattabomman and handed him over to the English. Bannerman brought the chief to an assembly of poligars at Kayattar on 16th October. Vira Pandyan accepted the charges and declared that he did resist the Company's authority. Thereupon, the sepoys carried Kattabomman off and executed him in a conspicuous spot near the old fort of Kayattar. When Vira Pandyan was led off for excution, Bannerman addressed the poligars who witnessed all that had happened in silent awe and astonishment. He expressed an earnest hope that what had seen would convince them and their posterity that no rank of them acting in contempt of British authority would in future escape punishment.[33]

However, it may be questioned whether the Company was justified in taking such as extreme step as the execution of the chiefs. By virtue of the treaties English Company was a render while the Nawab was still the sovereign and the poligars were his subjects. As such execution of the rebels without his sanction overstepped the authority that he granted to the Company. In a situation of suspicion and doubt liberality and kindness would have been the best means of securing the allegiance of the people, but on this occasion these were not tried on the otherhand Lord Clive applied coercive means and later events showed that they had their own reaction.

After the suspression of the rebellion the company in its attempt to prevent further outbreaks took different measures. It rewarded the allies, who assisted the Company in the military operations against the insurgents. The poligars of Ettayapuram, Maniachi and Mailandai were rewarded with the allotment of villages from Panjalamkurichi. The Governor presented a horse and an ornamental attire to Tondaiman of Pudukkottai as a mark of acknowledgment of the services,[34] that he rendered to the cause of the Company. In contrast rebel chiefs were subjected to harsh treatment. Accordingly the poligars of Nagalapuram, Ezhayirampannai, Kolarpatti and Kulattoor were put in prisons. The relatives of Kattabomman including Umaithurai were shut in the fort of Palayamkottai.[35]

The estates of the rebel powers were confiscated and brought under the direct administration of the Company.[36] The Madras Council assumed the military duties exercised by the poligars and the collection of taxes. In order to curtail the influence on the feudal chieftains it forced them to destory their forts, and prohibited them from retaining armed followers. The administration prohibited the use of fire arms on pain of death and forced the inhabitants to surrender them, but without giving any compensation. The Madras Council posted bodies of troops at centers of disaffection and overawed the inhabitants in its bud to prevent recurrence of outbreaks.[37]

These radical measures produced the most extensive changes in the affairs of the country. The enforcement of a series of drastic reforms in quick succession created internal tension. The southern poligars were a race of rude warriors, habituated to arms and independence.[38] But they found that their chieftains were either executed or condemned to a perpetual and ignominous imprisonment. This harsh treatment of a high spirited people reacted violently upon their sentiments. The Company in surprising the poligars subverted a time honored system of government, but without providing an effective parallel. The people were disarmed, their arms were confiscated and forts were razed to the ground. While no protection was given, the inhabitants were deprived of the means of rebelling the predatory incursions of their hereditory enemies residing in other territories and of resisting the unjust demands of the parties claiming the authority of the Nawab. They found their life subjected to constant supervision by British troops and interfered with by the Company's tax-collectors. These harsh measures had their natural reaction before long.

Notes and References

1. Madras Council, Political Despatches to England, 29, September 1794,Vol. 2, pp. 311-318.
2. Madras Council, Military Consultations,16 October, 1792, Vol. 167, p. 5109.
3. Madras Council, Political Despatches to England, 29, September 1794, Vol. 2, pp. 316-318.
4. Military Country Correspondence, Fort St. George, 10 May 1795, Vol. 46, pp. 44-46.
5. Madras Council, Revenue Consultations, 14 December 1798, Vol. 91, p. 4729.
6. Madras Council, Military Consultations,15 June 1792, Vol. 168, pp. 2603-2604.
7. *Ibid.*, 7 September 1792, Vol. 166, pp. 4422-4431
8. Madras Council, Political Despatches to England, 30 January 1793, Vol. 2, pp. 133-150.
9. Madras Council, Military Consultations, 9 October 1792, Vol. 16, p. 4860.

10. Madras Council, Political Despatches to England, 29 September 1794,Vol. 3, pp. 316-318 and 332-333.
11. Mohammad Ali, 23 June 1794, letter to Setupati, Military Country Correspondence, translation, Vol. 45, p. 198 and Madras Council Mililtary Consultations, 8 July 1794, Vol. 187, p. 2992.
12. Mohammad Ali, 28 May 1794, Letter to Madras Council, Military Country Correspondence, Vol. 45, p. 153.
13. Madras Council, Revenue Despatches to England, 24 April 1795, Vol. 2, pp. 350-355.
14. Madras Council, Revenue Consultations, 18 July 1795,Vol. 64, pp. 2541-2547.
15. Madras Council, Political Despatches to England, 4 March 1795,Vol. 2, pp. 338-341.
16. S.R. Lushington, 21 August 1799, Letter to Board of Revenue Proceedings, Vol. 231, pp. 3903-3905.
17. Board of Revenue, Report to Madras Council, 10 January 1792, Vol. 2, pp. 94-96.
18. Madras Council, Revenue Consultations, September 1799,Vol. 88, pp. 3110-3112.
19. Edward Lord Clive, later on Lord Towis, was the son of Robert Clive Governor of fort William. Jackson was dismissed from service on charges of mismanagement.(Madras Council, Revenue Consultations, 21 December 1798,Vol. 92, pp. 5415-5417).
20. Board of Revenue, proceedings,18 June 1799, Vol. 229, pp. 4890-4893.
21. Madras Council, Revenue Consultations, 8 November 1799, Vol. 98, pp. 3321-3322.
23. Madras Council, Revenue Consultations, September 1799, Vol. 97, pp. 2418-2420.
24. *Ibid.*, 12 August 1802, Vol. 112, p. 2690.
25. J. Webbe, Secretary to Government, Orders to John Bannerman, 19 August 1799, Secret Sundries, Vol. 26, pp. 386-391.
26. Madras Council, Military Consultations, 11 June 1799, Vol. 253, pp. 3246-3255.
27. James Webb, *Military Reminiscences*, Vol. 1, p. 62.
28. Madras Council, Revenue Consultations, 22 November 1799, Vol. 98, pp. 2777-2785.

29. *Ibid.*, 8 November 1799, Vol., pp. 2706-2711.
30. Revenue Consulations, Bannerman, 5 September 1799, letter to Secretary Webbe, Vol. 98, pp. 2706-2711.
31. Madras Council, Revenue Consultations, 8 November 1798, Vol. 98, pp. 2713-2727.
32. *Ibid.*, Vol. 988, pp. 3767-3780.
33. Madras Council, Revenue Consultations, Bannerman, 17 October 1799, Vol. 98, pp. 2877-2884.
34. Madras Council, Revenue Consultations, 8 November 1799, Vol. 98, pp. 2796-2797.
35. James Webb, *op.cit.*, Vol. 1, p. 51.
36. Madras Council, Revenue Consultations, 8 November 1799, Vol. 98, p. 2766.
37. *Ibid.*, pp. 2864-2875.
38. James Welsh, *op.cit.*, Vol. 1, p. 57.

CHAPTER - 7

DRIFT TO IMPERIAL SWAY

The wars against the feudal powers and suppression of their resistance coincided with a steady and gradual drift of the Tamil provinces to the imperial authority of the British. The poligar wars weakened the influence of the sovereign as well as his auxiliary powers. As these wars were waged with the support of the Company, they weakened the Nawab's authority for they increased his public dept and ultimately contributed to foreign intervention. The poligars offered a second line of defence in the land and when it was dismantled by the Company in the name of the sovereign, the Nawab found himself isolated from his tributaries. At the same time he had no allies either among the Indian powers or among the European powers tó shield him against the imperial designs of the British. Such a situation led him to his eclipse and replaced the system of dual control by a single authority, that of the British.

The Tamil Country during the last decade of the eighteenth century was divided among several powers. The Nawab of Arcot held possession of most of the country which included the provinces of Tirunelveli, Madurai, Tiruchirapalli and Arcot. The Marathas held possession of Thanjavur in the east. Tipu Sultan of Mysore ruled once the districts of Dindigul, Karur, Baramahal and Coimbatore in the north west. The English East India Company in 1767 acquired possession of the jaghir of Chengalpattu from Nawab Mohammad Ali of Arcot in return for the services it did in the wars against the Nevayets and the French. The French retained possession of Pondicherry on the east coast. As a result of wars and settlements, the Company brought the entire Tamil Country except the French possessions under its imperial sway. From a feudal order marked by divisions and conflicts the land of the Tamils passed under the British control and came to have a uniform system of administration.

The Mysore War and Annexation of Narth West

The north western region usually called a Kongu Nadu comprised the districts of Salem, Dharmapuri, Coimbatore, Satyamangalam and most of Dindigul. It formed part of the Nayak Kingdom of Madurai but had been annexed by the Wodayars of Mysore. After the fall of the Wodayars, these territories together with Mysore passed under the rule of Haidar Ali and Tipu Sultan. Mysore and the English fought against each other four major wars. During the First War (1767-1769), the Company's forces ravaged parts of Kongu Nadu but failed to occupy it. As the Second War broke out in 1780, the British forces moved into this territory. They captured Coimbatore, Karur and Dharapuram but restored them to the possession of Mysore in 1784 under the Treaty of Mangalore. In 1782 when this war was in progress, Haidar Ali passed away and Tipu Sultan succeeded him to the throne. The invasion of Travancore, an ally of the Company, by the forces of Mysore led to the outbreak of the Third Mysore War (1790-1792). Lord Cornwallis, the Governor General, formed an alliance with the Marathas and the Nizam and embarked on military operations against Mysore. Kongu Nadu served as the principal theatre of conflict. General Meadows, advancing from Tiruchirapalli reduced Karur and Coimbatore to submission while Colonel Stuart besieged Dindigul and forced the garrison to surrender. But in September 1790 Tipu, at the command of 40,000 troops, drove the British forces from their forward positions including Erode and moved swiftly through Toppur into the Carnatic. Lord Cornwallis as a counter-move, led an expedition to Srirangapatnam. As his capital was threatened and the fall of his stronghold appeared certain, the Sultan sued for peace. By the Treaty of Srirangapatnam signed in 1792 Tipu surrendered half of his territory. Together with Malabar, the English obtained possession of the Tamil districts of Dindigul, Salem and Baramahal in the north west. The poligars in this region not only sided with Tipu but also supported the rebel powers southward. Now they found themselves brought under the jurisdiction of the Company.

In 1798-99 the English fought the fourth war against Mysore. The cause was the hostile attitude and mutual suspicion of Tipu Sultan as well as of the English. Governor General Mornington declared that the Sultan sought an alliance with the French and refused to accept the protection of the British. On these grounds he went to war against Mysore with the support of the Nizam. Lord Mornington reached Madras to supervise the conduct of war. He entrusted the command of the forces of Madras as well as of Bombay with the General Harris Commander-in-Chief of the Forces of Fort St.George, a general who was well suited for post by virtue of his experience and local Knowledge. Also, he constituted a commission to assist the commander-in-chief in accomplishing the great task in view. It consisted of Colonel Arthur Wellesley, Colonel close, Lt Colonel Agnew and Captain Malcolm. General Staurt took the command of the Bombay detachment marching from Malabar. Colonel Wellesley led a detachment from Hyderabad, but the General command of the subsidiary forces and the Nizam's troops was entrusted with Captain Malcolm. The total strength of the grand army came to about two and a half lakhs. This army, properly equipped with arms and provisions it entered Mysore on 5th March, 1799.

In an attempt to defend the Sultan marched against the forces of Madras, which were then advancing into his territory from the east under the command of General Harris. At Malavelly on 27th March, the enemies came to a clash, which soon developed into a general engagement in which the forces of Madras won a signal victory. The Sultan retreated. Resuming the march, General Harris crossed river Cauvery at Sosilla and occupied the strong positions on the bank of the river at a distance of about fifteen miles from Srirangapatnam. On 5th April the Company's army encamped within two miles southwest of Srirangapatnam. The next day, after a bitter struggle in which the troops of Mysore made a stubborn resistance, the British forces occupied Sultanpettah. From there a strong detachment under the command of Major General Floyed advanced to Periapatnam, where it was joined by the Bombay detachment. Meanwhile Lieutenant Colonel Read occupied the districts north of Royacottah while Lieutenant Colonel Brown occupied the territory south of that place. He took possession of Karpur and Erode and reduced the strong fort of Avarakurichi.[1] On 4th May General Harris commenced an assault of Srirangapatnam. Major Baird commanding the storming party effected a breach on the Fort. With admirable gallantry, the assailants moved into the inner fort and overwhelmed a heroic resistance, put up by the Mysorean forces. The Sultan sought to reorgainse the defences, but he himself fell in the battle. Thereupon the broken ranks of the Mysore army fled and the Fort fell into the possession of the Company. With more of military operations, the out lying provinces of Mysore were brought under the control of the victorious powers.[2]

Lord Mornington, who directed the military operations from Fort St.George appointed a commission headed by General Harris to take effective steps for the restoration of peace and order in the conquered territories. In an attempt to conciliate the military chieftains, it granted an allowance for their support.

The commissioners made provision for the maintenance of the families of those who died in war.[3] These measures were intended to reconcile the feudal and military chiefs to the Company's authority. The important task that the commission encountered was the division of the conquered territory between the victors and the arrangement for the future government of Mysore. For the settlement of these questions, the commission framed two treaties- the partition treaty of Mysore and the subsidiary treaty of Srirangapatnam. Lord Mornington and his Council approved these treaties and accordingly implemented the provisions.[4] By the Treaty of Mysore concluded between the Company and the Nizam on 22 June 1799, these powers acquired vast territories. To the share of the English fell Coimbatore, Dharapuram and the territory lying below the Ghats in the Tamil Country. In addition to these, the Company took possession of all strategic forts and places including the island of Srirangapatnam.[5]

The successful termination of the war against Tipu Sultan and the political settlement of Mysore were attended with far-reaching consequences upon the affairs of the Tamil Country. Till the extinction of the military power of Mysore, the vicinity of hostile country was a source of constant alarm to the security of the eastern coast. During times of peace between the Company and Mysore, the intrigues of Tipu Sultan among the feudal powers served as a cause of commotion in the Carnatic. The auxiliary powers under the Sultan offered refuge to the offenders and rebels.[6] In the event of war, the troops of Mysore quickly descended upon the Carnatic and in collution with the poligars wrought havoc. The English now totally destroyed the military power of Mysore and turned a hostile country into an ally of the Company. The expansion of the Empire at the expense of Mysore gave a strong geographical barrier. As the defensive barrier of the Carnatic was pushed from the open country to the mountainous tracts, various forts like Arni, Tiruchirapalli and Thanjavur lost their relevance.[7] However, it cannot be said that all the consequences of the conquest of Mysore were beneficial to the Tamil Country. The equipment of the grand army necessitated the collection of provisions from a territory which laboured under a tyrannical system of dual administration of the Nawab and the Company, It caused widespread suffering to the inhabitants. Even after the conquest of Mysore the Tamil Country had to divert its resources for the consolidation of British authority. The state of affairs of the newly acquired provinces embroiled the Company in more of rebellions and more of wars. As a result, the new conquests continued to be a source of severe strain on the economy of the land.

Treaty of Thanjavur Annexation

Soon after the conquest of Mysore, the Company proceeded to annex Thanjavur, the granary of the Tamil country. It was ruled by Rajah Serfoji who replaced Amir Singh in 1798. Even before the accession of Serfoji, the Company had established its influence in the state. The Treaty of 1792 deprived the ruler of his political powers and reduced him to virtual subservience to the English. The accession of Serfoji at the instance of the Campany further tightened up the British held over the principality. Thereafter it adopted such a policy as to leave for the ruler no alternative other than the surrender of his territory. The history of the state under Serfoji coincided with the eclipse of the Marthas of Thanjavur by the rising power of the Company.

In 1798 the Madras Council made an endeavour to take over the administration of Tanjore from Serfoji. It felt that the administration was inefficient and the authority of the Rajah was feeble. As the finances of the state were in a state of disorder, the tribute to the Company fell in arrears. Rajah Serfoji himself was young and inexperienced. Taking advantage of these difficulties of the ruler the English sought to take over the control of the principality at least for a short period. However as no justifiable or reasonable excuse could be found for such a drastic step, the Supreme Government instructed the Presidency of Fort St.George that it could resort to such a step only if the Rajah himself expressed a desire for it. But paradoxically, within a few days, Serfoji himself stated that on account of his inexperience in the transaction of public business, it was difficult for him to relieve his government from the existing embarrassments. On that ground, he requested the Madras Council to take over the administration of his state for a period not exceeding two years. It seems that the servants of the Company had exerted pressure on the young ruler for the expression of such an idea, that was quite detrimental to his interests.

Now no obstacle prevented the Company from taking over the control of Thanjavur at least for two years. But General Harris, the acting Governor of Fort St. George, hesitated. He felt that a temporary exercise of British authority was quite inadequate to settle the problems, which faced the country. Added to this difficulty by 1798 the prospect of a war against Mysore loomed large. Hence Lord Mornington counted upon an alliance with the Marathas against Tipu Sultan. Rajah Serfoji was a Maratha and any step against that prince would have deterred the Marathas from entering into an alliance with the English. Hence the Governor General felt that the assumption of the administration of the principality at that moment would destroy the confidence of the Indian powers on the Company. These considerations deterred the Company from assuming the immediate control of the state.[8]

Yet the Company's administration was not prepared to extend any support to the government of Serfoji either in a spirit of Co-operation or as a matter of obligation. On the other hand, it tolerated its servants in humiliating and degrading the authority of the Rajah. The British forces stationed at Thanjavur exercised over-riding authority over the administration of the state. Major Innes, the commanding Officer at Thanjavur, expelled the servants of the prince from his palace and prevented people from attending the public offices. On account of these the Rajah could not collect the revenue from the people. In this state of helplessness, Serfoji appeared to Governor Clive for the redressal of his grievances.[9] He stated "I am as if imprisoned, which is cause of much disgrace to me in the world..."[10] Yet there came no relief. It appeared that the Madras Council wanted to prepare the ground for the annexation of the state.[11] The Anglo-Mysore War in 1799 added to the difficulties of the Rajah. In order to appease his imperial masters, he had to furnish provisions for the forces. The exportation of grain created famine conditions in his state. The employment of the carriage bullocks with the armies caused stagnation of traffic and the consequent loss of revenue under the head of customs.[12] Notwithstanding these bitter experiences the young ruler cherished an expectation that he would be allowed to survive as a ruler, but it proved wrong before long.[13] In 1799 Lord Clive instructed Torin, the Resident at Thanjavur, to take prompt steps for the annexation of the state. Accordingly, the Resident took the necessary steps. In a conference with Serfoji Torin explained to him that the disorders prevalent in his country could be rectified only by a through reform of the existing system of administration. Such a reform could be effected only through a new settlement with the Company. He announced to the prince that the more he relished the novelty of the scheme which the British Government had in view, the more he himself would approve it. The impact was sudden and the Rajah realised his inability to escape from the design of the Company that was in view. Therefore he requested that he should be given a little time to consider the suggestion of the Resident. A few days later the Rajah replied that he was fully convinced that the English in suggesting a new settlement, were solely motivated by their desire for the permanent prosperity of himself and his people. On that ground he expressed his acquiescence to the surrender of his territory.[14] Thus with the consent of Serfoji. Lord Clive executed a treaty on 25th October 1799. It was given a strange title "Treaty for cementing the friendship and alliance between the Company and the Rajah of Tanjore and for establishing the Government of Tanjore on a permanent Foundation", However, in compliance with the desire of Serfoji. Lord Clive included a provision for the transfer of the control of the Fort of Thanjavur to the Rajah and provided for the receipt of the Danish peishcush[15] by the Rajah.[16] The Treaty contained fifteen articles. Accordingly, the Company was entitled to establish a permanent system of reforms for the collection of revenue and the administration of justice. It was at liberty to ascertain, determine and establish rights of property and to fix a reasonable assessment. The English could administer justice according to such ordinances and regulations enacted by the Governor in Council of Fort St. George but with due regard to the existing laws and usage of the country. The Rajah was entitled to receive one lakh star pagodas a year from the Company in addition to one fifth of the revenues of the state.[17] He could receive as usual the tribute from the Danes of Tranquebar for the lands that they held from him. Besides, the Rajah was entitled to take possession of the Fort of Thanjavur but in the event of a war in the Carnatic, the Company could use it was a military post.[18] In effect the Treaty provided for the permanent transfer of the administration of Thanjavur from the Rajah to the Company. It added to the Presidency the resources of a fertile territory and a territorial extent of about 4000 square miles in the Tamil Country.[19] After the conclusion of the Treaty, the Governor stated that he achieved it "not only with the full consent, but with the zealous co-operation of the Rajah for the permanent benefit of his people."[20] But it does not appear that the statement of Lord Clive is in agreement with the procedure that he adopted.

Treaty of Carnatic Annexation

After Thanjavur, it was the turn of the Carnatic which comprised most of the Tamil Country. The history of the relation of the Company with the Carnatic from 1798 to 1801 was one of determined and repeated efforts made by the English to annex the territory despite the opposition of the Nawab. Lord Mornington on his arrival in India in 1798 suggested a modification of the Treaty of 1792 to Nawab Umdut-ul-Umara, who succeeded his father Mohammad Ali in 1795. But the Nawab firmly refused to agree to it, for he was afraid that it would result in the ultimate loss of his territories. Thereupon the Governor General directed Lord Clive to await a favourable opportunity.[21]

The outbreak of the Mysore War in 1798 appeared to offer an opportunity to the Madras Council to demand the transfer of the control of the territories of the Nawab to the English. The third article of the Treaty of 1792 stipulated that in the event of war breaking out in the Carnatic and the countries appertaining to either party, the Nawab or the Company, and dependent on the Carnatic or contiguous there to, the Company should possess full authority over the Carnatic except the Nawab's jagirs and charities.[22] However, it was expected that the Mysore War would not continue for long. In that case the assumption of the administration of the country was inexpedient, for the Company was to restore it to the Nawab soon after the end of the War, as demanded by the Treaty.

Therefore Lord Mornington, who was at Madras during the Mysore War, suggested that the Nawab should cede all his territories except North Arcot and his jagirs in lieu of his annual payment to the Company.[23] As an inducement to the Nawab for complying with his demand, the Governor General offered to recognise his claims over the revenues of Madras, Ramnad and the Pearl fishery of Tutukudi.[24] But here too the English did not succeed. The Mysore War ended within two months after its commencement due to which the English could not push through their scheme of annexations.[25]

Soon after the end of the Mysore War, there was discovered a voluminous correspondence of the Nawab with Tipu Sultan among the palace records at Srirangapatnam. This gave a new dimension to the entire scheme. Edmonstone, with whom was entrusted the translation of the correspondence, submitted his report on it in April 1800. In his report he made the following allegations against the Nawab: that Mohammad Ali maintained a secret correspondence with Tipu Sultan through the medium of Ghulam Ali Khan and Ali Raza Khan, the deputies of the Sultan,[26] that the purpose of the correspondence was to establish a connection with Tipu Sultan adversive to the interests of the English in India that Umdut-ul-Umara, the son of Mohammad Ali, was the principal channel of communication between his father and the Sultan, that even after his accession to the throne Umdut-ul-Umara continued to maintain the correspondence with the Sultan and that in the correspondence he used the vague expressions of "the writing known of" and "the affair known of" and also a cypher in figure of some secret meaning.[27]

With a view to establishing further proof against the Nawab and clarifying the doubts, Lord Mornington decided on a more detailed enquiry. Accordingly, Lord Clive appointed secretary Webbs and Colonel Close as commissioners to conduct the necessary oral examination of the persons, who were associated with the Nawab and the Sultan in their correspondence. The commissioners separately examined the prime suspects Ghulam Ali Khan, Ali Raza Khan, Dewan Purnea,[28] Mir Sadr and Habibullah among others. However, the result of the enquiry, from the English point of view, was disappointing. It was made clear that the correspondence was intended only for a matrimonial alliance between the ruling houses of Mysore and the Carnatic. The expressions "the writing known of" and "the affair known of" appeared to refer to that proposed marriage.[29] The key to the cypher revealed that Mohammad Ali was designated "Wellwisher of Mankind", the Nizam as "Nothingness", the Marathtas as "Despicable" and English as "New comers". As a result, the oral examination worked against the contention of Edmonstone that the Nawab maintained a secret correspondence with the Sultan for the purpose of forming a connection adversive to British interests.

Inspite of these, lord Clive suggested to the Governor General that the Nawab cherished hostile designs and as such the Company should assume the administration of his territory. In his attempt to establish that the Nawab was the enemy of the Company, he stated that the proposed matrimonial alliance was an explanation devised for the purpose of satisfying suspicion if the correspondence were discovered.[30] However, in defence of the Nawab, it should be pointed out that he did not maintain any direct correspondence with the Sultan. The letters contained only the expressions of the deputies of the Sultan, though they were attributed to the Nawab. Even here, the authenticity of their statements is to be doubted, for there was an instance in which a speech made by Colonel Deveton in his conference with the deputies to the Sultan. Even if the reports of the deputies were as the authentic expressions of the Nawab, it should be admitted that they contained only vague expressions of goodwill. Mohammad Najib Salar Jung and Tuckia Ali Khan, two sirdars of Umdut-ul-Umara, asserted that the correspondence contained nothing but expressions of civility and compliment and that the correspondence was begun only on instructions from Lord Cornwallis for cultivating the friendship of the Sultan. However, Lord Clive made no attempt to examine the truth of that assertion. It must also be pointed out that the Nawab, being a sovereign had the authority to violate the treaty-it at all he did so. At the most, the violation of a treaty by one party would place both parties in a state of relation which existed prior to the conclusion of the treaty. It would not stand to reason if one party proceeded to annex the territory of the other if at all the latter violated an agreement.

Still Lord Mornington directed Lord Clive to open negotiations with the Nawab inducting him to surrender his territories. However the Nawab was seriously ill and that dissuaded Lord Clive from announcing the instructions, which he received from the Governor General. On 15th July 1801 Umdut-ul-Umara passed away.[31] Before his death, the Nawab nominated his son Ali Hussain, a young prince of eighteen years, as his successor. He also appointed Mohammad Najib Khan Salar Jung and Tuckia Ali Khan as the deputies to the young prince.

Soon after the demise of Umdut-ul-Umara, Lord Clive deputed secretary Webbs and Colonel Close to the palace of the Nawab.[32] In a conference with the deputies the commissioners informed them of the nature of the documents that were discovered at Srirangapatnam and the determination of the Company to annex the Carnatic. But the deputies asserted that the correspondence contained nothing but expressions of civility and compliment and requested that they be granted an opportunity to reply to the charges.[33] But strangely enough, the commissioners declared that "the British Government, being satisfied of the sufficiency of its proofs, had no intention of constituting itself a judge of the conduct of its ally".[34] They impressed upon Ali Hussain and his deputies that as the Nawab entered into a secret correspondence with Tipu Sultan, the Company was determined to enforce a new settlement for the administration of the Carnatic. On that ground they demanded acquiescence of Ali Hussain to implement that scheme in view. But Ali Hussain and his deputies refused their consent for the annexation of their territories. Thereupon Lord Clive explained to Ali Hussain that in consequence of the breach of the Treaty of 1792 by his father, the Company had the right to annex the Carnatic. On that ground Lord Clive announced in the most serious and formal manner that if he did not agree for an amicable settlement, the result would be disastrous to his family. Inspite of this, Ali Hussain categorically refused to give his consent for the annexation of the Carnatic.

In consequence of this development the governor decided to identify another member of the House of Mohammad Ali, who would agree to surrender the territory in return for a title and an allowance. Accordingly, his commissioners consulted one Azeem ul Doula, son of Amir Ul Umara, who was the second son of Mohammad Ali. On consultation with that prince, he readily agreed to give his consent for a new settlement if he were declared as the Nawab of the Carnatic; for he had nothing to lose, but everything to gain. Subsequently, Lord Clive ignored the hereditary rights of Ali Hussain[35] and his place recognised Azeem ul Doula as the Nawab of the Carnatic-but without territory. On 31st July 1801 Lord Clive elevated him to the throne, with every display of pomp and splendour.[36] Though the new Nawab was deprived of his power and territory, Lord Clive allowed his some of the appendages of sovereignty. Thus he was given the right to receive ususal *peishcush* from Travancore, and to take possession of the palace at Tiruchirapalli.[37]

Before the enthronement of Azeem ul Doula Lord Clive settled with him the provisions of a new treaty for the annexation of the Carnatic. The Supreme Government at fort William ratified the treaty and it was called the Treaty for settling the succession of the Soubahdary of the Territories of Arcot and for vesting the administration of the Carnatic Payenghat in the United Company of Merchants of India Trading to the East Indies. The Treaty contained 12 articles. The Nawab on his part vested the civil and military administration of the Carnatic with the English. In return the Company was to pay one fifth of the net revenues of the Carnatic for the support of the house of the Nawab.[38] However, if the revenues of the Carnatic exceeded 25 lakhs of star pagodas, the Nawab was not entitled to any share from the surplus.

Though the procedure taken by Lord Clive for the acquisition of the Carnatic could not be justified, it should be noted that the ultimate results of the annexation were beneficial to the English. The Treaty of 1801 added a territorial extent of 17,250 square miles to the Presidency. Henceforth the English were at liberty to establish a uniform system of administration for the Tamil Country.[39] Perhaps the significant benefit which the Treaty bestowed upon the people was the end of a double government. Ever since the establishment of British influence in the Carnatic, the people laboured under a system of authority exercised by the feudal powers, rulers of the land and the Company's administration. However, the suppression of the poligars and settlement of the treaties of annexation prepared ground for imperialist consolidation under a uniform system.[40]

Notes and References

1. Lord Mornington, Letter to the Court of Directors, 20 April, 1799, Marquess Wellesey's Despatches, Vol. I, pp. 528-534.
2. General Harris, Letter to Lord Mornington, 4 May 1799, Maruess Wellesley's Despatches, Vol. I, pp. 529-577.
3. Madras Council, Sectret Consultations, 25 July 1799, Vol. 8, pp. 680-685.
4. Madras Council, Political Despatches to England, 13 August 1799, Vol. 5, pp. 53-55.
5. Apart from these districts, the Company took Canara and subsequently Harpanahalli that was rescued from the Marathas, while the Nizam took Gooty. The rest of Mysore was restored to the Wodayars as a princely state under a subsidiary treaty.
6. Lord Mornington, Letter to the Court of Directors, 3 August 1799, *Marquess Wellesey's Despatches*, Vol. 2, pp. 97-98.
7. Madras Council, Military Despatches to England, 14 April 1800, Vol. 30, p. 751.
8. Madras Council, Political Despatches to England, 15 October 1798, Vol. 4, pp. 199-207.
9. Military Country Correspondence, Fort St. George, 16 November 1798, Vol. 49. pp. 321-328.
10. *Ibid.*, Raja Serfoji, Letter to Lord Clive, 9 November 1798, Vol. 49. p. 316.

11. Madras Council, Military Consultations. 21 December 1798, Vol. 246, pp. 8064-8065.
12. *Ibid.*, 6 August 1799, Vol. 256, pp. 4782-4789.
13. Lord Clive directed Torin to open communication with the Rajah for the annexation of Tanjore in compliance with the wishes of Lord Morington.
14. The description of certain historians that Lord Wellesley (Lord Morington) enthroned Serfoji on the condition of his surrendering the territory, is not supported by facts. (Madras Council, Military Consultations letter from Torin, 26 September 1799, Vol. 259, p. 6765.)
15. The Danes of Tranquebar held a few villages from the Rajah of Thanjavur. For these villages, they paid an annual tribute of 2000 chakrams (one rupee is equivalent to 28 chakrams).
16. Madras Council, Military Consultations, 26 September 1799, Vol. 259, pp. 6769-6773.
17. One fifth of the revenue was calculated after deducting all charges of collection and a sum of 25000 star pagodas, which was appropriated for the support of Amir Singh.
18. Treaty of Thanjavur, 25 October 1799, Military Consultations Vol. 259, pp. 6785-6796. Serfoji died in 1832 and was succeeded was Sivaji. The next ruler was Serfoji II, Who died in 1855 without a mal heir. Taking advantage of the situation, Lord Dalhousie occupied the Fort and abolished the Rajahship.
19. Madras Council, Military Consultations. 5 November 1799, Vol. 259, pp. 6775-6777.
20. *Ibid.*, pp. 6745-6747.
21. Lord Mornington to Lord Clive, dated 29th July 1798, *Marquess Wellesley's Despatches,* Vol. 2, pp. 226-228. Lord Mornington instructed that "it is very neceeary that we should be prepared to decide the eventual question of the succession to the Nawabship in the probable event of his highness's early death. Your Lordship will have the goodness to assertain the respective pretensions of those who might lay claim to the Musnud in such an event. Upon such information as I shall receive from you, we may be enabled to anticipate the mischiefs of a disputed succession and to avid the disgrace of adoptiing a premature decision, which we might be compelled to revoke".

22. According to the Treaty of 1792, the Company hold the carnatic during the War. In that case the Nawab was entitled to one fifth of the revenue of his territories.
23. Madras Council, Secret Consultations. 23 July 1799, Vol. 8, pp. 1243-1245.
24. *Ibid.*, 24 April 1799, Vol. pp. 1213-1220.
25. Lord Mornington, letter dated 25 January 1800, to the Secret Committee of the Court of Directors, *Marquess Wellesley's Dispatches*, Vol. 2, p. 198.
26. The deputies sent by the Sultan to Madras to attend on the two princes who were entrusted with the Company as hostage for the fulfilment of the terms of the Treaty of Srirangapatnam (1792).
27. Madras Council, Secret Consultations. 25 July 1801, Vol. 12, pp. 376-378.
28. Purnea was the Minister of Tipu Sultan. After the fall of the Sultan, he was appointed Dewan of Mysore.
29. Madras Council, Secret Consultations. 25 July 1801, Vol. 12, pp. 469-472.
30. *Ibid.*, 23 May 1800, Vol. 12, pp. 553-557.
31. On hearing the illness of Umdut-ul-Umara, Lord Clive stationed troops at chepauk Palace on the plea of maintaining peace in the palace and preventing the removel of the treasure. In fact the Nawab was not allowed to die in peace.
32. It is stated that lord clive sought to annex the Carnatic by negotiation and not by a proclamation because of the critical state of affairs. It is possible that he feared the spread of the rebellion, which broke out in the southern districts in 1801 to the north. One of the objects of the rebels was to restore the Nawab to his former dignity.
33. Madras Council, Secret Consultations. 31 July 1801, Vol. 13, pp. 664-668.
34. James Mill, *The History of British India*, Vol. 6, p. 236.
35. A few days after the enthronement of Azeem ul Doula, Ali Hussain died under suspicious circumstances.
36. Madras Council, Secret Dispatches to England, 3 August 1801, Vol. 2, pp. 92-107.

37. Madras Council, Political Dispatches to England, 17 February 1802, Vol. 6, pp. 39-41. The Rajah of Travancore paid *peishcush* for Shencottah and Kanyakumari.

38. One fifth of the revenue was calculated after deducting the charges of collection, the revenue of the jagir lands, which worked at 2,13,421 star pagodas and a sum of 621,105 star pagodas, which was alloted as the amount required for the liquidation of the private depts as Mohammad Ali, every year. These were declared as permanent deductions from the revenues of the Carnatic. However, it was decided that the monthly payment to the Nawab should not be below 12,000 star pagodas and if the revenue of the Carnatic exceeded 25 lakhs of star pagodas, then the fifth part of the surplus revenue was to be applied to the repair of forts and for the defence of the Carnatic.

39. Madras Council, Secret Despatches to England, 1 October 1802, Vol. 2, pp. 103-106.

40. *Ibid.*, 17 February 1802, Vol. 2, p. 138.

CHAPTER – 8

RESISTANCE MOVEMENT AND ITS VIOLENT END

Through military operations and political settlements the English East India Company reduced the Tamil Country to unity. With the annexation of Kongu Nadu, Thanjavur and the Carnatic the imperial order replaced the dual system of control. In 1799 the company, despite the dual authority shared with the Nawab, waged military operation against the poligars. But it was of limited scope, for its rights came into conflict with those of the sovereign and it was confinced to parts of Ramnad and Tirunelveli. However, in consequence of the settlement of the Carnatic Tready of 1801 the British gained complet jurisdiction over the poligars and found themselves free to deal with these powers as they wanted.

The Campany's administration looked upon the poligari system as essentially feudal and opposed to the central authority and its existence as detrimental to its interests. Still, such a view was not shared by all the administrators. For instance, B.Hurdis, Collector of Salem, in his report to the Board of Revenue dated 4th May 1797 observed: "...the character of the poligars, I do not conceive to be fairly understood. The Europeans have received their impression from the *amuls* of the Nawab of the Carnatic and have enquired no further. As they have been plundered by the administration, they have deemed it essential to plunder others; this does not show their character but their act. The poligars are called refractory and detachments moved against them to overcome their resistance by terror and when it is satisfied in its full extent, the instrument by which it was enforced was withdrawn. However, no attempt was made to win their confidence; we understand from the official papers that demands were made for tribute, we hear the demands were refused and we hear that fire and sword exacted, what was refused".[1] In comparison with the British system many of the inhabitants found the poligari system more beneficial.[2] In 1799 the inhabitants of Rajapalayam in Tirunelveli represented to the Madras Council that when the poligars exercised their jurisdiction over them, they treated them with respect and extended assistance and protection. They helped in the settlement of disputes between the inhabitants and public servants and obtained for the ryots the circar's permission for the cultivation of public lands. If the administration in its demand exceeded the terms of the revenue settlement, the poligars intervened on behalf of the inhabitants and forced the circar to do justice.[3]

In fact many of the inhabitants considered the poligars as guardians of public welfare. This was because these chieftains enforced police authority, undertook protection of private property against robbery, paid compensation for losses through theft, administered justice, founded villages, conducted religious festivals, maintained temples, promoted cultivation and contributed to charities. These factors created and promoted a bond of local affinity between the poligars and the inhabitants. Inspite of this and in disregard their status in traditional society, the British forces engaged them in a long series of campaigns for more than half a century, executed many of them and annexed their estates.[4] In 1799 the British administration asserted that the power of the poligars was annihilated to such an extent that they were deprived of the power of resistance.[5] This was because their forts were dismantled, their armed establishments were disbanded and their resources were taken over. Yet the Company found it not possible to curb resistance against its authority.

In subsequent periods headmen of the villages, the broken ranks of the rebel powers and the emissaries of the French

Directory joined together in organising opposition to British imperialism.[6] At different places the opposing forces organised regional leagues to apearhead astruggle agaisnt the British. Marudu Pandyan, a minister in the service of Sivaganga, sent his emissaries on missions to Ramnad, Kallar Nadu and Tirunelveli, won the suppoort of discontented headmen and chiefs. This led to the formation of a Ramnad League. Mean while the alliance system of the poligars, that was formed by the rebels of Tirunelveli, maintained its association with different rebel groups to work out the escape of the chiefs who were imprisoned at Palayamkottai. While Gopala Nayak of Virupakshi in Palani organised a rebel group in Dindigul, Kerala Varma in Malabar, Krishnappa Nayak in Karnataka and Dhondia Waug in Shimoga created their own alliance systems. The records of the Company indicate that the headmen of the villages in Kongu Nadu and the emissaries of the French Directory went on missions to the centres of disaffection and kept the rebel groups in contact with each other.[7] Much because of their effort, representatives of the rebal leagues held a conspiracy, presided over by Gopala Nayak, Poligar of Virupakshi, in his fort by the end of April 1800. In this conspiracy the rebel powers decided to launch a general offensive against the British with the storming of Coimbatore. The possession of Coimbatore appeared as a strategic necessity so as to provide a vital link to the rebels operating in the Tamil country and those in the Karnataka region. June 3, 1800 was decided upon for capturing Coimbatore, for the Mohammadan sepoys stationed by the Company to guard this fort, were expected to be busy with Muharram Feast. The rebels decided to destroy the exhausted regiment late in that night, when it would go an a procession around the town and occupy the fort.[8] Accordingly, armed columns on June 3, 1800 took up their positions in the vicinity of Coimbatore. However, the Tahsildar of the area received information about the rebel design and passed it on to Lieutenant Colonel Macalister, stationed in the fort. Thereupon, parties went in search of the hiding rebels. Among the suspects who were brought to trial, forty two insurgents were executed publicity at different centers of disaffection. This marked a serious blow to rebel strategy.[9] Despite the failure of the projected assault on Coimbatore, the rebel parties worked out the escape of the rebels, who were imprisoned at Palayamkottai and waged a determined struggle against the British forces.

Escape of Poligar Prisoners

The relatives of Kattabomman, seventeen in number, condemned for perpetual imprisonment, were confined in a small enclosure in the Fort of Palayamkottai. Rebels of consequence, they were kept in iron, rigidly guarded. Three of them died in ordeal, while the rest languished in prison. However on the 2nd of February 1801 by a clever strategem they made their escape. Among the escaped prisoners were Sevatish and Kumaraswami Nayak, also Called Oomathurai, the brothers of Kattabomman. After the failure of an attempt made by Marudu Pandyan to work out the release of the prisoners, Oomathurai entered into a correspondence with the rebels of Panjalamkurachi. Potti Pakada, a servant employed for the collection of firewood for the prisoners, carried his letters wriiten on palmyra leaves to the rebels, who met him in the nearby jungles. Through the excahnge of letters the strategy was worked out. Accordingly, in January 1801 a party of rebels numbering about 200 disguised as pilgrims going to Tiruchendur Temple started from Panjalamkurichi. Playing 'Kavadi'[10] blowing the conch shell, distributing holy ashes, receiving offerings and chanting spells, all reached Palayamkottai. On hearing the chanting of spells, the prisoners to their relief understood that the relieving party had arrived. As sellers of plantain leaves, fruits and firewood, the party now approched the gate of the fort. Oomathurai in the mean time won the sympathy of the wife of the superintendent of the fort and secured permission to perform the ceremonies for the dead. He offered to purchase the fruits, leaves and firewood for the same. The prices were setteled and all the people were permitted to carry the loads into the fort. They excised no suspicion but they kept arms concealed inside the loads.

At the right moment the prisoners privately sent away their women, who were allowed to stay at liberty within the fort.

Large parties of insurgents, armed with country weapons lay in wait. They brought a few horses to provide quick means of escape to their imprisoned leaders. At the appointed hour soon after sun set on the 2nd of February 1801, the prisoners sprung forward. They disarmed the sentinels, overpowered the guard and got safely off. The quickness of the assault and the war cry raised by them took the troops by complet surprise. Jointed by more columns of armed men on their way, the fugitives moved rapidly to the Vallanad Hills, near Panjalamkurchi. The rebels annihilated the authority of the English, reoccupied Panjalamkurichi and proclaimed Sevathiah as the poligar.

With the escape of rebels, pillaging parties surprised and subdued British military posts and released the prisoners. Before the end of February they occupied all the territories extending from Panajlamkurichi to Srivaikuntam and Alwar Tirunagiri. They converted the *palayams* of Kulattoor, Kadalkudi, Nagalapuram, Kolarpatti and Yezhayirampannai into their strongholds and reconstructed the demolished forts.[11] In March the insurgents marched to Tutukudi, upon which the garrison surrendered. They permitted Edward Ormsley, the English commander of the fort, to take away his properties and to go away in safety. They imprisoned Baggot, the Master Attendent but as the prisoner's wife followed the rebels and appealed to their chief for his safety, they released him from custody and restored to him his properties. After the fall of Tutukudi, the rebels made irruption into Ramnad and made preparations in Vallanad hills to capture Tirunelveli.[12]

Colin Mecaulay, the Company's commandiing officer at Palayamkottai, issued a proclamation warning the people of exemplary punishment if they were found in arms of rendering aid to the rebels. He sent express directions to the poligars of amicable disposition like those of Sivagiri and Ettayapuam to remain on their guard and to convey information about the rebel movements.[13] In February 1801 Macaulay launched operations against the rebels. Mobilishing the whole disposable force of the province, he marched to Sankaranainarkoil, then to Kayattar and reached Kadayanallur, six miles short of Panjalamkurichi. As the troops pitched their camp and prepared for a hearty meal after a tedious march, they found their camp suddenly attacked on all sides. Advancing under cover of a deep ravine, the armed men made a simultaneous attack from different directions. The British troops killed forty of the rebels and then formed into a square with guns at angles and baggage in the centre remaining in their position the whole night, subjected to repeated alarms. The next day, the forces encamped near Panjalamkurichi. To their astonishment they found the demolished fort"raised as it were by magic in six days" and every part of it was well manned by thousands of armed men.[14] The rebels foiled an attempt to capture the Pagoda of Ottapidaram and boldly appeared on the rear and flank of the forces. Macaulay for fear that his column would be cut off by rebels both from Panjalamkurichi and Vallanad hills, retreated under the guise of preparing for an attack. As soon as the rebels understood their mistake, they overtook the troops with shouts and screams. In the clash that ensued the rebels lost 110 men. Still followed by them, after a severe march that lasted all the night the forces reached Palayamkottai on 10th February, Mean while Captain Hazard reinforced by a detail from Madurai attacked Kadalkudi, but was defeated. On 19th March the rebels directed all their effort for the reduction of the Company's post at Srivaikuntam, overwhlemed a body of troops led by Major Sheppard and took the post.[15]

While the Company's forces were suffering reverses in different quarters, fresh troops poured into Tirunelveli under the direction of General Brathwaite, the Commander-in-chief of the forces of Fort St. George. Macaulay assembled these forces at Kayattar. Assuming the command of the forces, he reached Pusuvanthanai situated near Panjalamkurichi on the 30th of March. At this place the troops of Ettayapuram joined the English forces. Soon afterwards, the forces found themselves surrounded by a formidable phalanx of insurgents. Macaulay charged them and killed ninety six of these "brave but unskilful pedestrians".[16] The rest of them effected their escape through a nearby wood. On the 31st March Macaulay concentrated his forces on the north west angle of the Fort, throwing out the cavalry to the south and the troops of Ettayapuram to the east. When the preparations were completed, the heavy guns commenced a sharp fire. At 3 p.m.the breach seemed perfectly practicable. The European details, supported by native infantry, moved forward to the breach "under the heaviest fire imaginable". But the gallant assault of the assailants did not dissuade the insurgents from their determination to resist. With intrepid firmness they engaged the assailants in a fierce encounter. They either picked or shot dead all the soldiers, who pressed their way to the breach. Repeated attempts were made to surmount the breach, but all ended in fiasco. The troops of Ettayapuram who attacked the east wall of the rebel stronghold sheered the fate of their allies.[17] Thus, the British troops, as Governor Clive himself admitted: "after sustaining an unequal conflicts, against a superior force, with unshakable bravery and discipline, were repulsed with heavy loss.[18]

Reaction in Dindigul and Coimbatore

In Dindigul and Coimbatore the poligars took the lead in organising the rebellion. Allied with the rebels of Malabar, Mysore, Sivaganga and Tirunelveli the resistance movements in this region formed link between the rebels of the north and of the south. The rebel chieftains assembled not only their peons but also all the inhabitants to take arms against the English.[19]

When the forces that were encamped in Dindigul were withdrawn for the suppression of a rebellion in Malabar, the armed men of Virupakshi under the leadership of Gopala Nayak rose in rebellion. The escapee of the rebels who were imprisoned at Palayamkottai and the subsequent rising in Tirunelveli in February 1801, gave encouragement to the rebels of Dindigul and Coimbatore.[20] The poligars of Dhili, Mangalam, Periapally, Chenchode, Julipatty, Tondamattoor and Somandory soon joined the insurrection. All threw of their allegiance to the English and made incursions into the territoies of the company.[21]

The administration took speedy measures to isolate the rebels from those of northern and southern powersand to suppress them. The success of British arms in Malabar and Wynaad enabled the Company to expedite the military operations. Lietutentant Colonel Innes, assuming the command of a detachment from Malabar, attacked the rebels' posts from the north. On 21st March, 1801, he defeated Gopala Nayak and occupied Virupakshi. After posting a body of troops for the defence of Virupakshi, the British troops, took Dhili without much opposition. Theses reverses forced the rebels to flee to the jungles. Descending from the hills, they made incursions into the territories of the Company.[22] But Innes marching through a close jungle west of Anamalaikottai attacked the rebel strongholds. The insurgents pulled down huge stones on the advancing troops and inflicted losses. Yet on 13th April, Innes won a signal success over the united forces of Virupakshi and Delhi.[23] The rebels, determined as they were made a second attempt to establish themselves and raised barriers on the hills. On the 20th April Innes moved against them through a thick forced for about eight miles and arrived at Attoor. He captured the barriers that were held by the rebels and dispersed them. Thereupon the fugitives led by Muthu Vella Nayak, son of Gopala Nayak, evacuated the terrain and joined the rebel camps in Sivaganga and Ramnad.[24] While the Poligar of Dhili escaped to the western hills, where he died, Gopala Nayak of Virupakshi fell into the custody of advancing troops. The rebellion in Dindigul was suppressed and fifteen rebels of note including the poligars of Virupakshi and Jellipatti were hanged to death.[25]

Capture of Panjalamkurichi

After the failure of a determined attempt on Panjalamkurichi, the attacking forces instituted a blockade. There followed skirmishes day after day. While the blockade was on, the Madras Council rushed reinforcements from fort St.George, St. Thomas Mount, Arcot,Malabar and Tiruchirapalli to the south. He entrusted the command of the grand army with Lieutenant Colonel Agnew, the Adjutant General and an officer well qualified by his gallantly, integrity and experience, for the task.[26]

On 23rd May Agnew commanded the army from Kovilpatti to Panajalamkurichi. The 53 day blockkade ended and a regular siege began. The troops opened fire at the bastion of the south west angle of the citadel. On 24th a breach being effected, an attack was ordered. Coloumns moved forward, supported by the field pieces, while the big batteries by a heavy fire covered the advance. Notwithstanding the formidable array, the rebels did not shrink back, but received the enemy with renewed vigour. Armed with musquetry and pikes, the rebels kept up a heavy fire on parties, while others sallying forth from the broken bastions engaged the approching troops. An the storming arduoud contest ensued, in which both the parties suffered heavy loss. Their herioc resistance continued till all of them who gathered on the breach fell dead or wounded. The British troops emerged triumphant. Shortly after the decisive hour, th rest of the rebels numbering about 3000 assembled on the eastern sector of the fort. They rushed rapidly in an eastern and northern direction; soon forming into two columns and retreated, 'beset but not dismayed'. The English cavalry supported by the troops of Ettayapuram attacked the rebel columns in flank and rear and killed about 600. Four hundred and fifty of the dead insurgents were found inside the fort. Those who were killed in former occasions were found deposed outside the east face. The rebels, whom Agnew took prisoners, were executed on the 24th May, near the fallen fort.[27]

As a result of this victory, British forces took the fort of Panajalamkurichi for the first time by storm. Therupon the rebels evacuated theri centres at Vallanad, Tutukudi and Kadalkudi. The mass of the insurgents fled to the north, while the rest of them scattered themselves in various parts of Tirunelveli. Dalaway Pillai, a chief associate of the rebels of Panajalamkurichi, fled to Nanguneri where he organised a rebellion but Lusington suppressed it in October 1801.[28]

Spread of the Rebellion to Sivaganga

The rebels of Tirunelveli were allied with the disaffected inhabitants of the region northward. As the fugitives escaped to Sivaganga, the rebel forces joined them in strength. In may

1801 the Marudu brothers, Vella Marudu and his more influential brother Chinna Marudu, who served as ministers of the estate uniting themselves with the disaffected chieftains, assembled a formidable force. They equipped their armed men with all available weapons and trusted themselves on the jungle recesses.[29] The pagodas of Kalayarkoil located in the heart of the Sivaganga forest become the rallying point of the insurgents, obviously because they attached a religious significance to their struggle. From the sheltered posts in the jungles, the rebel forces laid waste the neighbouring districts in defiance of British authority.[30]

From Sivaganga the rebellion spread to the adjoining territories. In May 1801 the rebels seized the fort of Tirupatore and occupied Natham and Melur held by the Company's forces.[31] They proclaimed Muthu Karuppa Tevar as the Rajah of Ramnad. Led by the Rajah, the armed inhabitants occupied the Company's post at Kamudi. At this place the fugitives from Tirunelveli, led by OomathuraI, joined the rebels of Ramnad. Reinforced by these rebels, armed men took Palamanerri and captured Company's garrison at Tiruchuzhi on 16th July. Melappan, leading the rebels souhtward, freed the southern parts of Ramnad from British control while Puttur, another rebel chief, occupied thenorthern territories of Ramnad.[32] The success of the rebels in Ramnad greatly contributed to the strength of the struggle. The country being famine striken, the people joined the rising in large bodies. Besides, it secured for the rebels the command of the sea coast.

They employed boats in the Bay of Tondy and obtained supplies of grain, arms and ammunition.[33] Oomathurai, after his recovery, led the rebels to Palaynad, where he established himself. In July the Kallar tribes of Annoor rose in revolt, taking possession of the western part of Madurai. A large body of the rebels marched to the Fort of Madurai, but finding it well defended, retreated to Kadaracoil.[34]

In the mean time rebel forces under the command of Shevata Tambi, the son of Chinna Marudu, marched to Thanjavur where the inhabitants rallied to the standard of revolt. The rebels occupied the subah of Pattukottai.

Establishing their posts at Arandangy and Audiarkudi, they advanced as far as Mangudy. They remained in force in the Kaveri delta till the British operations in other quarters put them on the defensive.[35]

The renewed struggle on such a widespread and violent proportion took the Company's administration by surprise. The outbreaks were connected with the Political designs of the rebels in different areas of South India.[36] Though it was feudal in content, the common people of different areas swelled the rebel ranks. The unity of purpose rendered their resistance determined. The guerrilla tactics employed by the rebels were calculated to harass the attacking forces.

However, the Company found it possible to combat the hostile combination. This was because it controlled the communication system, received the support of local rulers and possessed well equipped forces.[37]

In a bid to overcome the odds, the English gained the support of the princes, particularly the Tondaiman of Pudukkottai and the Rajah of Thanjavur and rushed in reinforcements, brought from Bengal and Malaya. They resumed operations on a large scale in May 1801. Agnew in consequence of his success in capturing a number of rebel strongholds, checked the rising tempo of rebellion in Ramnad and relieved Madurai Fort from threat of assault. A force under the command of Major James Graham marched from Tiruppuvanam to Madurai. The rebels in considerable strength attacked Graham, but another detachment under Major Sheppard reached to his rescue.[38] On the 11th of June the detachment of Agnew marching through Manamadurai and Parthibanur, reoccupied Paramagudi. The armed bodies hovered round the English troops throughout their march. They cut a party to pieces at Tiruppachetty and pressed vigorously on British lines; but withdrew after a clash in which seventy of them died. On the 10th near Manamadurai columns of rebels lined behind high banks, water-courses and jungles on the opposite bank of river Palamaneri. They made a dash across the river and charged the British troops with pikes. In the clashes that followed both sides suffered considerable losses

Still the forces continued their advance and reaced Ramnad on the 14th of June.[39]

Leaving Ramnad, Agnew reached Madurai on the 9th of July. On the 24th he stormed the rebel stronghold of Tirupatore and waited for the arrival of a detachment, led by Colonel Innes from Malabar. After suppressing the rebels of Dindigul, Innes advanced towards Madurai. Reinforced, he attached Piranmalai on the 18th of June, but was defeated. Retreating to Natham, he marched to Manapacherry on the 4th of July. But the Columns led by the Mardu brothers pressed vigorously on his troops, again forcing his retreat to Natham. Subsequently taking the route through Piranmalai, Innes on the 25th arrived at Satturusamharakkottai. The next day, while he was marching to Tirupatore through a thick wood, the rebels again attacked him using rockets, but was rescued by Agnew.[40] The combined forces of Agnew and Innes now reduced Okkur and attacked Siruwayal, the headquarters of the rebels of Sivaganga. After a futile resistance, the insurgents retired to the jungles.[41] Marching from Siruwayal, the forces of Kalayarkoil. Driven to desperation,the rebels fought for every inch of land. Though the English succeeded in beating off the crowds every hour, they found themselves completely and constantly surrounded by hordes. As no alternative presented itself, Agnew retreated to Siruwayal and abandoned his project of advancing to Kalayarkoil from that direction.[42]

However the Company's troops gained more victories in Ramnad and Thanjavur. Captain Blackburne, with the assistance of the Rajah of Thanjaur, reoccupied the southern bank of the Kaveri. A detachment commanded by Lieutenant Maclean routed the rebels led by Puttur at Worior. In September Blackburne drove the insurgents from Arandangy and desolated the villages of Terboinad. He proceeded within twenty miles of Sirwayal, then advancing eastward, detached the forces to join Maclean in Ramnad. The rebels about 3000 strong, led by Oomaithurai, marched to attack Maclean's troops, but finding the task risky, retreated. Blackburne reached Karaikudi in October and captured the rebels strongholds in the jungles of Singampinary.[43] Mean while Macaulay directed his operations against the armed men the southern region of Ramnad. Lieutenant Miller, whom he detached to Kamudi, won a victory over the rebels on 13th August.[44] On 27th August Macaulay, supported by the troops of Ettayapuram routed the rebels led by Melappan at Abiramam. The forces under Martins and Miller dispersed a body of insurgents, who assembled near the fort of Ramnad. In September Macaulay marched to the west to assist Agnew for suppressing of the rebels of Sivaganga.[45]

The Madras council had long been contemplating upon the tactics to divide the united force of the rebels into opposite camps. Failing to turn the Marudu brothers against eaach other, it found Padamattur Woya Tevar, a member of the royal house, as its candiate to the rajahship of Sivaganga. Agnew proclaimed him as the Rajah of Sivaganga at Cholapuram with the display of every mark of respect and splendour.[46] This had the decisive effect on the rebels. The inhabitants of Nalukottai, Okkur, Erekur, Pattimangalm and Paghenery soon paid homage to the new ruler. Thus the Company's administration divided the insurgents into two camps of opposing interests-that of Vengum Peria Wodia Tevar and Padmattu Woya Tevar.[47] This development weakened the resistance movement.

Battle of Kalayarkoil

Supported by the rival ruler of Sivaganga, Agnew began a second offensive against Kalayarkoil. A detachment occupied Piranmalai on 18th of September;[48] while another reduced Nandikkottai to submission. By the end of September Agnew, marching through Vanimkudi and Collumbum took Muthur situated on the western side of Kalayarkoil. In the midnight of 30th September he sent a detachment under Lieutenent Colonel Spray, another under Sheppard and a thrid under Innes against Kalayarkoil. In the mean time, Blackburne pressed the rebels from the south. The dawn of 1st October witnessed the simultaneous approach of the British forces from different directions against the pagoda of Kalayarkoil. The insurgents, though taked by surprise, fought with determination; but were routed. Spray took possession of the pagoda of Kalayarkoil a handsome buliding surrounded by a stone wall, 18feet in height. This marked the end of the revolt in Sivaganga. Soon after this decisive event, a body of rebels led by Sevathiah, Oomaithurai and Muthuvail Nayak, son of the Poligar of Virupakshi, marched in a northern direction through Tirupatore. The Marudu brothers with their selected followers took shelter in the jungles of Singampunari.[49]

Rebel Reverses in Dindigul

However, in October 1801 wiith the arrival of rebels from the south rebellion broke out again. Soon after the fall of Kalayarkoil, a body of their armed men numering about 600 led by Oomaithurai, Sevathiah and Muhtu Vella Nayak fled to Dindigul. A force was despatched to intercept their march, but did not succeed.[50] The fugitives carried with them neither ammunition nor provisions, After a long march, they made good their way to the hills of Virupakshi.[51]

Soon after the arrival of the fugitives, the people of the neighbouring country flocked together and rose in arms. The inhabitants of Chetrampatty and the adjoining territory joined the rebels in large number. Alarming reports reached the English camps that the strength of the insurgents was becoming more and more formidable. The inhabitants reconstructed barries especially the Great Stone Carmon Dhilli Barrier and embarked upon depredations into the Company's territories.[52] They attaked the troops stationed at Chetrampatty and forced them to retreat to Iagoody. A force under the command of Jones marched against the rebels but it was also forced to retreat.[53]

On 12th October Innes recommenced military operations on a large scale. The rebels under the leadership of Oomaithurai engaged the English army on the plain of Virupakshi but were defeated and dispersed. They made another stand at Chetrampatty but again suffered reverse. The Company's detachment followed up their victories by a close pursuit of the rebels. Innes, marching through a thick wood, occupied Cowdhilli, a rock commanding the view of Cormen Dhili Barriers and moved ahead.[54] A body of the insurgents led by Oomaithurai after descending from the hills again moved to the valley of Dindigul. Major Burrows, whom Innes sent against them, drove the rebels upto Vettilagundu for about fifty one miles. As the country seemed unfavourable for charging the insurgents, Burrows sent parties in pursuit. After a fierce encounter, Oomaithurai with sixty five of his followers, fell under the custody of the English.[55] Doraiswamy, who was at large, was taken a prisoner from a place near Madurai.[56] Sevethiah and Oomaithurai were brought to Panjalamkurichi, where they were beheaded.[57] The fall of Oomaithurai marked the end of the Rebellion which began with the revolt of his brother Kattabomman.

Muthu Vella Nayak also graced gallows.[58] The handsome youth of Doraiswamy evoked the compassion of Agnew and Governor Clive; hence his life was spared. However seventy three principal rebels including Doraiswamy were banished to the Prince of Wales Island, Penang.

Reconstruction of British Authority

With the suppression of the insurrection the Madras Council concentrated his attention on measures aimed at the consolidation of British authority on a stable foundtion. By his proclamation of 1st December 1801, the Governor clive expressed his deep regret that the. Desperate resistance offered to British troops was attended with so much loss of life and material He announced a general annesty to the people and their chieftains in order to relieve them from any further solicitude and apprehension.[59] Lord Clive assured the people that the British Government would honour the rights of property and life, religious usages and customs of the people. He announced his intention of reorgainsing the administration of the country on a permanent basis; but respecting the traditions of the people. The Governor declared his decision that a permanent assessment of revenue would be instituted on principles of zamindari tenure by which hereditary rights would be granted to the poligars on their estates. He explained that the permanent assessment would secure to the chieftains the possession of land under the operation of limited and definite laws, which would restrain the servants of the

Company from unnecessary interference.[60] By this proclamation, Lord Clive sought to concilate the chieftains and the people. In 1799 he confiscated the estates of the rebel chieftains, but by his proclamation of 1801 he assured them that they would be granted hereditary rights on their lands. The British offer that the Company would respect the rights and customs of the people and that it would free them from unnecessary interference by the English servants, was indeed an inducement to the rebels to return to the cultivation of the arts of peace.

The same time Lord Clive rewarded the allies for their sevice and restored the possessions to the chiefs. He conveyed his feelings of pride and satisfaction to the friendly cheiftains in their strady attachment with the Company and guaranteed to them of augmented security, favour and wealth. True to his promise, he ceded a strip of territory called Kelanelly from Tanjore to the Tondaiman of Pudukkottai.[61] The Governor also conciliated the rebel chieftains. In 1802 he restored the estate of Ramagiri to Vengiri Nayak, who appeared as the rightful claimant.[62] In 1803 he restored the zamindary of Sapatore to Warra Kannaiah Nayak, the son of the rebel poligar Kannaiah Nayak. Besides, he ordered the restoration of the zamindary of Ramnad to Mungul Eshwar Nauchayar, the sister of the deceased Rajah. However, Lord Clive did not restore the palayams which were sequestered in 1799 to the families of the rebel cheiftains. On the other hand he declared them as *havelly* or public lands and in a spirit of vengeance ordered the name of Panjalamkurichi to be expunged from all public records. The name 'Panjalamkurichi' being associated wiht the humiliating reverses of the English, the Governor abliterated the very name of that rebel stronghold.[63]

Further, Lord Clive sought to improve the government of the southern provinces by cradicating the system of rapine and oppression that crept into the adminstration. He understood that one of the sources of the misery of the people was a system of exaction, practised by the European adventurers who claimed protection from the Company. The Governor withdrew by a proclamation the protection which they claimed.

He placed under restraint those who were engaged in coercion of the inhabitants. These measures removed a form of oppression which endangered the foundations of public security.[64]

In addition, Lord Clive disarmed the chieftains and their armed inhanbitants. By a proclamation he directed the people to surrender their fire-arms.

This resolution for disarming the inhabitatnts was tempered with every practicable degree of attention to the hereditary customs of the chieftains. Thus the Governor allowed the chieftains to retain a certain number of peons carrying pikes in order to enable them to maintain those ceremonies of state, to which they had been accustomed. Besides, he ordered the payment of compensation for the loss of fire-arms surrendered by the inhabitants. On a comparison with the situation in 1799 these measures appeared conciliatory; for in 1799 Lord Clive refused compensation for the loss of the personalproperty of the people. He also ordered the destruction of hte forts of the poligars and institued periodical inspection of the palayams to prevent the reconstruction of demolished forts.[65]

The company carried out these measures successfully taking advantage of the favourable circumstances. In 1799 similar measures did not meet with success on account of the divided system of control of the country by the Nawab and the Company and the inadequacy of military strength to coerce the powerful poligars. But in 1801 these obstacles no more existed and hence it could effevtively disarm the country and reconstruct the administration.

Notes and References

1. Board of Revenue, proceedings, 7 June 1797, Vol. 178, pp. 2924.
2. After the acquisition of territories, the Company greatly increased the taxes in Dindigul by 25 per cent Gudalur 96 per cent, Kambum 11 per cent to 93$^{3/4}$ per cent over Tipu's assessments. Nowonder the people considered these revisions as oppressive. (general Report to the Board of Revenue, 1 October 1797, Vol. 2, p. 13).

3. Board of Revenue, proceedings, 14 January 1799, Vol. 217, p. 374.
4. K. Rajayyan, *Administration and Society in the Carnatic,* pp. 93-94.
5. Madras Council, Revenue consultations, 29 November 1799, Vol. 99, pp. 3249.
6. K. Rajayyan in his work *South Indian Rebellian* the first War of Independence (chapter 4) has discussed the details, which appear relevant for reference.
7. Madras Council, Military Consultations, 17 August 1798, Letter from Manaparai, Vol. 241, p. 5088.
8. K. Rajayyan in his work *South Indian Rebellion,* pp. 129-130.
9. *Ibid.,* pp. 134-142.
10. *Kavadi* is a wooden frame carrying the image or the weapon of Lord Subramania and taken on the devotee's shoulders to the shrine of the deity.
11. Madras Council, Military Consultations, 15 March 1801, Vol. 280, p. 1644.
12. *Ibid.,* 17 February 1801, Vol. 279, pp. 880 and 1616.
13. *Ibid.,* 7 February 1801, Vol. 280, pp. 281-282.
14. *Ibid.,* 17 February 1801, Vol. 279, pp. 886-887.
15. Madras Council, Secret Consultations, 14 April 1801, Vol. 2, pp. 231-232.
16. James Welsh, *op.cit.,* Vol. p. 61.
17. Madras Council, Military Consultations, 7 April 1801, Vol. 281, pp. 2007-2008.
18. Madras Council, Secret Despatches to England, 2 May 1801, Vol. 2, p. 81.
19. Madras Council, Military Consultations, 23 May 1801, Vol. 283, p. 3500.
20. Madras Council, Secret Consultations,14 April 1801, Vol. 2, pp. 230-231.
21. Madras Council, Military Consultations, 22 May 1801, Vol. 283, pp. 3500-3504.
22. Madras Council, Secret Despatches to England,1 April 1801, Vol. 2, pp. 78-80.
23. Madras Council, Revenue Consultations, 23 April 1801, Vol. 109, pp. 851-855.

24. Madras Council, Military Despatches to England, 17 February 1802, Vol. 2, pp. 269-270.
25. Madras Council, Secret Despatches to England, 3 June 1801, Vol. 2, p. 89.
26. Madras Council, Secret Despatches to England, 15 October 1801, Vol. 31, p. 157.
27. Madras Council, Military Consultations, 2 June 1801, Vol. 284, pp. 4220-4229.
28. K. Rajayyan, *South Indian Rebellian*, pp. 80-89.
29. Madras Council, Military Consultations, 26 May 1801, Vol. 26, pp. 3820-3821.
30. *Ibid.*, 12 June 1801, Vol. 284, pp. 4840-4971.
31. *Ibid.*, 1 June 1801, p. 2820.
32. *Ibid.*, 21 June 1801, Vol. 285, p. 4603.
33. *Ibid.*, 20 October 1801, Vol. 288, p. 6934.
34. *Ibid.*, 7 July 1801, Vol. 281, pp. 5051-5053.
35. *Ibid.*, 4 August 1801, Vol. 281, pp. 5352-5370.
36. K. Rajayyan in his work *South Indian Rebellion, The first War of Independence, 1800-1801* has established that this rebellion in the Tamil Country was not an isolated developments. On the other han it was the outcome of a concerted move, made by the rebel powers of different regions of the peninsula.
37. Madras Council, Military Despatches to England, 15 October 1801, Vol. 31, pp. 152-157.
38. Madras Council, Military Consultations, 9 June 1801, Vol. 284, pp. 4339-4341.
39. *Ibid.*, 21 June 1801, Vol. 285, pp. 4603-4604.
40. *Ibid.*, 4 August 1801, Vol. 286, p. 5367.
41. *Ibid.*, 4 August 1801, Vol. 286, pp. 5348-5349, 5367-5370.
42. James Welsh, *op.cit.*, Vol. 1, pp. 89-92.
43. *Ibid.*, 20 October 1801, Vol. 288, pp. 6925-6973.
44. Madras Council, Revenue Consultations, 4 September 1801, Vol. 110, pp. 1692-1693.
45. Madras Council, Military Consultations, 20 October 1801, Vol.288, pp. 6850-6861.
46. *Ibid.*, 7 July 1801, Vol. 285, p. 4975.

47. *Ibid.*, 20 October 1801, Vol. 288, p. 6845 and 6908.
48. *Ibid.*, 20 October 1801, Vol. 288, p. 6865 and 6936.
49. *Ibid.*, 20 October 1801, Vol. 288, pp. 6844-6895.
50. *Ibid.*, 20 October 1801, Vol. 2888, pp. 6891-6895.
51. *Ibid.*, 1 December 1801, Vol. 289, p. 7212.
52. *Ibid.*, 27 October 1801, Vol. 288, pp. 6896-6905.
53. *Ibid.*, 1 December 1801, Vol. 288, p. 1708.
54. *Ibid.*, 22 December 1801, Vol. 290, p. 8080.
55. *Ibid.*, 27 October 1801, Vol. 288, p. 7116.
56. *Ibid.*, 1 December 1801, Vol. 289, p. 7615
57. *Ibid.*, 1 December 1801, Vol. 289, p. 7726.
58. *Ibid.*, 1 December 1801, Vol. 289, p. 7740.
59. Madras Council, Military Despatches to England, 17 February 1802, Vol. 31, p. 272.
60. Madras Council, Military Consultations, 17 February 1802, Vol. 31, p. 272.
61. Madras Council, Political Consultations, 5 July 1803, Vol. 10, pp. 833-834.
62. Madras Council, Revenue Despatches to England, 19 March 1802, Vol. 7, p. 262.
63. *Ibid.*, 9 May 1803, Vol. 7, pp. 528-530 and 538-540.
64. Madras Council, Secret Despatches to England, 14 April 1800, Vol. 2, pp. 12-14.
65. Madras Council, Military Despatches to England, 29 May 1802, Vol. 32, pp. 454-456.

CHAPTER - 9

REVENUE SETTLEMENT-ZAMINDARI TO RYOTWARI

The unification of the Tamil Country under British rule required the enforcement of a uniform system of administration for all its regions. Accordingly the Madras Council implemented administration by the collectors. The system was already in operation in Dindigul and Ramnad. After the end of the Mysore War in 1799 the Company formed three divisions-Dindigul, Baramahal and Coimbatore-out of the north western acquisition from Mysore and placed each of these districts under a separate collector.[1] By the Treaty of Tanjore the Company acquired possession of the subahs of Kumbakonam, Tiruvadi and Pattukottai. They were formed into two divisions and subsequently into one division, Thanjavur, under a collector.[2] After the settlement of the Carnatic Treaty of 1801 a similar system was applied. Accordingly, Tirunelveli was placed under the charge of the collector of Southern Poligar Peishcush with headquarters at Ramnad. The administration of Madurai was entrusted with the collector of Dindigul. Tiruchirapalli was made a separate division under another collector. Arcot and the adjoining areas were organised into a separate collectorate. While Pulicat and Satmedu were entrusted with the Collector of Chingalput, the territory situated between Palar and Nellore with the collector of Western Poligar Peishkush. With the Board of Revenue exercising control over the collectors and the collectors over the local officials, the administrative reorganisation obliterated the traditional authorities and gave a common pattern to the entire land of the Tamils.[3]

When the East India Company assumed control of the administration, the revenue collection varied from place to place and from time to time. The administration was interested in raising the maximum revenue and the upkeep of the necessary hierarchy of officials and armed forces for the collection of that revenue. In different areas revenue management was relegated to local chieftains, poligars, renters and headman of the villages.[4] Even if they exercised the most arbitray authority within their jurisdictions, the Government allowed them so long as the revenue was forthcoming.[5] As a result the vested interests vitiated the working of the system.

In 1769 the Government of Fort St. George set about making improved settlements. The first step was to appoint provincial councils to supervise the collection of revenue by the zamindars. This did not prove a success as it was not effective. Therefore in 1781 the Court of Directors appointed a special commission called the Circuit Committee.[6] This too was not able to achieve much, because of the manipulations that were attempted by influencial zamindars. Thereupon, collectors were appointed in charge of different divisions. To supervise the work of these collectors the Board of Revenue was constituted in 1786 with the sanction of the Court of Directors.[7] The main function of the Board was to secure the collection of revenue. In addition it recorded statistics with regard to population, agriculture, exports and imports, the condition and advancement of the country. It managed the expenditure of special funds and took charge of the estates of minors in its capacity as a court of wards.[8] Yet it imposed no limit to the demands made by the revenue officials, as a result of which they went on increasing their demand upon ryots from year to year. There was nothing to prevent the zamindars from rock-renting the tenants under their control.[9] Whenever the government raised its demand, the zamindars in their turn imposed more of a burden on the tenants. Such a practice rendered the position of the tenants intolerable.[10]

Finding no other way, the Court of Directors instructed the Company's administration to assess the revenue on a permanent basis as it was done in Bengal. In 1799 Edward Clive the Governor of Madras, directed the Board of Revenue to make a detailed enquiry as to the manner of landholding in the Presidency. After pains taking investigation the Board prepared a report and in 1801 definite orders were issued from England on the basis of the report to introduce permanent settlement in Madras Presidency. In pursuance of this order, the Board of Revenue formulated the rules, stipuled the class of landholders, specified the rent and defined the rights and duties of the tenants as well as the zamindars.[11]

Permanent Revenue Settlement

The Madras Council appointed a special commission with William Petrie as president and Cockburn and Webbe as commissioners. It was entrusted with the task of arranging the settlement of revenue on a permanent basis. Accordingly, the southern districts of Ramnad and Sivaganga were parcelled out into estates and permanently assessed. By 1802, the revenues in parts of Salem and Baramahal were assessed on a permanent basis.[12] In September 1802 Lushington, Collector of Tirunelvelli submitted to the special commission a comprehensive scheme. Accordingly lands were assessed on a permanent basis and the scheme was implemented in 1803.[13] In Madurai the systematic survey and assessment were completed by 1804-1805. As per this reform permanent contracts were entered into between the zamindars and the government. The rent payable by the zamindars was technically called the *peishcush*. Some of the zamindars looked upon this form of rent collection with suspicion and saw some political motives. Therefore many of the zamindars avoided settlements. These estates were known as *havelly* or unsettled *palayams*.[14] The unsettled lands were parcelled out into *mittas* and they were sold by auction to the highest bidders. Those who gained possession of estates through the auction were called *mittadars*.

The zamindars were declared as "proprietors of the soil". The assessment that was made for their lands was termed as perpetual. The rent that was fixed related only to land revenue, but not to other sources of income like excise and customs. The general standard by which the *jumma* or land rent to be paid by the zamindars, was regulated on two thirds of the gross collection from the cultivators.[15] The zamindars and mittadars were to give pattas to the tenants or ryots, clearly specifying the rent that they were to pay.[16] In case of any failure on the part of a ryot to pay his dues to the zamindar, his personal property was liable to be dispossessed. In case it was not sufficient to make good the arrears of rent, he could be ousted from the occupancy of the land, that was cultivated by him. The zamindar was at liberty to put another ryot into the possession of it on the usual terms. On the other hand, if the zamindar himself failed, the government could confiscate his property and take over the possession of his estates. The ryots as well as the zamindars were free to seek justice against arbitary proceedings from the law courts.[17]

The Company with an idea obtaining a stipulated sum of rent for ever and perhaps to free itself from a complicated system of collection introduced the permanent settlement. But it showed signs of failure even from the beginning. In some estates it was over assessment, in others as in South Arcot, it was failure of crops due to drought, but in most of the cases it was mismanagement and extravagance on the part of the remainders. The result was that within about ten years several estates accumulated large arrears and the Board of Revenue found that for realising them, they had either to attach these estates and manage them for some years or to put them for sale.[18] Apart from these, the settlement represented a compromise with the feudal interests, but it did not do justice to the interests of the peasants. The Company deprived the peasants of their rights on land, grouped their holdings into estates and sold them to the highest bidders. This was advantageous to the rich individuals for they were enabled to become landlords over independent villages and to entrench themselves in the feudal set up. By the Regulation XXX of 1802, the peasants were given the right to seek justice from the courts but practically this was not that easy. The condition of the agricultural classes in the estates was deplorable. The poverty stricken people, ignorant of the proceedings of the court, found it impossible to defend themselves against the powerful zamindars. As a result the ryots were left to the oppressions and exactions of the feudal interests.[19] The Company could have done justice, provided it had concluded individual settlements with the peasant proprietors. But to its selfish motives more that popular sentiments counted. After having waged a series of wars, it was not prepared to do any thing more alienate the rank and file of feudal interests. Therefore it effected a compromise with the feudal chiefs and associated them with the revenue administration in their capacity as zamindars. In other words the Company deprived the feudal lords of their armed strength but was not prepared to destroy their economic influence.

Lord William Bentinck, the Governor of Madras (1803-1807) and successor of Lord Clive was against the permanent settlement.[20] According to him the system was unsound. For it did not in any way directly improve the position of the ryots or actual cultivators and it was unwise to create landed aristocracies.[21] A ryot might be converted into a zamindar at any time but a zamindar could not be so easily altered it found unsuccessful. In one of his minutes he had recorded "the more I consider this important question, the stronger is my conviction that the present system is not the best that might be adopted".[22]

In its report dated 22nd February 1807 the Tanjore Committe suggested the introdction of villages settlement. Hodgson, a member of the Board of Revenue, and of the Tanjore Commission having toured the districts of Coimbatore and Tirunelveli submitted two reports to the Government. He pointed out that the country consisted of numerous villages each with its own boundaries, settlements and tracts of land both arable and waste. The circar share or land rent was usually received from the *nanja* lands or wet lands in kind at rates varying from forty to sixty per cent of the gross produce, after deducting a certain portion needed for harvest expenses before every threshing season. The share of the circar from punja or dry grain lands was usually received in cash either at so much for a fixed measure of land or so much for the same measure of land varying with the produce.[23] On these grounds Hodgson favoured a settlement with the mirasdars of a village on the basis of the extent of cultivation and the rates of taxes in the previous years. The mirasdars were to be encouraged in every instance to undertake remittance of the rents of the villages and it was only they refused, the villages were to be formed into *muttas* and sold to the highest bidders.[24] The lease was to be limited to a period of three years instead of five years. Yet it cannot be denied that the proposal carried astrong feudal content.

On the other hand Thomas Munro Suggested a ryotwari settlement. He declared that the existing assessment was to be reduced by twenty five per cent so as to proved against crop failure and shortage in productivity. The balance was to fixed as the share of the state. He proposed a tax or rent which was to be paid annually by the cultivators or the ryots. The idea was to guarantee a settled income for the Government and to provide for further increase of rent with the extension to cultivation. The settlement was to be made from year to year with each ryot. However, Munro had to contend with the opposition of a number of officials in Madras and also the authorities in Bengal. The government could not part with any part of its revenue and found his proposal unacceptable.[25] It was not sure whether the benefit would go to the peasants, as the revenue servants were capable of collecting the same old rates under one pretext or the other.

In view of these proposals, Lord William Bentinck, Governor of Madras, (1803-1807) made several experiments, beginning with village settlement. The Board of Revenue acquired a partiality for the time honoured village system, which was believed to be the best suited to the country. Accordingly, the Government directed the introduction of the village lease system on ground that it would be less oppressive and more beneficial to the inhabitants.[26] So between 1804 and

1814 the village lease system, first triennial and then decennial, was implemented in the districts of Tirunelveli, Tiruchirapalli, Thanjavur, Coimbatore, South Arcot and North Arcot. Collectors were instructed to introduce it on an experimental basis but with a view to make it permanent ultimately.[27]

Accordingly, the Board of Revenue farmed out the lands of a village to the cultivators of the village, whether they were head inhabitants or mirasdars or to the village community. They further divided and leased the land to the individual ryots.[28] This settlement was to be made for ten years. The village system was permanently fixed at a standard rent called "kist" with reference to average collections during the previous years and the permanent resources of the villages. In those villages, where the inhabitants were poor and cultivation was low, a temporary settlement might be formed on a moderate progressive rent. The inhabitants were told that on their agreeing to pay the *sist* they would be placed on the footing of permanent renters. The Board considered that the *sist* would amount to one-third of the gross produce of the land, whereas it then stood at about one-half.[29]

In contravention to individual rights the Government, while introducing the village lease system, had its assumption that it owned all the lands; those who cultivated them were its tenants and those who agreed to pay the levies were renters. The decennial leases were expected to improve matters by introducing comparative stability. It expected that through the operation of the village settlement private property would be established and land would become salable.

However, the village lease system functioned under unfavourable conditions of over assessment, lack of co-operation between the authorities, adverse seasons and poor state of agriculture. The famine that ravaged the country from 1809 to 1816 created more of difference between the permanent revenue settlement that failed in Bengal and the village settlement that was implemented in the Madras Presidency. In view of bitter experiences the Court of Directors felt that the interests of the state as well as of the agricultural classes could be secured best only under ryotwari settlement. Already this system had been with so much success introduced in Baramahal - Salem and the Ceded Districts by Colonel Read and Thomas Munro. Therefore in 1814 they ordered that in all the districts the ryotwari settlement should be introduced.[30]

Ryotwari Settlement

Munro's ryotwari settlement of land revenue, that is, a settlement made d directly with the cultivators, dispensing with middlemen, was of abiding interest. When the assessment for each individual owner was fixed separately, there could be no question of joint ownership of the village.

In 1808 the Board of Control in England was reconstituted and James Cumming became the head of the Revenue Department. A friend of Col. Munro, he turned a critic of the Cornwallis system of revenue and ardent champion of the ryotwari system. Colonel Munro visited England, met the Directors and prevailed upon them not to extend the permanent system of revenue. According to him though the system relieved the English of the trouble of the onerous duty of investigation and writing long reports, it perpetuated their ignorance of the Indian system of revenue and gave no protection to the peasants. It was believed that the ryotwathi system was intricate and expensive. Col. Munro on the other hand contradicted this view and said that if well managed it would be simpler and more efficient than any other kind of settlement. He asserted that it helped better contact with the people and gave a sense of security to the peasants. Added to Colonel Munro's arguments the Select Committee on revenue recommended in 1810 the substitution of the permanent settlement by ryotwari system. The English utilitarians, who gained influence in the India House, supported the introduction of the ryotwari system. They argued that in making the revenue of the state permanent it was denying itself the future improvement of collections.[31]

These developments brought about a change in the Company's attitude. The Directors were no longer enamoured of the permanent settlement and were convinced that the interests of the state as well as of the agricultural class would be best served only under the ryotwari system, which had worked with considerable success in Baramahal and in the Ceded Districts. So the Court decreed that no more permanent settlement should be concluded and that the ryotwari settlement should introduced in all the districts, lately acquired from the Nawab of Arcot. In accordance with this directive, the ryotwari system was introduced in the circar lands and in the estates that were assumed for arrears of revenue.[32]

The roytwari system introduced in the year 1814 had its origin in Baramahal. When Baramahal was ceded by Mysore to the English in 1792 during the Third Mysore War Colonel Read was made the Collector of the district. He was asked to proceed wiith the quinquennial system. While he was surveying the lands, the idea of settling wiht the ryots directly, occured to him. During the first two years of his administration the districts were under the rending system on annual tenures. To protect the ryots Col.Read instructed the village headmem to issue pattas or contract documents to the ryots in the villages.[33] Thomas Munro, who was then in charge of a sub division under Col.Read, was implementing annual village settlements. As there were abuses in the system, he adopted the practice of ascertaining the value of the lands of those who paid a rent and contracted a patta or agreement. A copy of it was given to the village headman who was given the authority to collect the rent and also to raise or lower it. This system prevented the headman from altering the demands at will subsquently as he had been in the practice of doing it. Munro brought the ryots under his direct authority and did away with the intermediaries. This system registered an increase of revenue and the Board was impressed with the result. Read issued a proclamation in 1796 to the ryots of a system which was ryotwari in principle. These experiments became the basis for the future ryotwari system. Munro, who had not much faith in this system at the beginning, became an ardent beliver, when the experiments of Colonel Read yielded favourable results.[34]

However, the outbreak of the Fourth Mysore War in 1798 interrupted experiments in the ryotwari system. After the war, Munro became the Collector of the Ceded District in 1800. He introduced the village rents in these districts during the first year and began a survey, after which he implemented a ryotwari settlement. Though the revenue decreased in the initial years, it registered an increase within a short period.[35]

However, Hodgon, the President of the Board of Revenue, and an ardent admirer of the peprmanent system. Submitted a memoir in 1808 in support of the permanent system.[36] Munro refuted the arguments of Hodgson and remarked that as the latter system gave them proprietorship and sense of pride in possessing land the ryots would rarely abandon their lands unlike as under the zamindari or mutahdari system and that it wuold also facilitate extension of cultivation. He pointed out that though charges of collection might good by the increase of revenue derived in the course of years. Against the argument that it needed great details of accounts and constant interference Munro said that it would be much counter balanced by the through knowledge it afforded about the state of cultivation and resources of the country and that constant interference would become uncessary in course of time. Munro also pointed out that the communal harmony in the village society would be violeted if people other village headmen were made the mutahdars in the village.[37] Munro remarked that under the permanent revenue system the tenants were not likely to cultivate their farms so well as to draw so great a produce from them as they would have done otherwise as owners of land under the ryotwari system. As the mutahdars of Madurai mismanged their estates, many of them ceased to exist.[38] William Bentinck, the Governor of Madras upheld the views of Munro and desired very much for the introduction of ryotwari system. Accordingly, he directed one Thackaray to go round the zamindari areas and submit his report. But before the report was received, Bentinck was recalled from office over the issue of the Mutiny at Vellore. Munro too left for England. As the advocates of the ryotwari system were away, Hodgson's views won the day. From the political point of view the Government decided to establish the villlage lease system to achieve its goal of permanent settlement. Accordingly, the ryotwari system that Munro introuced in Baramaghas was abandonded. The permanent settlement continued till 1812. By 1812, the auhtorities in India and England realised the futility of the permanent system and decided to replace it whereever it wherever possible by the ryotwari system.

The ryotwari system provided for direct settlement of rent wiiht the syots and exclusion of intermediaries. About forty per cent of the produce was calculated for the purpose of taxation. Several methods were tried for valuing the produce-one method was to estimate the grain produce for the particular year. The rent was fixed based upon current prices. In another method grain value was fixed with the aid of the former accounts. Estimating the government's share from the nature of the soil was yet another method. Unlike under the permenant system, the government retained the waste lands with it and rented them, when the ryots wanted them for cultivation. As and when the ryots came forward to accept these lands for cultivation, they were rented out. The ryots were free to hold or abandon the lands at will. As the land was not taxed under this system, the value of the land increased.[39]

Besides the intial assessment of the land revenue, an annual settlement called *jamabandi* was also held. This important work of the revenue department was entrusted to a group of revenue officials. The village headmen assisted by the *karnam* and other officials furnished to the tahsildars all the details relating to the village land settlements. A band of ministerial staff aided the tahsildar in each taluk to consolidate the accounts on lands and send them to the Collector's authority. The Collector received the details from the various divisions of the district and sent all the reports to the Board of Revenue which in turn reported the details to the Revenue Department at Fort St. George.[40]

The system seemed to involve a complicated process yet it did not appear so in practice. At the end of the *fasli*[41] the headmen of a villages ascertained from the ryots the extent of land that each one cultivated, while the *karnam* prepared an account showing the demand of collection an d balance for the whole year and prepared the *jamabandi*[42] report relating to the revenue, season and crops. At the begining of the season the tahsilar assembled the ryots in their respective villages and ascertained from them what lands the ryots had already cultivated or undertook to cultivate during the year. When the crops ripened, he went round again and verifed the declartion given by the ryots. The Collector set out on his circuit in September or October, when the early crops were to be reaped and the late to be sown. This was called the *jamabandi* tour. A group of officials from the collectorate as well as the concerned subdivison accompanied the Collector to scrutinise the statements given about the cultivation of the field, nature of the holding, increase or decrease in crops and other details connected with the land revenue. The Collector assembled all the ryots and four or five from the nearest villages and ascertained the details about the progress of cultivation in the current year and compared them with those of the previous year. The terms of contract for the newly cultivated lands were determined by the accounts of former years or by the opinions of ryots generally assembled at the time of the *jamabandi*. The publictry made for every operation in the *jamabandi* helped much in expediting the settlement. If a peasant claimed concession on insufficient grounds he could not succeed so easily because his neighbours who were present would possibly raise objections. Thus popular participation in the *jamabandi* settlement was a note worthy feature of the ryotwari system.[43]

In this process the preliminary work of the settlement was done by the ryots themselves. In most of the cases the Collector confirmed the work that was done by the village headmen. When the season advanced, the assessments were made on basis of the prospects of the crop. However, the headman promised them that the previous year's settlement would continue, but for unavoidable altertions. The ryots, who were satisfied with this promise, received betel from him as a token of confirmation and began the cultivation. In addition to these accounts regarding land revenue, the karnam had to send an account on rainfall, inflow of water in the village tanks, mortality of cattle and similar details. Besides this, special reports were also prepared by tehm now and then. The *jamabandi* report related exclusively to the revenue from land, season, effects of season on crops and product of the land.[44] Nevertheless this required patience and expertise.

The adminstration was to ascertain what fields were cultivated and by whom they were held. The Government was to enter into a settlement with each ryot directly with regard to the rent that he had to pay. The waste lands were to be regarded as circar property but was to be assessed, when it was brought under the plough. Each ryot received a *patta,* in which particulars about the extent of the field that he held and the amount of rent that was to be paid were recorded.[45] When the holding of each ryot was ascertained and the rent was fixed, he was not required to pay more but was to be granted an abatement in the event of calamities.[46] Thomas Munro held that the ryotwari system was the most simple to be followed. No serious difficulty had arisen owing to any difference of opinion as to the interpretaion of the ryotwari contract, for in the ryotwari contract the Government dealt with an individual who was technically assumed to be acting on his own account. If he became a defaulter, the Government sold such portion of his land as was sufficient to cover the amount due.[47]

Merits and Defects

The system aimed at rectifying the defects associated with the zamindari system, insecurity of tenure, oppression and rack renting. It gave proprietorship to individual peasants, brought them under the direct control of the Government and faciliated extension of cultivation.[48]

However, when the system began to operate certain flaws were discovered. The authors of this system provided for a survey and specified that the assistance of the surveyors from Baramahal might be sought. But a fresh survey was not taken up. Therefore, the settlement was based on a previous survey. It was a defective survey and hence the new settlement based on it tended to be excessive, especially in the region of Dindigul. The mode of assessment varied within the same district. In Dindigul divison the assessment was based on the nature of the soil, while in Madurai, in certain places, it depended on the produce. The survey registers were not maintained and the fields were not numbered. In Dindigul the assessment of each field was inserted in the land register so that each ryot could know exactly what he had to pay to the Government. In Madurai the fields were registered under different classes, commensurate with their quality. The extent of each land was shown but not its money assessment. These anomalies gave scope for corruption. Little care was taken to preserve the survey accounts.[49]

Defects in survey and classification badly affected cultivation. Many fairly good lands were left uncultivated as the assessments fixed on them appeared excessive. In several cases the peasants abandoned such lands after finding their agricultural operations ending up in losses. So also there was no uniformity in classification. Settlement depended on the discretion of the Collector of the district. Collector Peter of Dindigul wrote to the Board as early as in 1812 requesting permission to resurvey and reclassify the lands of Dindigul, as it would help many of the inhabitants, who fled the district on account of fever and other causes, to return and the revenue could gradually increase to equal if not exceed, the revenue of former years. Peter pleaded in 1814 that the assessments on such lands might be reduced in order to encourage cultivation. But the Board of Revenue did not comply with his suggestion.[50] Though his suggestion for resurvey and settlement was not accepted, he was given discretionary powers to make such reductions in the *teerva* or settlement, whenever it was found necessary. But as lands in Dindigul had been irregularly classified and highly assessed and the revenue expected there amounted at times to the entire produce of the land, the reductions did not much relieve the tenants of their burden. The relief given by Peter did not reach all the peasants, suffering from the problems of over assessment. Only a few were benefitted and even to them the releif was not adequate.

Yet the Company took various measures to encourage agriculture. It abolished a tax called 'pathai kaval' that existed from the time of the Nayak rulers. It was paid by the peasants to the poligars for watching highways. After assumption of the palayams it was continued to be collected. Also it took various other attempts for extending the area of cutivation. Fertile lands near the jungles on the slope of hills remained unoccupied, as these lands were subjected to frequent ravages of the wild animals. The administation leased the lands for nominal rents and appointed armed watches to scare away these animals and protect the crops. They beat ton-toms through the nights and shot at the animals, when they approached the fields. As a result more lands of the bottom of the hills came under the plough.[51] In several instances the collectors of districts realized that the ryotwari assessments were quite heavy and tried to reduce them. Yet it could nor be denied that these measures had only limited effect on the condition of the ryots. This was because of frequent droughts. This mode of ryotwari settlement based on the defective survey was not altered till 1885 when the modern method of ryotwari system was introduced.[52]

The authors of the ryotwari system expected that it would be a better alternative to the previous systems. But when it began to operate the fears of Hodgson that scope for oppression in different forms might be inherent came true. In fact the revenue history of the land during the first half of the nineteenth century reveals overassessments and exaction whether it was in respect of zamindari settlement of ryotwari settlement and it exhausted the resources of the country. The vagaries of monsoon and the poor farming techniques demanded a moderate assessment. Yet because of the financial difficulties of the Madras Government, the rents were kept high. Such high rates of land tax proved harmful to the interests of the peasants.[53] The irregularities in the assessments adversely affected the extension of cultivation. As assessments were based on defective surveys, better sort of lands continued to be assessed excessively. In fact rate of assessments on these lands was not in proportion to that levied on inferior sort of lands. The peasants repeatedly requested for remissions and when they were not granted adequately they abandoned them and took up inferior sort of lands for cultivation.

The system also brought about fluctuations in the price of grain and loss to agriculturists. Under the village lease settlement the village community was able to regulate the price of grain by holding their stock till they could get a fair profit. But under the ryotwari system the ryots were forced to sell grain often at an unfavourable price to meet the demands of the revenue officials, as they could neither wait nor borrow money.[54] Also the working of the settlement led to agricultural indebtedness. Though the system permitted the grant of loans, in most cases the loans reached the peasents after inordinate delay, depriving them of their benefits in using them for agricultural purposes. So the ryots were to borrow money from the money lenders at a high rate of interest for supporting themselves as well as for buying seeds, grain agricultural implements and also for paying rents to the Government. At the same time they collected public loans and frittered them away on social expenditures. All these made them live in perpetual debt. Another reason that drove the peasants to money lenders was the economic depression that caused steep decline in prices for about two decades from the thirties and the repeated ravages of droughts. The ryots could not find market for their grains but at the same time they were forced to borrow money from usurers in order to pay their dues. Any adverse fluctuations in prices caused by famine, epidemic or depression hit them hard. They were forced to sell their property and become farm labourers.[55]

Though the system provided that the ryots could take up lands for cultivation or give them up at will, this freedom was denied to many ryots. They were not allowed to surrender their lands even when they expressed their inability to pay the taxes. On the other hand, they were forced to retain possession of the lands allotted to them and compelled to cultivate the prescribed area of land and consequently they had to pay the full revenue on all lands registered in their names. The system also contributed to forced labour. The officials employed the peasants to plant trees by road sides, keep watch over highways at nights and construct roads. When the ryots declined, they, were beaten up or were deprived of the produce from their fields. The ryotwari system increased the importance of revenue officials as the success of this settlement depended much on their efficiency. The rank and file of these officials were native personnel. The power given to revenue officials in classifying land gave them opportunities of oppressing hte ryots, when they refused tribes. Reports about corruption of the officials like the *karnam*, *nattamkar*, *tahsildar* and other categories abounded soon. An honest *karnam* was almost a contradiction in terms.[56] On representation by tahsildars, hereditary *karnams* were removed from offices and with a view to checking corruption the same experiment was tried in the case of appointment of *nattamkars*. But it did not work satisfactorily as the strangers never acquired an interest in the villages and so it was given up.

The revenue officials resorted to torture to enforce collection to extract forced labour and to obtain contributions. The fraud and oppression practised by the low-paid officials was pointed out to the concerned authorities and efforts were taken now and then to check such practices. Regulations were passed empowering the Collector to punish corrupt officials. But these regulations failed to put an end to the praactice of torture in revenue cases. Legal redress from torture was almost impossible either due to the ignorance of the ryots or fear of the ryots about the consequences and the cost and time involved in it. Munro was aware of the oppressions that the ryots suffered at the hands of the revenueu officials and he wanted to make law effictive so as to check misuse of authority. But before he could implement his scheme, he died in the yeaar 1827. Since no effictive step was taken to correct the situation and as such it continued to be a source of oppression throughout the Company's rule. For, Bourdillon, an experienced civil servent, in his report on public works submitted in 1833 observed that because of the oppressive exactions a large majority of the ryots had a hand-to -mouth existence.[57] A Commission appointed in 1854 to go into the cases of torture revealed the existence of the practice in its rigorous form in the collection of revenue and inability of the aggrieved parties to get any redress. It exposed the fact that cases of torture were frequent wherever the lands were highly assessed and it was very much a part of the ryotwari system during the Company's administration. The report showed that flogging by tamarind switches, the sun treatment, the horse and the rider method, the driving the devil method, the squeezing of the limbs in diverse ways, kittle and fastenting the body of a man to a branch of a tree under which a fire had been kindled for the purpose of suffocating the victims wiht the smoke were all very usual mehtods of torture.[58]

Nevertheless, the ryotwari system was well meant to be a good substitue for the Bengal system of revenue. But with the inherent defects unrectified, it brought all its woes with it. True that benign administrators endeavoured to ameliorate the condition of the peasants and to contribute to the extension of cultivation and increase of revenue. Yet the irregularities caused by faulty survey and over assessments remained unremoved throughout and when it was combined with the corruption of the officials, they caused unlimited harm to the inhabitants.

Yet, it cannot be denied that the ryotwari system eliminated middle men and established a definite contact between the administration and the people. The frequent tours that were undertaken enabled the English officials to learn more about the customs and habits of the people. This led to a better understanding between the rulers and the ruled. The system diffused the right of property more extensively than any other settlement. The flaws experienced in the mode of operation were more due to the persons than to the system. When the settlement was revised subsequently in 1885, in the light of th experiences it proved to be a much improved one and helped to promote the welfare of the ryots.[59] Accordingly, the ryotwari system was extended to North Arcot, South Arcot, Tiruchirapalli, Coimbatore, Madurai and Tirunelveli but also "in the estates which had reverted to the government owing to the failure of the zamindars".[60] However, in areas where feudal vestiges remained, the zamindari system continued to operate.

Notes and References

1. Madras Council, Revenue Consultations, 5 July 1799, Vol. 95, pp. 1150-1157.
2. Do, Military Consultations, 17 December 1799, Vol. 261, pp. 7592-7600.
3. Do, Revenue Consultations, 31 July 1801, Vol. 110, pp. 1437-1440.
4. Madras Council, Revenue Consultations, 4 September 1799, Vol. 95, Para 1-5.
5. S. Sarada Raju, *Economic Conditions in the Madras Presidency, 1800-1850,* Madras, 1941. P.4
6. C.D. Maclean, *Standing Information Regarding the Official Administration of the Madras Presidency,* p. 58.
7. J.W. Kaye, *The Administration of the East India Company,* London, 1853, p. 205.
8. Regulation XIII of 1803, (State Archives, Madras).
9. Fifth Report on the Affairs of the East India Company, Vol. II, p. 15.
10. B.R. Chakravarthi, *A Handbook of Land Tenures in the Presidency of Madras,* p. 18.
11. Madras Council, Revenue Consultations, 4 September 1799, Vol. 96, pp. 1804-1806 and P. Gana Sundara Mudaliar, *Note on the Permanent Settlement,* Madras, 1940, p. 32.
12. Fifth Report on the Affairs of the East India Company, Vol. II, p. 53.
13. H.R. Pate, *op.cit.,* Vol. II, p. 273.
14. Madras Council, Revenue Despatches to England, 23 March, 1804, Vol. 8, pp. 16-18.
15. Madras Regulations, Section II of Regulation XXV, 1802 and Fifth Report on the Affairs of the East India Company, Vol. II, p. 54.
16. Srinivasa Raghava Iyengar, *Memorandum on the Progress of the Madras Presidency during the last 40 years of British Administration,* Madras, 1893, p. 227.
17. Madras Council, Revenue Despatches to England, 9 May 1803, Vol. 78, pp. 528-546.
18. Ramasamy Naidoo, *Memoir on the Internal Revenue System of the Madras Presidency,* Madras, 1908, p. 24.

19. Madras Council, Revenue Despatces to England, 16 December 1812, Vol. 5, Paras 6-13.

20. Madras Council, Revenue Consultations,26 April 1806, Vol. 149, pp. 1178-1191.

21. Fifth Report on the Affairs of the East India Company, Vol. II, p. 117.

22. Madras Council, Public Consultations, 28 February 1807, Vol. 332, p. 1096.

23. General Report of the Board of Revenue, 5 October 1808, Vol. 16, pp. 170-171.

24. The Asylum Press, *Almanac and Directory of Madras and Souht India,* 1931-1932, p. 203.

25. Madras Council, Revenue Consultations, 4 December 1807, Vol. 160, p. 9380.

26. H.R. Pate, (ed.) *Tinnevely Gazetteer,* Vol. I, p. 281.

27. General Report of the Board of Revenue, 5 October 1808, Vol. 16, pp. 172-176.

28. Madras Council, Revenue Consultations, 12 April 1808, Vol. 163, p. 1036.

29. General Report of the Board, 5 October 1808, Vol. 16, pp. 178-181.

30. Revenue Despatch from England, 16 December 1812, Vol. 5, Para 4-14.

31. Madras Revenue Selections, Madras, 1916, p. 617.

32. Revenue Despatches from England, 16 December 1812, Vol. 5, Para 4-47.

33. Mukerji, Nilamani, *The Ryotwari System in Madras,* Calcutta, 1962, pp. 7-8.

34. Baramhal Records, Colonel Read to David Hamilton, 10 August 1794.

35. General Repords to the Governor-in-Council, Vol. 7-9, January 1802, p. 180.

36. Fifth Report, Vol. III, Part IV, pp. 470-471.

37. Parliamentry Papers, 1831-1832, David Hill's Evidence, 18 March 1822, p. 735.

38. Fifth Report, Vol. III, Part IV, pp. 470.
39. Powell, Beden, *Land Systems of British India,* Vol. III, Delhi, 1972, pp. 38-39.
40. Ruthnasamy, M. (1939), *Some Influences that made the British Administrative System in India,* Madras, pp. 290-291.
41. Year from harvest to harvest. Karnam was the village accountant.
42. In addition to the accounts regarding land revenue, the Karnam sent accounts of rainfall, inflow of water into the village tanks, mortality, cattle and similar details and sent special reports now and then.
43. Munro's Report, 30 November 1806, Board's Proceedings 8 January 1807.
44. Nelson J.H. Manual of Madurai, Vol. III, Madras, 1868, p. 132.
45. Madras Council, Revenue Consultations,10 April 1804, Vol. 135, p. 1905.
46. Board of Revenue Proceedings, 5 January 1807, Vol. 25, pp. 5-6.
47. B.S. Baliga, *Manual of the Administration of the Madras Presidency,* Vol. I , p. 121.
48. Madras Revenue Selections, Vol. III, p. 600.
49. Madras Council, Revenue Consultations, 3 April 1827, Vol. 324, p. 1069.
50. Board of Revenue, Proceedings, 20 June 1814, Vol. 644, p. 7882.
51. K. Gowti, *Madurai Under the English East India Company,* Madurai, pp. 129-131.
52. A tax was levied on certain special kinds of produce under the head *Vanapyir*. They were betelvines, plantains turmerics, chillies and brinjals and where they ere grown on nunjah lands the above tax was levied on them. Collector parker explained to the Board that the levy of the tax checked initiative on the part of the ryots in developing cultivation of Gardens. At the request of parker this tax was abolished. (K. Gowri, *op.cit.,* p. 132.)
53. Dharma Kumar, *Land and Caste in South India,* Cambridge University Press, 1963, p. 83.
54. Dubbois, Abbe, *op.cit.,* p. 183 and first Report of the Select committee of the house of Commans, 1853, p. 286. The enquiries conducted by the Parliamentary committee in 1862 revealed that

the heavy assessments had sapped the morality of the people and totally impoverished them. Abbe Dubois who gave a graphic description of the poverty of the people, ascribed it to the revenue system of the company's Government.

55. There were reports against the tahsildars and sub-collects that there were cases of oppression, ill-treatment and compulsion to do things against their will. Collector R.D. Parker sent a report to the Board charging such offences against his sub-collector. (Madurai District Records, Vol. 5322, pp. 162-164).

56. K. Gowri, *op.cit.*, p. 135.

    Drury who was the commissioner of Madurai for sometiem charges Collector Blockburne with harsness towards the Ryots, which included exaction of many kinds of forced labour. A tahsildar had the entire control of assessments. Whenever a tahsildar visited a village the ryots endeavoured to buy to get a low assessment.

57. Bourdillon's Account of Madras Ryot quoted by Dutt, R.C. in his *Economic History of India,* Vol. II, pp. 50-61.

58. Muskets were turned down by maing the man support them with muzzles resting on his great toes and continuing in this position for hours together in the heat of the mid-day sun.

    Torture Commission Report, Appendix C No. 16. One man is made to support another exposed to the heat of the sun in the position of horse and rider for a few hours, and the rider dismounts and is ridden by the other man for the same length of time.

    Torure Commission Report, Appendix C. No. 16 A man is made to sit outside in the hottest part of the day with his head hair all lose and made to undergo a curious operation of turning his head in a whirling position, which is known in the tahsildar's cutcheries as extracting the devil; assisted with flagellation, if not performed quick, for th edriving out of the evil spirit.

    Torure Commission Report, Appendix C. No. 14, CXIV 'Kittle' was an instrument of torture. By this instrument the fingers are gradually bent backwards towards the back of the hand until the wretched sufferers being no longer able to endure the excruciating pain, yields to the demands of his tormentors.

59. Madura District Records, Vol. 5334, p. 370.

60. General Report of the Board of Revenue, I January 1814, Vol. 7, Paras 1084-1049.

CHAPTER – 10

LAW AND ORDER SYSTEM

Together wiht the reorganisation of revenue administration, the English East India Company took measures to create the needed institutions to enforce to law and order in its attempt to consolidate its imperial sway. This required organisation of law courts, police force and prison administration. It appeared that no where the feudal distinctions were so pronounced as in the working of traditional institutions. It cannot be denied that the inhabitants by tradition recognised the need for justice and courts. Yet in practice they operated them in a crude form. The general tendency was to overate the pretensions of influential people and to uphold the unequal claims of superior castes. As a result the weak and poor fell victims to inequality before law. In these circumstances the Company found it essential to rely upon its western tradtions and practies wherever necessary, for the enforcement law and order. Through the needed reforms the British consolidated and extended its authority.

Organisation of Law Courts

On the establishment of its auhtority over the country the Company found that there existed a traditional system of judicial administration. The laws followed were based upon religious tenets and social customs. The village was managed by a headman, who combined in himself the powers of magistrate, judge and tax collector. Assisted by a jury called *panchayat,* he decided the cases. His judgement was subject to appeal to the district *amuldar* and then to the provincial *amildar* and form him to the ruler, whether he was a poligar or rajah or nawab. In each town there were a *kazi* and a *pundit* to decide civil and criminal cases involving the Muslims and the Hindus respectively. Despite these, there were no organised law courts, no legal language, no counsels, and no legal code other than customs and conventions. In such a situation arbitrary methods and well and pleasure judgements were the order of the day.[1] Therefore, the machinery of justice required reorganistion and improvement.

As the acquisition of territories needed the establishment of courts, British Parliment enacted legislation either for improving the existing courts or for establishing new courts of law. The city of Madras had its court with Mayor and Aldermen under the royal charter of 1687.[2] In the beginning it was called Mayor's Court. The Recorder's Court took the place of the old Mayor's Court in 1798. It had jurisdiction over civil, criminal, ecclesiastical and admiralty cases within the limits of the city of Madras.[3] However the jurisdiction did not extend beyond the territorial limits of Fort St. George.[4] British Parliament held that the judiciary in India should be separated from the executive. Accordingly, Lord Cornwallis, the Governor-General of Bengal (1786-1795), separated the department of justice from revenue, by depriving the collector of all authority as judge and magistrate and vesting it in the hands of a distinct court.[5] The needs of the times demanded more of reforms. Accordingly in 1801 by an act of Parliament, the Supreme Court was at Madras, superseding the Recorder's Court. It consisted of a Chief Justice and two puisne judges.[6] Sir Thomas Strange became the first Chief Justice of this court with Henry Guillim and Benjamin Sullivan as the puiene judges.[7]

The jurisdiction of the supreme Court at Madras extended over all civil cases. Till then these cases were tried by the Mayor's court and the Recorder's Court at Madras. The court could exercise civil, criminal, admiralty and ecclesiastical jurisdiction, both as to the local inhabitants and British subjects.

It was to be invested with such power and authorities, privileges and immunities for the better administration of the same and subject to the same limitations, restrictions and control within Fort St.George and town of Madras and the factories subordinate thereto and within the territories of Madras.[8] Cases of the local people were to be tried according to their laws and usages, ie., cases of the Hindus were to be decided according to the laws and usages of the Hindus and cases of the Muslims according to the laws and usages of the Muslims.If a Hindu and a Muslim were the contending parties, it was to be decided according to the laws and usages of the community of the defendant. Every case was decided by the majority vote of the judges present. The appeals from the Supreme court lay to the King-in-Council.[9] The Sheriff of Madras was "to execute all units, orders, rules, commands, warrants and process of the court and make return of the same together with the manner of the execution thereof to the court".[10] The Supreme Court at Madras exercised its powers independent of the Governor-in-Council.[11]

The modification of the court at the top level, neede changes in the administration of justice at the lower level. Most of the duties performed by some minor courts like the Master in Equity were taken over by the Supreme Court. So the powers and income of the Court of the Master in equity decreased and it appointment of two professional men for discharging the duty of Master in Equity. Accordingly in 1802, the Court of Request was reorganised and called "The Court of Commissioners for the Recovery of Small Debts". It functioned under the superitendance of the Master in the Supreme Court. This court was expected to provide for speedy easy remedy for recovering the rights of the people.[12] While the Supreme Court made no distinction between a suit which was intended for the recovery of fifty pagodas and that of five thousand pagodas in the fixation of fees, the Court of Commissioners fixed the table of fees at a comparatively low rate for the small cases.[13] Court of Wards for the protection of the rights and property of the incapacitated persons was also created.[14] The inherited properties of those incapacitated by minority, sex or natural infirmity were usually placed under the charge of other people, but the managers frequently abused and disregarded the rights of the incapacitated persons. Now legal provisions were made for the due preservation of the property of the incapacitated persons, the education of minors and the care of the lunatics and idiots.[15]

Till 1802 the Company's administration made no organised effort to improve the judical administration in the districts. What was provided was just haphazard. The collectors of the districts decided the civil cases and appeal lay to the Board of Revenue.[16] Criminal cases were tried by the military tribunals. However, in 1802 a series of regulations were passed to create a hierarchy of civil and criminal courts and to define their powers. Thereby three types of courts came into existence–

(i) The zillah courts having both civil and magisterial jurisdiction,

(ii) Provincial and Circuit Courts each having jurisdiction over a group of districts and

(iii) Sadar and criminal jurisdiction.[17]

Accordingly, Lord Clive constituted zillah courts in the districts where assessment of revenue on a permanent basis was completed. The jurisdiction of the zillah court extended over all civil cases. A native Commissioner, attached to it, heard and decided petty cases. The zillah judge also served as the magistrate for the district. In that capacity he controlled the 'thanadars' and 'darogas' who were posted at important places for doing police duties and the 'kavalkars' who were directed to watch the villages.[18] With the establishment of the zillah courts, the collectors ceased to exercise any judicial or police functions. Governor Clive followed the example of Bengal in setting up the zillah courts, yet he made the necessary adjustments so as to suit the system to the circumstances of the country. The association of the native machinery for the performance of police duties was an instance of such an adjustment. The creation of a separate police force would have resulted in the unemployment of a large number of village guards. Therefore the Madras Council instead of dispensing with their services, associated them with the new set up.[19] The appeals from the zillah courts lay to the Provincial Court of Appeal, which was the highest civil court for the province. Appeals from the provinicial courts lay to the Madras Council, who acted as Court of Appeal to the Sadar Adalat or chief court of civil judicature. Along with Provincial Court of Appeal, there came into existence Courts of Circuit to try criminal cases. Appeals from the circuit courts lay to the Foujdary Adalat or chief criminal court at Fort St.George.[20] Territories of Fort St. George were divided into four divisions the Northern, Southern, Central and Western for the purpose of administration of justice.[21] The zillah magistrate, who was the head of the district police, apprehended individuals alleged to have committed crimes and committed them to take their trial before the judges of the courts of circuit[22] The criminal law was based on principles of Muhammadan Law. Law officers called qazis or Muftis were appointed to assist the judges in delivering judgements. In all cases of murder, where a sentence of death or imprisonment for life was passed, proceedings of the court should be transmitted to the Foujdary Adalat and the Circuit Court was to wait for the decision of the Foujdary Adalat. The judges of the circuit courts were vested with certain administrative duties also. Thus exercised control over the zillah magistrates and should report to the Foujdary Adalat, if they found the magistrates guilty of neglect or misconduct in the discharge of their duty. They should visit the jails in every circuit and isuse such orders as they considered necessary for the security of the prisoners or for their better treatment and accommodation. They were to submit such rules as in their view would promote the better administation of justice and the improvement of police.

Four Provincial Courts of Appeal were eestablished at Dindigul, Krishnagiri, Ellore and Chicable. They heard appeals from decisions passed by the zillah courts.[23] Each court was superintended by three judges. The courts were held in large and convenient halls, three days in a week. The provincial courts of Appeal tried and determined in the first instance suits of complaints or any matter of civil nature, which were transmitted to them for this purpose by the Sadar Adalat.[24]

The Sadar Adalat was the highest civil court in the Presidency. The begin with the Governor and Member of his Council of Fort St. George were made judges of the Sader Adalat. They were made judges of the Court of Foujdary Adalat as well.[25] Both the courts were practically one. When it sat for the adjudication of civil cases, it was called Sadar Adalat and when it heard criminal cases, it became Foujdary Adalat.There were three judges, the chief, second judge and third judge of the Sader Adalat.[26] The Governor of Fort St. George acted as the chief judtice of the court till the Regulation III of 1807 was enacted. By Regulation III of 1807, the court was placed under a chief judge, who was to be a member of the Council. Sadar Adalat had both original and appellate powers. Only the English men were appointed as the judges of this court. It was empowered to receive the suits from the provincial courts of appeal. The Sadar Adalat had powers to decide finally all suits upto Rs. 45,000/- and above that sum, an appeal lay to the Governor-General-in-Council. The Foujdary Adalat was the final appellate court for all criminal cases. The court consisted of the Governor and Members of his Council. It was assisted by the qazi. The Governor functioned as the chief judge, assisted by three judges, who were appointed by the Governor-in-Council from among the covenanted civil servants of the Company, not being members of the Governor's Council.[27] By the Regulation III of 1807, this court underwent significant changes. Accordingly it was given a separate a chief judge and three puiene judges. Also it dealt with all matters relating to the adminisration of justice in criminal cases. The court was empowered to propose new regulation, alteration and additions to the Muhammadan laws. In cases of murder the head Qazi and Mufti were to give their opinions. This court was empowered to pass sentence of death punishment, if the criminals were found quilty as per law.

Thus there came into existence two court systems-the Supreme Court set up by the Crown and the graded system of courts set up by the Company. For the first time in the history of the country an elaborate system of couts was institued. In reorganising judical administration, due consideration was given to the customs and practices of the people.[28] Still the system had its own defects. The local people had not much of a say in the administration of justice. The courts were guided by the British rules of procedure, which were foreign to the country. To the inhabitants who were ignorant and illiterate courts remained out of thier reach. Inability to proceed to the court, complexity of the processes and uncertainty of results were factors which would dissuade the aggrieved from seeking redressal of grievances from court. In effect the East India Company assumed little command over the local or village judicial system upto 1815. Traditionally, the village headmen who were called as potails used to deal with the cases under their jurisdiction. They were supposed to know the state of the matter better than anybody else and were, therefore, always summoned.[29] Only after the introduction of Thomas Munro's reforms in the Madras Presidency in 1816, the British began to involve the local authority in their judical system. Yet it cannot be denied that the judical system was made more systematic and organised than what it had been. It was extended to the provinces, where it had never been heard of till then.

Prison Reforms

The Comapny inherited from the past an irreguler system of prison administrartion. The convicts were summarily tried whipped soundly or set free or confined in miserable choultries.[30] However, with the introduction of law courts-the Sadar Adalat, provincial courts of circuit and zillah criminal courts,[31] it became essential to erect proper prisons and to frame rules for their Management. In this important work, the European administrators were to a considerable extent influenced by humanitarian ideas of the west. They wanted to codify and simplify the criminal proceedings in order to reform the criminals and prevent crime. Accordingly they tried to give medical aid, segregate men from women, debtors from felons and novices from hardened criminals in the prisons.[32]

The company's administrators found that the were prisons not been constructed on any regular plan. Some old tents, a couple of hired houses or a dilapidated wing of the court-house constituted the zillah prison. As a result, discipline could not be maintained in these places. There were often brawls, riots and escapes.[33] The places used as prison afforded neither security to the public nor health to the prisoners.[34] Therefore attempts were made from time to time to provide for separate accommodation for the different descriptions of prisoners. It was laid down that separate cells in each prison should be allotted to those who were under sentence of death, those who were sentenced for long terms, those committed for trial before the circuit judges and those sentenced for petty crimes by the magistrates. Yet these rules could not be enforced until proper prisons were erected.[35]

By 1815-16 substantial prisons were built according to plans. Each prison as enclosed by a wall ten to twelve feet high and it was provided with several wards.[36]Each ward consited of a number of cells. A whole ward or one or more cells were allotted for the confinement of hardened criminals, females and juvenile culprits. Every prison was equipped with a hospital, a dispensary, a manufactory, guard rooms, lunatic cells, store rooms, kitchens, wells and latrines.[37] Medical care and morale of the prisoners received due attention.[38] Each zillah prison was placed under the charge of a jailor, who was generally an Indian but sometime a European. Prison guards were posted to assist the jailor in his work. The zillah surgeon was asked to visit the prison periodically, while a resident Indian doctor worked in the prison hospital and the dispensary. The zillah crimanal judge supervised the duties of the jailor, the surgeon and the doctor. At first he was required to visit the prison aat least once a month, but later once a week, to investigate and redresscomplaints of ill-treatment, preferred to him by the prisoners against the jailor or any other officer.[39] He was especially asked to be "attentive to the health and cleanliness of the prisoners and to see that the surgeon of the station attends and administers to the sick". Also he was made answerable to the judges of circuit, who were asked to visit the prisons in their divisions on every circuit and to issue to the criminal judges such orders as might be necessary "for the better treatment and accomadation or security of the prisoners".[40] The circuit judges after such half-yearly or quarterly circuit were to report on the state of the prisons to the Sadar Foujdary Adalat,[41] Which in turn was made responsible to the Government.

Measures were also adopted for the internal management of the prisons with proper attention to food, clothing, sanitation, labour and discipline.[42] In regard to food, the prisoners were taken care of properly. In addition to common food, they were provided wiht betel and tobacco and when sick wine and liquor.[43] The prisoners were given extra rations, when they performed hard labour. This liberality shown to the prisoners made imprisonment lose its terror and the result was over crowding of the prisons. The Government was therefore compelled to prohibit what appeared as luxuries expect on medical care.

Labour in the prison was not made very rigorous. Even those who were sentenced to hard labour were generally engaged in the work of common artisans and craftsmen.[44] The object was to reform the prisoners and to train them in arts and crafts in order to make them useful earning members of the society after their release. The credit for introducing plans based on these noble sentiments belonged to an able civilian, Newnham, the Judge and Magistrate of Cuddapah. It was he who for the first time systematically employed the prisoners for manufacturing different items like tools, carpenters and masons bricks, mats, cumblies and coarse cloth. The last three items were for the use of the prisoners themselves.

The Madras Council recommended his plans to all criminal judges of the Presideency for implementation.[45]

In course of time, these items of labour were considered too light to be allotted to convicts sentenced to hard labour. From the beginning minor public works such as erecting small bridge heads or repairing minor roads were occasionally entrusted to the prisoners.[46] In 1816 Wright, the Criminal Judge of Chittoor discovered the immense possibilities of convict labour for constructing large irrigation tanks and repairing trunk roads. Accordingly, the Government ordered the systematic employment of convicts on such public works in all districts. Since then the convicts of a whole division or a group of districts were regularly employed on public works under proper supervision.[47]

Generally strict vigilance was kept in order to maintain discipline. The prison authorities were empowered to hold summary esquires into all matters relating to discipline and to punish refusal to work or willful defiance of rules by stripes upto sixty and by reduction of diet allowance. Resistance to the jailor, abusive language, riot, insurrection, attempt to escape or tempering with irons were punished by awarding stripes upto 150 and, as far as practicable, even by solitary confinement. Whippers were not to strike on any part of the body except the upper part of the back. The prison doctor could step them whipping it he deemed it necessary.

Reorganisation of Police

It was essential to have an efficient police system not only for the working of the judicial system but also for maintaining law and order in the country. The police duties performed by the kavalkars in the villages and kotwals in the towns were not of the mark. Therefore the East India Company tried to dispense with this system in 1801. In the districts the collector was given *sibbandy* peons. He empolyed his *sibbandy* peons under the control of revenue servants for the apprehension of criminals and for the maintenance of law and order.[48] in 1802 the policing of the village was restored to the village taliaries under the supervision of the collector.[49] The poligar was relieved from all the police and military duties.[50] Thereupon the Government carried into effect reforms for the administraation of pollice in the districts.

Accordingly series of regulations were passed in 1802 for reforming the police administration. They transferred the control of the police and the functions of the district magistrate to the collector. After investing the collector with the authority of a magistrate, the Sadar Adalat issued regulations to give effect to the directions of the Court of Directors. The first regulation in this regard restored the management of the village police to the heads of the villages and of the district police to the tahsildars or amuldars under the collector.[51] The hereditary village officials were allowed to perform police duties. The headmen of the villages were empowered to hear and decide petty cases. The competence of Indian judical officers was promoted through a simplification of various rules that were framed for practising in law courts. *Panchayats* or courts of arbitration were created for villages and larger areas. As a result the police came to perform many of the duties for which kavalkars, sibbendies and sepoys were formerly employed.[52]

It was found necessary to arrange for a regular police in order to preserve order and promote and safety of the inhabitants.[53] Therefore in 1815 the Madras Council appointed a commission to suggest reforms. On the basis of the report of the commission, the Madras council enacted the Regulation of 1816. It entrusted the responsibility of police duties with the village headmen, the tahsildars, the kotwals and the zillah magistrates in their respective areas of jurisdiction. They were assisted by clerks and peons.[54] This reform represented a compromise with the traditional system, for by this reform the headmen of villages and kotwals of towns regained a status in the administration of law and order.[55]

In spite of these reforms there was not much of improvement in the crime situation. The police administration continued to be inefficient, corrupt and oppressive much due to the combination of revenue and police authority in the same agency. The village headsmen and the tahsildars concentrated their effort on the collection of taxes and neglected the police duties. Nevertheless the police forces served the needs of imperial authority for law and order were its main concern.

Conclusion

In the evolution of a feudal system in the Tamil Country the organisation of the Nayankara system represented a significant event. By 1465 A.D. the forces of Vijayanagar Empire overran the southern regiọn defeated the Sambuvarayas of Tondaimandalam and the Sultans Afghans of Madurai and annexed the Tamil provinces. In view of the local opposition the Emperors needed the support of chiefs, who appeared ready to serve. Then is times of war as well as in peace. Also they wanted to win over the allegiance of local chieftains and descendants of ancient ruling families for the consolidation of their authority. These considerations led them to reorganise the administration on a feudal basis and the result was the rise of the Nayankara system. However, with the decline of Vijayanagar Empire, the Nayankara system transformed itself into independent Nayak monarchies of Jinji, Thanjavur and Madurai.

As the Nayaks declined and disappeared from the political scene, the order of the Poligars emerged prominent in the feudal set up. In the three tier polity of vijayanagar the rayas, the nayaks and the poligars presented the constituents, each in its turn supporting and sustaining the other. The rayas who were emperors declined and as they declined the nayaks emerged as independent monarchies. When these monarchies went out of the slave, the poligars came to the forefront. They were in fact lesser nayaks but were called Palayakkarans or poligars, as they were holders of palayams or armed camps. If the Nayaks held possession of large territories, the poligars held possession of different tracts of land, needed to support an armed establishment. Like the nayaks they served the rayas and subsequently the nayaks. The had to encounter a new situation as the nayaks went out power and external powers established their sway.

Under the Nayaks the country was dotted with feudal estates of the poligars. Most of them were concerned in Tirunelveli, Madurai, Ramnad, Thanjavur, Tiruchirapalli, Dindugal and Coimbatore. The resources of the territories decided the political status of the respective poligars. After the decline of the vijayanagar and nayak powers, the aggressive Muslim powers gained control of the political system of the land. The poligar system too experienced the consequent vicissitudes in its fortune.

The poligars represented the feudal order in the Tamil Country. In fact the poligar combined in himself the authority of a ruler as well as the status of a subject in the local community. Accordingly, his functions included maintenance of armed men continually equipped for military service, protection of their own communities, suppression of criminals, punishment of offenders against person and property and payment of compensation in the event of their failure to restore property lost through theft. In return for the due fulfillment of these duties, the poligar was treated as the proprietor of the rent from his estate.

The poligars under the rule of the Wallajahs encountered a complicated situation created by conflicting interests. They were required to deal with the administration of the Nawab, of the English East India Company as an ally of the Nawab and of the rival powers. Assisted by the English, the Nawab sent expeditions against the chieftains and made a limited advance towards the consolidation of his authority. But this trend could not be sustained because of opposition of the rival powers, particularly Maphuz khan and Khan Sahib. The consequent wars created terror and turmoil, yet the feudal powers found it possiible to take advantage of the disorders to expand their influence. For a time Nawab instead of pursuing his policy of coercion, resorted to a policy of conciliation with a view to gaining their alliance and granted them more of rights. The rival and rebel powers sought their aid and they too gave them concessions. More of the circar villages accepted their protection and paid taxes. However, this situation did not last long for the auxiliary powers followed no uniform or common policy in relation with the new developments. Mohammad Ali on the otherhand was supported by his British ally. This let to the suppression of several poligars and the annexation of the palayams of Turiayur, Ariyalur, Wodayarpalayam, Sivaganga and Ramanathapuram. These gains were significant but the Nawab found himself more and more indebted to the English.

The Military operations of the Nawab against the feudal powers were marked by up and downs. The Madras council felt that the Nawab would collect the arrears of rent that the poligars owed to him and that he would clear his dept to the English East India Company and offer rewards. With this end to view it extended support to military operations. But it was disappointed, for nothing much could be collected and what was collected was inadequate to meet the expenses of the expeditions. In this situation the Company found it necessary to mobilise resources for the conduct of major wars against Mysore. These required to intervention of the Company not only in the internal administration of the country but also in Nawab's relations with the feudal powers.

The 'assignment' and the 'assumption' policies were two landmarks in the history of the British ascendancy in the Tamil Country. They were of considerable advantage to the Company when it was engaged in Major conflicts with other South Indian Powers, especially Mysore and the Martha's. The apparently common defense system of the region, as was envisaged in the treaties, served as an instrument to force the Nawab of Arcot and the Rajah of Thanjavur to furnish their resources for the support of large-scale military operations of the English, as and when they were required. Added to these the treaties of 1787 and 1792 formulated and established a dual system of administration in the Tamil Country. The English exercised military authority and controlled foreign relations. The Nawab of the carnatic and the Rajah of Thanjavur, on the otherhand, administered revenue and justice in their respective territories. The dual system infused illfeeling in the relations of the poligars with the English ,as there forllowed a direct confrontation. The enforcement of a series of drastic reforms of the British in quick succession excited internal tension. The Southern poligars were a race of rude warriors, habituated to arms and independence. But they found that their chieftains were either executed or condemned to a perpetual and ignominious imprisonment. This harsh treatment of a high spirited people reacted violently upon their sentiments. The Company in suppressing the poligars subverted a time honoured system of government, but without providing an effective parallel. The people were disarmed, their arms were confiscated and forts were razed to the ground. While no protection was given, the inhabitants were deprived of the means of repelling the predatory incursions of their hereditary enemies, residing in other territories and of resisting the unjust demands of the parties claiming the authority of the Nawab They found their life subjected to constant supervision by British troops and interfered with by the Company's tax-collectors.

The wars against the feudal powers and suppression of their resistance coincided with a steady and gradual drift of the Tamil provinces to the imperial authority of the British. The wars of the poligars the influence of the sovereign as well as the auxiliary powers. As these wars were waged with the support of the Company they weakened the Nawab's influence, for they increased his public dept and ultimately contributed to foreign intervention. The poligars offered a second line of defence in the lard and when it was dismantled by the Company in the name of the sovereign, the Nawab the latter found himself isolated from his triibutaries. At the same time he had no allies either among the Indian powers or among the European powers to should him against the imperial designs of the British. Such a situation led to eclipse of local powers and replaced the system of dual control by a single authority, that of the British.

The Treaty of 1801 added a territorial extent of 17,250 square miles to the Madras Presidency. Henceforth the English were at liberty to establish a uniform system of administration for the Tamil Country. The significant benefit of the Treaty was the end of double government. Ever since the establishment of British influence in the carnatic the people laboured under a system of authority exercised by the feudal powers rulers of the land and the Company's administration. However, the suppression of the poligars and settlement of the treaties of annexation prepared the ground for imperialist consolidation under a uniform system.

Through military operations and political settlements the English East India Company the Tamil Country to unity with the annexation of Kongu Nadu, Thanjavur and the carnatic the dual system of control came to an end. In consequence of the settlement of the Carnatic Treaty of 1801 the British gained themselves free to deal with these powers as they wanted.

The unification of the Tamil Country under British rule required the enforcement of a uniform system of administration for all regions. Accordingly the Madras Council entrusted the administration of the districts with the collectors. The system was already in operation in Dindigul and Ramnad. After the end of the Mysore War in 1799 the Company formed three divisions. Dindigul, Baramahal and Coimbatore out of the north western acquisition from Mysore and placed each of these districts under a separate collector. With the Board of Revenue exercising control over the collectors and the collectors over the local officials, the administrative reorganisation obliterated the traditional authorities and gave a common pattern to the land of the Tamils.

The ryotwari system eliminated middle men and established direct contact between the administration and the people. The frequent towers that were undertaken enabled the English officials to learn more about the customs and habits of the people. This led to a better understanding between the rulers and the ruled. The system diffused the right of property more extensively than any other settlement. The flaws experienced in the mode of operation were more due to the persons than to the system. When the settlement was revised subsequently in 1855, in the light of the experiences it proved to be a much improved one and helped to promote the interests of the ryots. Accordingly, the ryotwari system extended to North Arcot south Arcot, Tiruchirapalli, Coimbatore, Madurai and Tirunelveli. But also in the estates which had reverted to the government overing to the failure of the Zamindars. However, in zamindari areas feudal vestiges continued to operate on a restricted dimension.Together with the reorganisation of revenue administration, the English East India Company took measures to create the needed institutions to enforce law and order . This required organisation of law courts, police force and prison administration. It cannot be denied that the inhabitants by tradition recognised the need for justice and courts. Yet in practice they were operated in a crude form. The general tendency was to overrate the pretensions of influential people and to uphold the unequal claims of superior castes. As a result the weak and the poor sections of the society fell victims to inequality before law. In these circumstances the Company found it essential to rely upon its western traditions and practices wherever necessary for the enforcement of law and order. Through the reorganisation of traditional institutions the British consolidated and extended their authority.

In fact the reforms represented a compromise with the traditional system, for the headman of villages and kotwals of towns regained a status in the administration of law and order. Yet crimes were not controlled as expected. The police administration continued to be inefficient, corrupt and oppressive much due to the combination of revenue and police authority in the same agency. The village headmen and the tahsildars concentrated their efforts on the collection of taxes and neglected police duties. However, the police forces served the needs of imperial authority to maintain law and order and to preserve justice. Through the revenue and judicial regulations the British by 1816 destroyed the feudal authority and brought the country under a unified system. This transtion was of considerable significance to the political, social and economic life of the people of the Tamil Country.

Notes and References

1. A. Dubois, *Hindu Manners, Customs and Ceremonies*, Oxford, 1906, pp. 654-656.
2. C. S. Srinivasachari, *History of the city of Madras*, Madras, 1939, p. 204.
3. Madras Council, Public Despatches to England, 13 August 1799, Vol. 33, pp. 26-27.
4. Sir Thomas Strange was appointed the first Recorder. He had been for seven years Chief Justiceof Nova Scotia (Canada). He took an active in the public life of Madras. In 1817 he resigned office to return to England.
5. Madras Council, Judicial Consultations, 1 January 1803, Vol. 3A, pp. 1-2.

6. C.S. Srinivasachari, *op.cit.*, p. 204.
7. Madras Council, Public Despatches from England, 11 February 1801, Vol. 104, pp. 55-58.
8. Peter Auber, *An Analysis of the Constitution of the East India Company*, p. 253.
9. Madras Council, Public Despatches from England, 11 February 1801, Vol. 104, pp. 305-308.
10 C. D. Maclean, *Standing Information Regarding the Official Administration of the Madras Presidency*, p. 167.
11. Peter Auber, *op.cit.*, p. 253.
12. Madras Council, Public Consultations, 29 December 1801, Vol. 259, pp. 5380-5381.
13. *Ibid.*, pp. 5385-5387.
14. Madras Regulations, Regulation XIII of 1803.
15. Madras Council, Judical Consultations, 26 August 1803, Vol. 38, pp. 151-153.
16. Madras Regulations, Regulation I of 1803.
17. Lord Cornwallis' System of Courts for Bengal consisted of
    (1) Small courts presided over by native commissioners,
    (2) Zillah courts presided over by British judges and
    (3) Court of appeal or Sadar Diwani Adalat consisting of Governor-General and

    Members of the Council, Court of Circuit and Sadar Nizamat Adalat. A hierarchy of criminal courts was also set up.
18. The *thanadars*, the *darogas* and *kavalkars* were native institutions for preserving law and order in the country. Lord Clive associated them with new set up.
19. Madras Council, Judicial Consultations, 1 January 1803, Vol. 3, pp. 1-4.
20. Madras Council, Revenue Consultations, 9 July 1802, Vol. 117, pp. 2152-2167.
21. The Southern division extended from the Cape to Palar, central division from Palar to Krishna, Northern division from Krishna to Ganjam and Western division from the Ghats to the sea in the west.

22. Madras Regulations, Section IV of Regulation VII, 1802.
23. Madras Council, Revenue Consultations, 9 July 1802, Vol. 117, pp. 2156-2167.
24. Madras Regulations, Section IV of Regulation IV, 1802.
25. Peter Auber, *op.cit.*, p. 253.
26. Madras Council, Revenue Consultations, 9 July 1802, Vol. 117, pp. 2160-2167.
27. Madras Regulations, Section V of Regulation VII, 1802.
28. *Ibid.*, Section VII of Regulation VII, 1802 and Letter from Colonel Munro, First Commissioner to D. Hill, Chief Secretary to Government, 24 December 1814, p. 421.
29. Selection of Papers from the Records at the East India House, Vol. II, London, 1820, pp. 105-106.
30. Madras Council, Revenue Consultations, 19 April 1793, Vol. 58-A, pp. 449-451.
31. Madras Regulations, Regulations II, IV and V of 1802.
32. B.S. Baliga, *Studies in Madras Administration*, Vol. I, pp. 266-267.
33. Madras Council, Judical Consultations,24 September 1805, Vol. 12, p.1925 and 10 April, Vol. 50, p. 1329.
34. Madras Council, Public Consultations, 2 January 1806, Vol. 306, p. 18.
35. Madras Council, Judicial Consultations, 12 June 1807, Vol. 28, p. 3575.
36. *Ibid.*, 17 April 1816, Vol. 113, p. 1206.
37. *Ibid.*, 26 October 1816, Vol. 115, p. 4031.
38. B.S. Baliga, *Studies in Madras Administration*, Vol. 1, pp. 261-266.
39. Regulation VI of 1802, Section 10.
40. Regulation VII of 1802, Section 32.
41. *Ibid.*, Section 37.
42. C.D. Maclean, *op.cit.*, p.509.
43. B.S. Baliga, *op.cit.*, Vol. 1, p. 271.
44. *Ibid.*, pp. 269-270.
45. Madras Council, Judicial Despatches to England, 5 January 1816, Vol. 4, Paras 31-33.

46. Do, Judicial Consultations 12 April 1808, Vol. 34, p. 1097.
47. Do, Judicial Despatches to England, 5 January 1816, Vol. 4, Paras 26-30.
48. Judicial Sundries, Fort St. George, 29 April 1803, Vol. 13, p. 2081.
49. Fifth Report on the Affairs of the East India Company, Vol. I, 1885, p. 265.
50. Madras Council, Revenue Despatches to England, 22 January 1800, Vol. 7-A, p. 18.
51. Extract from the Letter of Colonel Munro, First Commissioner to D. Hill, Chief Secretary to Government, Madras, 24 December 1814, p. 422.
52. C.S. Srinivasachari, *History of the City of Madras,* p. 216.
53. Madras Council, Public Consultations, 6 August 1806, Vol. 315, pp. 5733-5734.
54. K. Rajayyan, *History of Tamil Nadu (1565-1982),* p. 258.
55. Police Department, *The History of the Madras Police,* Madras, 1959, p. 250.

BIBLIOGRAPHY

Primary Sources

Epigraphical & Manscript

Madras Epigraphical Reports for the Years 1906, 1908, 1909, 1911, 1912, Madras.

Kasinathan, N. (eds.) *Thirumalainayakar Cheppedukal,* Rajagopal S. and Vethasalam V. *State Department of Archaeology,* Madras, 1994.

Local Accoounts and Bellads

Chandrasekaran, T., (ed.) (1959), *Sivagangai Charithira Kummi and Ammanai (T), Government of Madras,* Madras.

Chaṇdrasekaran, T., (ed.) (1950), *Ramaiyan Ammanai (T)., Madras Governmental Oriental Series, No. XIL,* Madras.

Karnataka Rajakkal Savisthara Charitram (T), Oriental Manscript Library, (Mackenzie Collection, Part VII, Madras, 1959.

Kulanthaivelan, K., (ed.) (1981), *Palaiyappattukkalin Vamsavali (T), Vol. I and II, State Department of Archaeology,* Madras.

Kulanthaivelan, K., (ed.) (1981), *Palaiyappathukkalin Varalaru (T), Vols. III, State Department of Archaeology,* Madras.

Maduraiveeran Kummikatai, Madras, 1972.

Pachakmkurichi Alivu Charithira Kummi (T), Oriental Manscript Library, N.D.

Sivagangai Charithira Kummi (T), Oriental Manscript Library, Madras, N.D.

Vaiyapuri Pillai, S. (Ed.) (1951), *Ramappaiyan Ammanai (T), University of Madras,* Madras.

Vanamamalai, N., (ed.) (1971), *Veerapandia Kattabomman, Kathaipadal (T), Madurai University,* Madurai.

Vanamamalai, N., (ed.) (1972), *Khan Shahib Sandai (T), Madurai University,* Madurai.

Epistolary Sources

Bertrand, J., (Fr.) (1850), *La Mission Du Madurai,* Vol. III and IV, Paris.

Besse Leon (1914), *La Mission Du Madure,* Trichinopoly.

Lockman, J. (1762), *Travels of the Jesuits,* Vols. I & II, Paternoster Row, London.

Madura Mission Archives, Shenbaganur, Annual Reports, Photostate Copies of Correspondence exchanged between Jesuits in India and their Superior in home and Friends in Europe.

Diaries

Price, J.F., (ed.), (1904-1907), *Private Diaries of Anandaranga Pillai,* Vols. 1-3, Government Press, Madras.

Dod well, H., (ed.), (1916-1928), *Private Diaries of Anandaranga Pillai,* Vols. 4-12, Government Press, Madras.

Proceedings of the Madras Government

Military Department

Consultation Vols. 1 to 290.

Despatches to England-1 to 32.

Sundries–1 to 66.

Miscellancy-1 to 42

Political Department

Consultation Vols. 1 to 70

Despatches to England-1 to 6

Despatches from Engaland-1 to 6

Public Department

Consultations-111 to 180.

Despatches to England-1 to 42.

Secret Department

Consultations, Vols. 1 to 12

Despatches to England, Vols. 1 to 4.

Despatches from England, Vols. 1 to 4.

Sundries, Vols. 1 to 3.

Revenue Department

Consultations, Vols. 1 to 118.

Board of Revenue consultations Vols. 1 to 125.

Proceedings of the committee of Assigned Revenue 1780-1785.

Collectorate Records

Selections from the records of the collectorate of Trichnopoly, 1916.

Collector's Reports, Tinnevelly, Collectorate Press, Tinnevelly, 1916.

Madurai District Collectorate Records, Madurai from 1792 to 1803, Madurai, 1837.

Selections from the Records of the Collectorate of Tinnevelly, Madras, 1931.

Selections from the Records of Fort St. George, Madras, Revenue Series, No. XI, Madras, 1916.

Reports

A collection of Treaties C. Treaties between the East India Company, the Rajah of Thanjavur and the Nawab of the Carnatic and others, Madras, 1859.

Circular orders of the Board of Revenue, Vol. I and II, Madras, 1855.

Committie's Report on Local Self-Government, Madras, 1883.

Committee's Report on Tanjore Affairs, 1799, Tanjore, 1905.

Committee's Report on Revenue Survey of the Madras Presidency, Madras 1854.

Cotton, John (1816), *Report on the Ryotwari Settlement,* Tirunelveli.

Hudgeson, John (1914), *Report on the early History and Land Revenue of Tinnevelly,* 1807, Tinnevelly.

Lushington, S.R. (1916), *Report regarding the Tinnevelly poligars and Sequestered Pollan 1800,* Tinnevelly.

Lushington, S.R. (1802), *Report on Revenue Settlement.*

Lushington, S.R. (1800), *Correspondence on Permanent Settlement of the Southern Pollams of Ramnad and Sivaganga Zamindari* 24th December.

Correspondence

Correspondence Relating to the Revision Proposed in the Village Establishment of the Madras Presdiencey, Madras, 1867.

Correspondence Relating to the Settlement of Ramnad and Sivaganga Zamindari 1799-1803, Madras, 1983.

Military Country Correspondence, Vols. 1 to 46.

Political Country Correspondence, Vols. 1 to 4.

Public Country Correspondence, Vols. 1 to 4.

Journals, Manuals and Gazetters

Indian Antiquary, Bombay, Vols. 20, 23, 24, 28.

Baliga, B.S., (ed.) (1960), *Madras District Gazetters, Madurai*, Madras.

Baliga, B.S., (ed.) (1957), *Tanjore District Hand Book*, Madras.

Baliga, B.S., (ed.), *Madras District Gazetters*, Coimbatore.

Caldwell, R. (1881), *Tinnevelly District Manual*, Madras.

Francis, W., (ed.) (1906), *District Gazetteer, Madurai*, Madras.

Hemmingway, F.R. (1907), *The Trichinoploy Gazetteer*, Madras.

History of Land Revenue Settlement and Abohition of Intermediary Tenure in Tamil Nadu, Madras, 1977.

Maclean, C.D. (1881), *Glossary of Madras Presidency*, Vol. I, Madras.

Maclean, C.D. (1882), *Manual of Administration of the Madras Presidency*, Vols. I & II, Madras.

Pate H.R. (1917), *Tinnevelly District Gazetteer*, Madras.

Ramasami, A. (ed.), (1972), *Gazetteer of India, Ramanathapuram, District*, Madras.

Rajaram Row, T., (ed.) (1933), *Ramnad District Manual*, Madras.

Police Department, *The History of the Madras Police*, Madras, 1959.

Published Works

Secondary Sources

Aitchison, C.Y., (ed.) (1864), *A Collection of Teaties Engagement and Sandals*, Vol. I to III, Calcutta.

Annaswamy Ayaar, K. (1899), *The Sivaganga Zamindary,* Madras.

Baden-Powell, B.H. (1892), *The Land Systems of British India,* 3 Vols., Madras.

Beaglehole, T.M. (1966), *Thomas Munro,* Cambridge.

Besse, L. (1909), *Chanda Sahib and Beschi,* Trichinopoly.

Besse. L. (1918), *Father Beshi and his Writings,* Trichiropoly.

Bertrand (1850), *La Mission du Madura,* Paris, Vol. II.

Bishop Caldwell (1881), *History of Tirunelveli,* Madras.

Burhan (1939), *Tuzak-i-Walajahi,* Madras.

Burns, E.M. and Ralph, P.L. (1964), *World Civilizations,* Vol. I, Third Edition, Western and W. Gorc, New York.

Chandra Sekhara Reddi, *Vikramasimhapuri Mandalasaraswamy* (Printw)

Curry, J.C. (1909), *The Indian Policy.*

Danvers, F.C. (1894), *The Portuguese in India,* Vol. 2, London.

David Ludden (1979), *Peasant History in South India,* Vol. III, New Delhi.

Dodwell, H. (1920), *Dupliy and Clive,* London.

Duboia, *Hindu Manness, Customs and Cermonies,* Part III.

Dutt, R. (1906), *The Economic History of India Under Early British Rule,* Calcutta.

Elphinston, M. (1887), *The Rise of the British Power in the East,* London.

Family History of Ettaiyapuram, (Tamil MSS)

Foster, W. (1913), *The English Factories in India,* Oxford.

Fuller, J.B. (1902), *Land Revenue Policy of Indian Government,* Calcutta.

Ganapathi Pillai, W.E. (1980), *Ettayapuram Past and Present,* Madras.

Govindasamy, M.S. (1965), *The Role of Feudatories in Pallava History,* Annamalai Universtiy, Annamalai Nagar.

Griffith (1952), *British Impart on India,* London.

Heras, H. (1927), *The Aravidu Dynasty,* Madras.

Hill, S.C. (1885), Ysufkhan, *The Rebd Commandant,* London.

Indian Antianary, Bombay, 1914, Vol. 43, Vol. 46.

Jagaveeranar, K. (1950), *Panchalam Kurichi Virachartihram* Madurai.

Kathirvel, S. (1977), *A History of The Maravas,* Madurai.

Kaye, J.W. (1853), *The Administration of the East India Company,* London.

Krishnaswami, A. (1964), *The Tamil Country Under Vijayanagar,* Annamalainagar..

Mackenzie (1885), *Madras Manual of Administration,* Madras.

Mahalingam, T.V. (1955), *Administration and Social Life Under Vijayanagar,* Madras.

Maria John, B. (1994), *Linguistic Reorganisation of Madras Presidency,* Nagercoil.

Ma. Po. Si. (1942), *Virapandiya Kattabomman,* Madras.

Nelson, J.H. (1868), *The Madura Country,* Madras.

Nilakanta Sastri, K.A. (1952), *History of India,* Part III, Madras.

Nilakanta Sastri, K.A. (1956), *Colas ,University of Madras,* 2nd edn.

Nilakanta Sastri, K.A. (1957), *History of South India,* 3rd edn., Madras.

Nilakanta Sastri, K.A. (1929), *Pandyan Kingdom,* London.

Padmanabha Iyyar, V.S. (1933), *A Short Accouont of Tinnevely District Madras.*

Pillay. K.K. (1970), *Social History of the Tamils,* Madras.

Pillay, K.K. (1972), *South India and Ceylon,* Madras University.

Ponnambalam Regupathy (1987), *Early Settlements in Jaffna,* Madras.

Radhakrishna Ayyar, K. (1899), *The Sivaganga Zamindary.*

Radha Krishna Iyer (1916), *A General History of the Pudukottai State,* Pudukottai.

Raja Ram Rao, (ed.) (1933), *Ramnad Manual,* Madras.

Rajayyan, K. (1974), *Rise and fall of Poligars of Tamilnadu,* Madras.

Rajayyan, K. (1993), *Early Tamil Nadu,* Retna Publications, Rajambadi, Madurai.

Rajayyan. K. (1969), *A History of British Diplomacy in Tanjore,* Mysore.

Rajayyan, K. (1971), *South Indian Rebellion,* Mysore.

Rajayyan, K. (1974), *History of Madurai,* (1736-1802) Madurai University.

Rajayyan, K. (1966), *Administration and Society in the Carnatic,* Tirupati.

Ramasamy, N.S. (1977), *The Founding of Madras,* New Delhi.

Ramasamy Naidoo (1908), *Memoir an the Internal Revenue System of Madras* Presidency, Madras.

Report of the Tiruvandapuram Farm, 1775.

Saivasiddhantha Kazhagam (1943), *Puraporul Venba Malai*, Tirunelveli.

Sanjeevi, N. (1964), *Manamkatha Marudhu Pandiyar*, Madras.

Sanjeevi, N. (1956), *Marudhiravar*, Madras.

Sarada Raju, S. (1941), *Economic Conditions into Madras Presidency*, 1800-1850, Madras.

Sathianathier, R. (1934), *History of the Nayaks of Madura*, Madras.

Sathyanatha Iyer, R. (1956), *Tamilagam in the Seventeenth Century*, Madras.

Sathyanatha Iyer, R. (1952), *History of India*, Vol. III, Madras.

Sauliere, A. Fr. (1957), *Red Sand*, Trichinopoly.

Senart, E. (1930), *Caste in India*, London.

Sewell, R. (1900), *Forgotten Empire*, London.

Sharma, R.S. (1980), *Indian Feudalism*, The Macmillian Co., Madras.

Sharma, S.R. (1958), *The Making of Modern India*, Patna.

Srinivasachari, C.S., *A History of Gingee and its Rulers.*

Srinivasachari, C.S. (1951), *The Invardness of British Annexations in India*, Madras.

Srinivasachari, C.S. (1941), *Seluriaous from or me manscripts*, Madras.

Stuart, A.J., (ed.) (1879), *Manual of Tinnevelly*, Madras.

Subramaniam, K.R. (1928), *The Maratha Rajas of Tanjore*, Madras.

Subramanian, T.N. (1947), *Kattabomman*, Madras.

Subramanya Aiyer, K.V. (1967), *Historical Sketches of Ancient Dekhan*, Vol. II, The Co-operative Printing Press, Coimbatore.

Thiruvenkatachari (1959), *Sethupathies of Ramnad*, Karaikudi.

Thiyaga Rajan, M, (ed.) (1929), *Pudukottai Manual, Vols. I and II*, Pudukottai.

Thurston, E. (1909), *Castes and Tribes in South Inida, Vols. III & IV*, Madras.

Welsh (1830), *Military Reminiscences, Vols. 2* , London.

Wheeler, J. Talboys (1882), *Madras in the Olden Time Vols. 3* , Madras.

Wilson, Charles, Clive (1893), *(English man of Action Series,)* London.

INDEX

Q & R

U & V

W

Z